GW00459102

Testimonials

'I visited Dr (TCM) Attilio D'Alberto for baby brain, tiredness and to help me relax, all of which he assisted with. Towards the end of my pregnancy, I asked Dr (TCM) Attilio D'Alberto to help bring on labour, as I did not want to be induced in the hospital, and help with labour pains. My acupuncture appointment was at 7pm, my waters broke at 1am that night and I was in labour for 58 minutes. I safely delivered a baby boy. I definitely feel he helped to reduce the pain too.'
Mrs P

'I contacted Attilio as I was fast approaching my baby's due date and wanted to try acupuncture for labour induction. I'd never had acupuncture before, but it seemed completely safe as there are no chemicals involved and no chance of harming my baby. The session was incredibly relaxing. My husband was with me and Attilio took the time to teach him how to massage certain points on my body for relaxation, especially during labour. We were advised that acupuncture for labour induction might take a couple of days to work and, if not, that we may have to come back for another session. Amazingly, my contractions kicked in later that same day! My beautiful, healthy baby boy was born in the early hours of the next day.'
Mrs R

'Attilio made the acupuncture sessions relaxing and it didn't hurt at all having the needles inserted or removed. I was also given dietary and lifestyle advice to complement the acupuncture. The treatment worked very well for me and I felt more energised, rather than tired as I did before. I was so impressed with how well acupuncture had worked for me, I decided to have pre-birth acupuncture to help reduce the likelihood of requiring interventions during labour. I went into labour naturally 11 days before my due date and I had an active labour. I did a lot of walking and sitting on my birthing ball. The only pain relief I needed was gas and air, and the second phase of labour – the pushing bit – was only 30 minutes, which is very short for a first labour apparently.'

Mrs T

'I went to see Attilio after finding out my baby was breech at 36 weeks. My husband and I decided against an ECV procedure and we wanted to try moxibustion and acupuncture instead to turn the baby. Following treatment from Attilio, my husband and I were given moxa sticks to carry on the procedure at home for 10 days. After five days, the baby turned and we had a scan to confirm she was now head down!'

James and Sophie

My Pregnancy Guide

Ensuring a healthy pregnancy and labour

Dr (TCM) Attilio D'Alberto

www.attiliodalberto.com
www.myfertilityforum.com

Copyright © 2021 Attilio D'Alberto, London, UK

The moral right of Attilio D'Alberto to be identified as the author of this work has been asserted in accordance with the Copyright, Designs and Patents Act of 1988.

All rights reserved. No part of this book may be used or reproduced, stored in a retrieval system, or transmitted in any form or by any means, electronic, mechanical, photocopy, recording or otherwise without prior written permission of the author.

ISBN: 978-1-9162142-0-0

Though the majority of information presented in this book is sourced from hundreds of research articles, it does not replace your obstetrician's advice. Consult your health practitioner before changing any medication or dosage. The author does not accept any legal responsibility or liability for any personal injury or other damage or loss arising from the use of the information contained within this book.

To the family

Contents

My Pregnancy Guide by Dr (TCM) Attilio D'Alberto

Introduction

Congratulations! You have discovered that you are pregnant and are now carrying your baby. For a lot of women, this news can bring a mixture of emotions; joy, excitement and sometimes worry. Suddenly there are a lot of changes happening to your body and to your life. Try not to worry, as the information contained within this book will guide you through what will happen and help to ensure a healthier pregnancy and labour. I will give you lots of advice sourced from hundreds of research articles and share my decades of clinical experience to ensure that you have all the facts so that your baby has the best start in life.

Now that you are pregnant, a lot of changes will be going on physically, emotionally and mentally. I will guide you through all of these, outlining what to expect, what's going to happen and what to prepare for. I will also tell you how to protect your baby and how to optimise your lifestyle and diet to make sure your baby develops normally and healthily.

How this book can help you

One of the main reasons for writing this book is the lack of information available in one place, which means scouring the Internet and search engines, piecing different and sometimes contradictory information together. This can cause confusion and worry.

During my 20 years of experience, I have found that women are very knowledgeable about their pregnancy and require a lot more in-depth information than is often provided on websites or in other pregnancy books. I have therefore tried my best to include as much detailed information as possible in this book, but in a concise and easy-to-understand way.

I have added as much inside-track medical information as I can – the best route to take, what to avoid, what to eat, supplements to take, and how to change your lifestyle and diet to ensure a healthy pregnancy. This information is based on my unique understanding of Western and Chinese medicine combined, together with extensive research and the collective mass of thousands of my patients who have undergone their own pregnancy journeys.

Whether you have just found out that you are pregnant, are a few weeks in or near the end of your pregnancy, this book will inform and guide you towards a healthy pregnancy and labour.

How to use this book

This book is for women who are pregnant either by natural conception or from using assisted reproductive technologies such as in vitro fertilisation (IVF). It is intended to guide you through your pregnancy and labour for the best outcome possible, for you, your baby and your partner. I have also included a chapter for dads to help them understand the psychological changes they may be going through.

There is a lot of information presented in this book, most from fact-based research. You may already know pieces of information and would like to know more. 'Forewarned, is forearmed', as the saying goes. However, some women can find that too much information can be overwhelming and may cause anxiety. If you think this might be the case for you, I would recommend dipping into the book as and when needed rather than reading it from cover to cover.

You can get additional support from the book's forum **www.myfertilityforum.com**, where we host a range of pregnancy forums for women seeking advice and wanting to make new friends and grow their support network.

About the author

I have been practising since 2004, using acupuncture and Chinese herbs to help pregnant women. During this time, I have treated all types of pregnancy problems – from slow growth rate, pregnancy pain and carpal tunnel syndrome, to breech babies and labour inductions – for women in their early twenties through to those in their late forties.

My studies in acupuncture and Chinese herbal medicine started a long time ago, with a five-year full-time degree programme in Traditional Chinese Medicine jointly run by Middlesex University in London and Beijing University of Traditional Chinese Medicine in China. Since graduating I have had numerous articles published in medical journals and am the author of *My Fertility Guide: How to Get Pregnant Naturally*. I have learnt from some of the best acupuncturists in the world and now coach and advise other Chinese medicine practitioners.

I am passionate about acupuncture and Chinese medicine, the awareness it gives me and how I can use this to show people how to improve their health and have a healthy pregnancy. I blend ancient theories of Chinese medicine with modern scientific research to give a deeper insight into health and disharmony, creating a better awareness of how to improve one's health.

I believe it is important for people to understand their symptoms and address the disharmony they have, as it empowers them. This allows us to work consciously together to improve the health of both mother and baby.

Part One

The Fundamentals of Pregnancy

A lot of changes will happen during your pregnancy, some natural and some human-influenced. In this section I will explain the natural changes that you may go through and how to reduce the negative human influences to ensure your pregnancy is as healthy as possible.

Chapter 1

What to Expect

There are three stages of pregnancy:

1. First trimester: from week 1 to 13.
2. Second trimester: from week 14 to 27.
3. Third trimester: from week 28 to 40.

During each of the three stages of pregnancy, you may experience different symptoms.

What to Expect

A woman's body goes through a lot of changes during pregnancy, even from very early on. However, symptoms can vary from woman to woman and from pregnancy to pregnancy. Therefore, try not to worry if you do not experience any symptoms or just a few, even if this pregnancy is a subsequent one, as every pregnancy can be different. For those who have been struggling to conceive, feeling signs and symptoms of pregnancy can be reassuring, while for others it can cause distress. Whatever you feel, it is normal for you.

You may feel tired, bloated or suffer dizziness or lower back pain, or nothing at all. Some women will feel emotional as the increased level of hormones circulating in the body can play havoc with emotions. You may also experience other well-known symptoms such as nausea, a metallic taste in the mouth or a heightened sense of smell.

Tiredness

Tiredness is perfectly normal and can be a good sign. It means the pregnancy is viable and the baby is feeding off you. It is one of the first pregnancy symptoms a woman may experience, but try not to worry if you do not feel tired; it just means that you have more energy.

Growing the placenta, a new internal organ, requires a lot of energy and blood, which can lead to tiredness. Because of the increased demand for energy and blood, it is not good to allow yourself to become too tired as you can then become exhausted, and that's when problems can occur. This is where eating an optimal diet, taking supplements and even Chinese herbs can help to maintain good energy levels. Resting, eating and sleeping are the most important things a pregnant woman should be doing, as growing another human being is a full-time job!

Once the placenta is fully grown around weeks 10–12, energy levels often improve, hence why women tend to feel better in their second trimester.

Twinges and cramps

Experiencing twinges or cramps during pregnancy is perfectly normal. Even though your baby is very small at the start of pregnancy, lots of changes are happening around them, such as blood being redirected to the point at which your baby has attached to your uterus wall, your fallopian tubes being pushed back out of the way and the placenta growing. These changes all cause pressure on surrounding structures as everything tries to find a new home for the next nine months. You may feel bloated because of these movements. Some women may not feel any twinges or cramps and this, too, is perfectly normal. You can also feel discomfort after undergoing an ultrasound.

During the third trimester you may notice pains, which are most likely growing pains, as your skin and ligaments stretch. You may also feel pain when defecating as the baby restricts movement of the bowels.

Discharge

Some women will notice an increase in vaginal discharge during early pregnancy. This is normal and is caused by an increase in oestrogens, mainly oestradiol, within your body. The discharge forms part of the cervical plug that blocks the head of your womb, thereby protecting the womb from outside germs and viruses, which could potentially cause an infection and harm the baby.

These normal secretions should, however, be distinguished from vaginitis, which has symptoms of itching and discharge that is yellow in colour and has a bad odour. This should be treated as it can lead to preterm labour [1]. If you have these symptoms, tell your doctor, obstetrician or midwife.

At the end of your pregnancy, the cervical plug that created a barrier to harmful bacteria and viruses from the outside world will fall out before labour and is known as 'the show' (see page 226).

Bodily changes

Initially you may notice an extra band of fat around your lower abdomen, which may act as a shock absorber protecting your growing baby. This can make some women feel bloated. Others say they feel like their body has been taken over and, in some ways, it will be, for a short period of time.

You may notice that you are putting on weight, which is normal. Women can put on 11–16kg (25–35lb) of weight during pregnancy [2]. As you go further into the pregnancy, your body shape will change too.

Blood levels (haemoglobin) drop slightly due to an increased demand from the growing baby and placenta [3]. Taking low doses of iron is recommended to counter this. The recommended daily amount of iron increases in pregnancy from 14mg to 27mg. However, some women may need more if they are lacking in blood or have a history of anaemia (see page 30).

Further into the pregnancy it is common for a woman's breasts to increase in size, between 25 and 50 per cent. You may notice that your bra starts to feel uncomfortable as it digs into you. If you feel this, try using a bra that does not contain a metal underwire. Your nipples can become darker in colour as well as the midline of the stomach, below the belly button, which is known in Latin as the *linea nigra*[4]. You may develop darker skin on your face when you are pregnant, which is known as melasma or 'pregnancy mask'. The pituitary gland also increases in size by 135 per cent its pre-pregnancy level to accommodate the increased production of prolactin needed for breastfeeding, although you will not feel this[3].

Changes in appetite

A lot of women will experience changes to the foods they like to eat during pregnancy. For example, some will go off wanting to eat meat, salads and even chocolate, while others will crave carbohydrates and salty foods in the early weeks, such as crackers, toast, pizza and crisps, which is normal.

It is well known that for many women they will crave certain types of foods. These cravings are not always as strange as media lead us to believe. Cravings might be for foods that you have not eaten for a while, but your body remembers and innately knows that it needs. As a general rule, it is always better to follow your cravings and put aside the idea of trying to eat what we believe is a healthy diet, for example salads and meat.

Changes in appetite can also be affected by feelings of nausea (morning sickness). For those women who experience morning sickness, changes in appetite and preferences for certain foods may be greater (see page 42).

Digestion may feel sluggish and there may be a feeling of constantly being bloated. Apart from frequent urination, which is a well-known symptom in later pregnancy, some women will become constipated too as the heat generated by the pregnancy can make the colon drier and restrictions in space slow down bowel movements (see page 48).

Some women may experience a metallic taste in their mouth. The reasons for this are due to changes in your oestrogen levels. However, it is nothing to be worried about – it is normal. The metallic taste may affect your taste buds and preferences for certain foods, and may disappear after a while.

Sense of smell

Some women will experience an increased sense of smell. This may be a throwback to our ancient animalist survival skills that helped women to sense danger when they were in a more vulnerable state.

In today's modern world, an increased sense of smell can alert women to the effects of second-hand cigarette smoke, chemicals in perfumes and air pollution. Certain smells can make some women feel nauseous and reluctant to eat certain foods, for example after opening the fridge door.

Growing pains

During the third, and sometimes even in the second, trimester, you may feel pains in the outer edges of your baby bump as your skin stretches. This is normal and is literally growing pains. You can apply stretch mark lotions, such as green tea cream, to these areas in order to reduce the chances of developing stretch marks [5]. Green tea cream contains high levels of epigallocatechin gallate (EGCG), which protects the skin from UV damage and helps it to rejuvenate with enhanced collagen function [5].

Hair loss

After labour, some women may notice an increase in hair loss as many aged hairs will shed, which is partially caused by rapid hair growth during pregnancy [3]. Hair loss during pregnancy can be caused by a drop in blood levels due to the pregnancy draining the body. Normally, the hair loss is only temporary. If it continues, it can mean either the pregnancy or labour has drained the body. Taking iron supplements during pregnancy can help to maintain blood levels thereby reducing hair loss.

The uterus

The uterus goes through the greatest changes in size during pregnancy, as shown in the table below. Its shape will also change too. An ultrasound can be used to check the size and shape of your uterus.

	Non-pregnant uterus	**Full-term uterus**
Weight	50g (1.76oz)	950g (33.51oz)
Length	7.5cm (2.9in)	30cm (11.8in)
Depth	2.5cm (0.98in)	20cm (7.87in)
Shape	Flattened pear	Ovoid and erect

Table 1. The size differences of the uterus in pregnancy, pre- and full-term

Around 20 per cent of women will have a uterus that bends backwards, called a retroflexion or retroverted uterus. During the third trimester of pregnancy, a retroverted uterus can spontaneously correct its position, which is normal and will not affect the pregnancy [6].

The placenta

The placenta is a newly grown organ for the sole purpose of pregnancy. It is fully grown by week 12 and consists of two parts: the baby's portion and the mother's portion. The placenta provides the growing baby with life and protection. However, many drugs, alcohol and some substances can also pass freely. Certain viruses, such as those that cause AIDS, German measles, chickenpox, measles, encephalitis and poliomyelitis, can cross the placenta. The placenta's functions include:

- food
- hormonal synthesis
- respiration
- waste extraction

The placenta produces several hormones including oestrogens, progesterone and human chorionic gonadotropin (hCG). Certain human-made hormones can cross the placenta and affect the baby's hormones. These are discussed more in Chapter Three (page 20). The placenta stores nutrients, such as carbohydrates, proteins, calcium and iron, which are released to your baby when needed [7]. After giving birth, the placenta detaches from your uterus and is called the afterbirth and forms stage three of labour (see page 233).

Your baby is connected to the placenta via the umbilical cord, which is roughly 50–60cm (20–24in) long and 2cm (1in) wide [7]. The placenta itself weighs around 700g (1.5lb) and looks like a pancake [8].

Insomnia and sleeping

Some pregnant women may sleep for longer in their first trimester as they are tired, while others may find it hard to sleep at night. This is normal. It can be caused by a number of factors, for example feeling too warm at night as the pregnancy generates a lot of heat, which can make you feel hot and restless, or anxiety and worry about the pregnancy and the changes it will bring.

Being more restless at night can be a problem, especially if your partner snores. What was once tolerable can now become unbearable. This is normal. In such cases, you can use earplugs or send your partner to the spare bedroom. Getting enough sleep is important in pregnancy, so do not feel guilty about needing it!

Acupuncture is very good at relaxing the mind and aiding better sleep [9] [10] [11]. You can also use mind-relaxing techniques, such as breathing exercises, mindfulness or daydreaming (about positive things), as this will help transport you into the dream state of sleep.

As you go further into the pregnancy some women find it difficult to sleep due to the size of their bump or they wake up when their baby kicks or when they need to urinate.

You may have heard that it is better to sleep on your left-hand side while pregnant. For some women this is easy, while for others it may not be as they are used to sleeping on their backs or stomachs. Sleeping on your back is fine in the early weeks. You will know when it is no longer okay by the uncomfortable feeling you will have when the baby's weight presses on your major artery (inferior vena cava). If possible, sleeping on your side is best for your spine and for the baby, but do not worry if you cannot do so just yet.

When you get into your third trimester, you might find it is more comfortable to sleep with a pillow or a blanket in between your legs. This helps to give your hips more support. There are special pillows for pregnant women that you can buy which help to support you in bed.

Poor memory

Experiencing a poor memory during pregnancy is common and is often referred to as 'baby brain'. Cognitive performance can be reduced by a lack of iron in the body or tiredness. In Chinese medicine, poor memory and concentration is due to a lack of blood. I recommend taking an iron supplement throughout pregnancy, even if your iron levels are fine according to Western medical values.

Ensuring you have good levels of blood will not only reduce your risk of developing baby brain, but will ensure you have a healthy pregnancy, a good birth weight, less chance of a preterm delivery or pre-eclampsia, less restless legs syndrome and good breast milk levels.

Restless legs syndrome

Restless legs syndrome is an overwhelming urge to move your legs, usually at night-time when you are trying to sleep [12]. Some women feel strange sensations and may experience involuntary movements of their legs. It can be caused by tension in the muscle, which obstructs nerve signals. The body tries to relieve these nerve signals and tension by moving the legs. Walking, stretching, pregnancy yoga, heat and acupuncture can all help to relieve tension in the legs and the sensations of restless legs syndrome [13].

Braxton Hicks

From about week 34, you may be aware of your bump tightening. These are practice contractions known as Braxton Hicks contractions and are normal. They are called Braxton Hicks after the English obstetrician John Braxton Hicks who first noted them in medical literature in 1871 [14]. Practice contractions are often irregular and vary in intensity. They do not mean you are entering labour until they occur every three minutes and become painful with the discomfort radiating to your lower back and lower abdomen [4]. When this happens, you should contact your midwife or hospital as you may be entering labour.

Varicose veins

Varicose veins are common in pregnancy and usually reduce and disappear after giving birth. They are caused by the baby restricting blood flow. Wearing circulation stockings, raising the legs and having acupuncture treatment can help to provide short-term relief while pregnant [15] [16] [17].

Varicose veins tend to be more common in a second pregnancy, although some women can still experience varicose veins in their first. In such cases, I would recommend using arnica and witch hazel balm externally and keep the area cool, for example wearing dresses rather than trousers, and wearing cotton underwear. You can also drink mint tea to help cool you down and have cool baths. Alternatively, your obstetrician can treat the varicose vein by injecting chemicals, known as sclerosing agents, into the vein to shrink it – known as sclerotherapy [18] – although these agents have side effects such as an allergic reaction, ulceration of skin around the injection site, blood clot formation in the treated veins and inflammation around the injection site.

Vulvar varicosity

Around 10 per cent of pregnant women will experience genital varicose veins [18]. These can be caused by increased blood flow to the genital area together with heat and blood stasis – when blood slows down due to restriction of movement.

Coping with Pregnancy

Society makes women think that being pregnant should be a joyous and wonderful period in a woman's life, and for a lot of women this is the case. However, not all women will feel joyous. The emotions women feel about being pregnant can differ from woman to woman and from the type of fertility journey they have experienced in order to achieve pregnancy. Whatever you feel, do not judge yourself for it, as what you feel is normal for you.

Not a lot of women will talk about how they are truly feeling, even to their friends, family or partner; it is seen as a bit of a taboo. Just remember, it is perfectly normal to feel happy that you are pregnant and, on the other hand, to feel bad. It is not easy being pregnant!

Feeling nauseous can make pregnancy more difficult to cope with as there is sometimes little relief. An expectant mother's attitudes towards pregnancy often change once energy levels pick up, nausea reduces, hormones normalise and they feel the baby kick and feelings of motherhood start to emerge.

We have seen the various symptoms that you may experience during pregnancy. Let's now look at the psychological changes a man may be going through during your pregnancy.

Chapter 2

Pregnancy for Dads

Although the vast majority of fathers are either cohabiting or in touch with their pregnant partner, there is a vast lack of awareness and recognition of the father's importance during pregnancy from healthcare professionals [19]. It is often deemed that as the woman is pregnant, the man's job is done, and he is left to wait until the child arrives and for fatherhood to begin. This segregation can make it difficult for some men to make the transition to fatherhood.

Most fathers see themselves as partner and parent, with a strong desire to support their partners and to be fully engaged with the process of becoming a father. However, their experience of maternity care is often difficult and challenged [19] [20]. This can lead to some men finding themselves in a situation where they are in an interstitial and undefined space (both emotionally and physically) with the consequence that many feel uncertain, excluded and fearful [19].

This lack of inclusion of men in family planning, pregnancy and childbirth by healthcare professionals can leave many men to default into a traditional pattern of emotional development that can be based upon three phases:

1. Announcement phase.
2. Moratorium phase.
3. Focusing phase.

The announcement phase can vary in length from a few minutes to a few weeks. The variation of length can depend upon whether the pregnancy was planned or not.

The length of the second phase – the moratorium/reflection period – reflects their readiness for fatherhood. The moratorium phase can last for just a few days to several months depending upon the man [21]. This phase can be exacerbated by a lack of pregnancy symptoms in the expectant mother. Some men may carry on as normal, focusing on other life stresses, until the woman starts to experience pregnancy symptoms. As symptoms appear, this second phase often ends.

The focusing phase starts when the man has accepted his new role as a father and engages in parenthood. This can be expressed by attending midwife, obstetrician or neonatal appointments, or preparing for their new baby by purchasing items, setting up the nursery or even changing the car. The point at which they enter the focusing phase will vary from man to man. The speed at which the father passes through these phases can affect their adjustment to fatherhood [21]. The level of involvement during pregnancy predicts how well-equipped and involved the father will be after birth.

A man's health should naturally include the basic components of preconception health, such as sexual health, health promotion and psychosocial interventions, which can help identify challenges facing adolescents and barriers confronting boys in the transition to manhood, thereby helping them prepare for fatherhood [22]. These prenatal programmes can benefit their child's well-being [23] [24]. Attitudes are now changing in most modern countries, with the advancement of these new programmes designed to encourage male inclusion in prenatal care.

Fathers see themselves as much more than just passive supporters for their partners. They want to be authentically engaged and they tend to genuinely struggle with the need to try to balance their own unknown and uncertain journey to fatherhood with the desire to provide some certainty and support for the journeying mother. They see this process as being as life-changing and uncertain, and as potentially both traumatic and empowering, for them as it is for the woman they are supporting [19].

When there are specific antenatal groups focusing on men's needs, there are benefits in terms of reduced distress, increased ability to cope and improved relationship with their partner [25]. Women who were supported by their partner during pregnancy tend to have better health with fewer complications during labour, and may experience an easier transition to motherhood leading to a healthy child [21] [26].

Forty years ago, men were barred from attending births in hospitals. In contrast, expectant fathers are now expected to be involved in maternity care in most countries. In the UK, approximately 96 per cent of fathers attend the birth [27]. However, there is evidence that men still feel effectively excluded even though they are physically present. If men feel excluded, they may find it difficult to support their partner effectively in achieving the ideal transition from a successful pregnancy, to a joyful birth and parenthood experience unless they are themselves supported. This support may include being prepared for the reality of pregnancy and labour, and parenthood [19]. For this reason, I have included acupressure points which the father can stimulate on the mother during labour, see page 204. I would also encourage expecting fathers to ask any questions they may have to the midwife or obstetrician for example:

- How will my partner be affected by pregnancy?
- What can I do to support her during pregnancy?
- How can I prepare her for labour?

- What can I do during labour?

It is important for both you and your baby to ensure that your partner is included in all aspects of your pregnancy and has equal emotional and physical support. I would recommend that the father reads this book as it will offer them a valuable insight into your pregnancy and will allow them to feel informed and included during this magical process and transition into parenthood. You can also find antenatal classes that cater for both of your needs.

Chapter 3

Hormones in Pregnancy

Hormones are vital for pregnancy and your baby. Together they act like an orchestra, performing a symphony of bodily functions. The body is incredibly interconnected with many processes acting like a chain reaction. When they are performing in tune, your body is balanced and harmonised. Let's now look at the most important hormones in pregnancy and how they affect your body and the baby.

Foetal hormones

Your baby will start to produce its own range of hormones to support itself during pregnancy. These range of hormones include human chorionic gonadotropin (hCG), oestrogens and progesterones. Let's now look at each of them.

Human Chorionic Gonadotropin (hCG)

Once pregnant, the fertilised embryo produces the hormone hCG around eight days after it has implanted into your uterus wall [6]. The testing of hCG levels in your urine is how a home pregnancy test shows that you are pregnant. Levels of hCG rise dramatically in early pregnancy and double every 48 hours (see table 2 below).

hCG sustains the *corpus luteum* (the sack that once contained the egg) for a further three to four months, thereby maintaining the production of progesterone that is needed to maintain the uterus lining. From roughly weeks 8–12, the newly grown placenta contributes to the production of progesterone.

Week	hCG level (mIU/mL)
Week 3	5–50
Week 4	5–425
Week 5	20–7,250
Week 6	1,050–56,500
Weeks 7–8	7,500–230,000
Weeks 9–12	25,500–290,000

Table 2. The levels of hCG during the first trimester of pregnancy

Oestrogens

Oestrogens are made up of three hormones: oestradiol, oestrone and oestriol. The most abundant and therefore the most important one is oestradiol (also known as 17-beta-oestradiol or E2).

Levels of oestrogens rise rapidly in the first trimester of pregnancy (see table 3 below), which may cause nausea (morning sickness) [28]. Oestrogens help to thicken the uterus lining and prepare the breasts for milk production. Unfortunately, in our modern world we are all overdosing on man-made oestrogens (see page 102) for more on this).

Trimester	Oestradiol level (pmol/L)	Oestradiol level (pg/mL)
First	690–9,166	188–2,497
Second	4,691–26,401	1,278–7,192
Third	22,528–12,701	6,137–3,460

Table 3. The levels of oestradiol during pregnancy

Progestins

Progestins (also known as progestogens) are a group of steroid hormones produced by the *corpus luteum*. The most important progestin is progesterone (also known as P4). The normal level of progesterone in pregnancy is shown in the table below. If you have low levels of progesterone, you can request progesterone support from your obstetrician or doctor.

Trimester	Progesterone level (nmol/L)	Progesterone level (ng/mL)
First	32–140	10–44
Second	64–260	20–82
Third	207–922	65–290

Table 4. The levels of progesterone during pregnancy

Progesterone has several important functions, including:

- Aiding implantation of the embryo into the uterus wall [29].
- Turning off the production of new eggs.
- Thickening the uterus lining to feed the baby.
- Enlarging the mammary glands (breasts) for breastfeeding.
- Maintaining the pregnancy.

New research has shown that progesterone aids in the production of TH2 cells (part of the immune system), which protect an implanting embryo [29]. It also induces lymphocytes to release an immunomodulatory protein that enhances TH2 production, both of which are needed for successful implantation [30].

Hypothalamus

The hypothalamus produces corticotrophin-releasing hormone, thyrotropin-releasing hormone and oxytocin, which all control the pituitary gland.

Corticotrophin-releasing hormone (CRH)

During pregnancy, the placenta starts to produce CRH from around week 12 [7]. It stimulates the pituitary gland to produce adrenocorticotropic hormone (ACTH). However, too much CRH from around week 20 onwards has been linked with preterm labour [31] [32] [33] [34]. This may be caused by the mother feeling stressed and anxious. Acupuncture has been shown to reduce anxiety and CRH levels naturally [35] [36] [37] [38] [39] [40] [41] [42] [43] [44].

Thyrotropin-releasing hormone (TRH)

This causes the pituitary gland to produce thyroid-stimulating hormone.

Thyroid-stimulating hormone (TSH)

TSH triggers the production of thyroid hormones by the thyroid gland. The thyroid hormones it produces are thyroxine (T_4), triiodothyronine (T_3) and calcitonin (CT). During pregnancy, the thyroid gland enlarges and levels of thyroid hormones T_3 and T_4 increase, as does demand for iodine. Iodine is needed for proper T_4 and T_3 production as well as for the baby's growing thyroid [8]. A lack of iodine can result in a preterm delivery, intrauterine growth restriction (IUGR) and, in rare cases, miscarriage [8].

Vegetarians and vegans tend to be deficient in iodine [45] [46] [47] [48] [49]. Pregnant women who are vegetarian or vegan should be mindful of their iodine levels and their need for adequate iodine intake. This can be achieved by making changes to their diet or by taking an iodine supplement.

Levels of T_4 and T_3 increase in pregnancy to assist in the growing of the baby's brain. Levels of TSH during pregnancy should be closely monitored as higher than normal levels can be a cause of miscarriage. The ideal levels of TSH levels are shown in the table below. Women with a pre-existing thyroid disease will have their TSH levels monitored during pregnancy.

Trimester	Ideal range
First	0.1–2.5mU/L
Second	0.2–3.0mU/L
Third	0.3–3.0mU/L

Table 5. Ideal levels of TSH in pregnancy [50] [51]

Pituitary

The pituitary gland releases oxytocin and prolactin.

Oxytocin

Oxytocin is often known as the 'hug hormone', as physical contact i.e. a hug, a massage from a partner, sexual intercourse or acupuncture treatment increases its levels [52]. It is produced in the hypothalamus and released by the pituitary gland. It is important for social behaviour, bonding, appetite, anxiety regulation, labour and lactation. People with autism tend to have lower levels of oxytocin. It affects the uterus during labour by enhancing contractions of the muscles in the uterus wall, which pushes the baby out. Medical inductions use high doses of oxytocin to deliver the baby. The injection often given to women to deliver the placenta is a high dose of oxytocin. After delivery, oxytocin helps to stimulate the release of milk (not its actual production) from your breasts [53].

A high-fat diet is associated with low levels of oxytocin [54]. Low levels of oxytocin make us feel more emotionally down and make us more likely to comfort eat [55] [56]. Foods that are high in fat and sugar give a temporary feel-good factor (dopamine), but can cause people to put on weight. This weight gain can affect insulin levels, causing a rise in testosterone levels. High levels of testosterone commonly reduce levels of oxytocin, thus creating a vicious cycle. It is therefore important not to include too much fat and sugar in your diet while pregnant. See Chapter Twelve (page 124) for dietary information during pregnancy.

Prolactin

Prolactin stimulates your breasts to develop and maintains the release of milk, hence 'lactin' relates to lactation. However, breast milk is not released until levels of progesterone decrease after labour [7]. Prolactin also stops the menstrual cycle. Oestrogens, which rise rapidly in pregnancy, stimulate the release of TRH, which causes an increase in levels of prolactin, 10 times the pre-pregnancy level [3] [7].

Placenta

The placenta releases the hormone relaxin.

Relaxin

Relaxin is a hormone produced by the *corpus luteum* and the placenta for the sole purpose of labour. It helps to relax the pubic symphysis, hence the name relax-in. The pubic symphysis is a cartilaginous joint that is normally stiff. The hormone relaxin makes it relax, which allows the baby to pass through the birth canal. Relaxin also helps to dilate the cervix, which aids labour [7].

Insulin

Insulin is a hormone produced by the pancreas that decreases levels of glucose in the blood. Glucose is a type of sugar. The more sugar that is in the body, the higher the level of insulin. The normal level of insulin should be less than 6–7mmol/L (140mg/dL) [57]. As extra energy is needed for you and your growing baby, your metabolic rate increases by around 20 per cent during pregnancy, leading to an increase in sensitivity to insulin.

Insulin stimulates fat storage [58]. Women who are overweight tend to have higher levels of insulin, caused by eating too much sugar or fat. Artificial sweeteners, which are used as a sugar substitute, are now believed to interfere with insulin levels and can actually cause weight gain in both mother and baby [59]. Around 2–5 per cent of pregnant women will develop diabetes during pregnancy, known as gestational diabetes (see page 54) [4] [8]. High levels of insulin during pregnancy can be a problem for both mother and baby. Babies born from diabetic mothers are six times more likely to develop congenital anomalies, for example heart or limb deformities [4]. Out of 2–5 per cent of pregnancies, 40–60 per cent of mothers go on to develop diabetes later in life [8]. It is therefore important to maintain a balanced, nutritional diet that is low in processed sugars to reduce any problems during pregnancy. See Chapter Twelve (page 124) for more on eating a diet low in sugar. New research has demonstrated that acupuncture is also able to regulate insulin levels [60], which can help pregnant mothers.

Adrenals

The adrenal glands sit on top of the kidneys. The adrenals produce several hormones. The important ones in pregnancy are glucocorticoids.

Glucocorticoids

Glucocorticoids are made up of a group of hormones: cortisol (the most abundant of the three), corticosterone and cortisone. The hypothalamus sends CRH to the pituitary gland, causing it to release ACTH, which stimulates the adrenals to produce cortisol, corticosterone and cortisone. During pregnancy, a mother will have levels of cortisol 2–10 times higher than her baby [61]. In pregnancy, cortisol is needed for the maturation of the baby's lungs [7].

By understanding and being aware of the changes to your hormones, you are better able to balance and manage them, which in turn leads to the healthy growth of your baby and ensures a smoother labour experience. Let's now look at how your baby's growth is measured and monitored during pregnancy.

Chapter 4

Tests During Pregnancy

During pregnancy, your midwife or obstetrician will perform several tests to assess your health and that of your baby. There are also additional tests that you may need or want to have done as well.

Ultrasounds

Ultrasounds are sometimes called sonograms or sonography. They use high-frequency sound waves (5–7.5MHz for transvaginal and 3.5–5MHz for transabdominal) to create an image inside the body. The vast majority of ultrasounds are made using 2D. 3D or real-time 3D (known as 4D) ultrasounds are better at evaluating the baby's health and that of the placenta [57].

Ultrasounds are generally safe, although as a 3.5–7.5MHz sound wave is passed through the baby, there is a small risk of male babies being born with a lower birth weight or developing autism [62] [63]. It is therefore not advisable to have excessive ultrasounds, if possible.

First trimester ultrasounds

Ultrasounds are commonly used in pregnancy to see the gestational sac, yolk sac and embryo. The gestational sac is a fluid-filled structure surrounding the yolk sac and embryo during the first few weeks of your baby's development.

Using a transvaginal probe (an ultrasound wand that is inserted into the vagina), a 2–3-mm gestational sac can usually be seen five weeks from the last menstrual period (LMP). The yolk sac and the small foetal pole, which develops alongside the yolk sac, is usually seen by six menstrual weeks. From the foetal pole the heart starts to beat and is normally detected with an ultrasound around this time (see table 6 below).

Days from last menstrual period	28–35	35–42	42–49	49–56
Gestational sac	100%			
Yolk sac	0%	91%	100%	
Embryo with + heartbeat	0%	0%	86%	100%

Table 6. The appearance of your baby from your last menstrual period

Transvaginal ultrasounds have a higher sensitivity and produce clearer images than transabdominal ultrasounds. The gestational sac is usually seen when your hCG levels are around 7,000mIU/mL and the embryo is usually seen when your hCG levels are around 11,000mIU/mL [8].

The number of weeks of your pregnancy can be measured by the crown–rump length (CRL) in the first trimester within an accuracy of three to five days as compared to an error of +two weeks when measured in the second trimester and +three weeks in the third trimester [8]. The CRL is the measurement of the length of your baby from the top of the head (crown) to the bottom of the buttocks (rump) during an ultrasound. To establish the number of weeks you are, take the CRL figure and add 6.5 to calculate your baby's gestational age.

Second trimester ultrasounds

During your second trimester ultrasounds you will receive more detailed information about your baby and their gender, if you wish to know it. An anatomical survey will be conducted between weeks

18 and 22 to check that your baby is growing normally. The amniotic fluid volume will be estimated, the number of vessels of the umbilical cord measured and the placenta location identified.

During your second trimester ultrasounds, your baby's nuchal fold thickness will be measured along with the nuchal transparency (NT). This is used to determine whether the baby has a higher rate of being born with Down's syndrome (trisomy 21), Edwards' syndrome (trisomy 18), Patau's syndrome (trisomy 13) and Turner syndrome [4] [64]. The different nuchal fold thicknesses are shown in the table below.

Gestational age	Abnormal measurements
8–12 weeks	> 2.5mm
12–16 weeks	> 4mm
> 16 weeks	> 6mm

Table 7. Nuchal fold thicknesses in pregnancy

Third trimester ultrasounds

Third trimester ultrasounds are similar to second trimester ultrasounds. However, not all women will be offered an ultrasound in their third trimester. It varies depending upon the country you live in and the healthcare available. For example, in the UK, you are generally given one ultrasound at 12 weeks and then another at 20 weeks. You may only be given additional ultrasounds in the UK if there is a medical need for it.

If you are given an ultrasound at this stage, your baby's estimated foetal weight (EFW) will be measured from an average of three measurements from three different readings: femur length (FL), biparietal diameter (BPD) and the most important one – the abdominal circumference (AC). Measuring the baby's AC is not easy and there can be error rates of 15–20 per cent. Therefore, try not to be alarmed if the measurement is lower than you expected, as it may be slightly wrong.

Doppler Machines

After several weeks of pregnancy, a Doppler ultrasound can be used by your midwife or obstetrician. The combination of an ultrasound with a Doppler measurement can help identify the baby's heartbeat as well as being a useful non-invasive method of assessing blood flow to the uterus. You can buy a Doppler machine to use at home. However, if you cannot find the baby's heartbeat it may cause unnecessary anxiety, when the baby may have just moved position. It is often best when used by a trained medical professional.

Blood Tests

As part of your antenatal care, you will be offered several blood tests. Some are offered to all women and some are only offered if you are at risk of a particular infection or medical condition, such as you have a family history of diabetes. The blood tests you may be offered include:

- blood group
- anaemia
- diabetes
- rhesus disease

Blood group

It is useful to know your blood group in case you need to be given blood, for example if you have heavy bleeding (haemorrhage) during pregnancy or in labour.

Anaemia

If you have a blood test and the results show anaemia (ferritin ug/litre <30), you may be prescribed iron, usually 200–600mg a day. This level of iron may cause stomach cramps, tarry stools and constipation, which is normal.

Diabetes

Gestational diabetes is a reduced tolerance to carbohydrates and refined sugar in pregnancy. When digested, carbohydrates turn into blood glucose (a type of sugar). Gestational diabetes affects between 3.5 and 16 per cent of pregnancies [57]. Having gestational diabetes leads to an increase of glucose to the baby resulting in a large birth weight and possible complications during labour, for example the baby is too big for a vaginal delivery leading to a caesarean delivery [8] [57]. It can also lead to diabetes in 40–60 per cent of mothers in later life [8].

Women with pre-existing diabetes mellitus may have higher glucose levels in the first trimester during the baby's organ development [3]. Gestational diabetes is tested in the third trimester using a glucose challenge test (GCT), a glucose tolerance test (GTT) or a glucose load test (GLT) in women who are considered high risk [4].

A lot of women will crave carbohydrates in early pregnancy, which is normal and should not be excluded from your diet unless you are a diabetic. Carbohydrates become more of a problem in developing gestational diabetes in the third trimester. One way of keeping your blood sugar levels in the normal range is by monitoring the amount of carbohydrates and refined sugar in your diet. See Chapter Twelve (page 124) for more information on how to reduce your risk of developing gestational diabetes.

Rhesus disease

Rhesus disease is a condition where antibodies in a pregnant woman's blood destroy her baby's blood cells. It is also known as haemolytic disease of the foetus and newborn (HDFN). Rhesus disease happens when the mother has rhesus negative blood and the baby has rhesus positive blood. In the UK, it affects around 10 per cent of pregnancies [3]. You will be tested for this in early pregnancy with a blood sample [4].

Women who are rhesus negative do not have a D antigen on the surface of their red blood cells, which can lead to potential problems. If a small amount of the baby's rhesus positive blood enters a mother's bloodstream that is rhesus negative during pregnancy or birth, the mother will produce anti-D antibodies against the rhesus positive cell [57]. Injections of anti-D can prevent rhesus negative women from producing antibodies against their baby [3] [57]. Rhesus negative mothers are offered anti-D injections at week 28 of pregnancy, or earlier if the pregnancy is threatened, as well as 72 hours after delivery in case any blood crossed over during labour [3] [4] [57].

A rhesus negative woman can carry a baby who is rhesus positive if the baby's father is rhesus positive. If both parents are rhesus negative, then the baby too will be rhesus negative and will be unaffected [57].

Being rhesus negative usually does not affect the pregnancy, but if a woman who is rhesus negative has another pregnancy with a rhesus positive baby, her immune system will mount a greater response and she may produce a lot more antibodies [57]. This can lead to anaemia and jaundice in the baby [3] [4].

Urine Tests

Having your urine routinely checked during pregnancy is normal. Usually, every time you visit your midwife or antenatal clinic, they will check your urine. They are looking for any protein (albumin) or glucose that might be present [3]. Having small amounts of protein in your urine is common in pregnancy. Protein in your urine may also mean that your body is fighting a minor infection, such as a urinary tract infection (UTI).

In about 3–5 per cent of pregnancies, there can be large amounts of protein in the urine during the second and third trimester, which may be a sign of early pre-eclampsia (see page 46) [57]. If there are large amounts of albumin in the urine, it may mean that the kidneys are not functioning properly. This is called albuminuria. Albuminuria is most often caused by kidney damage from gestational diabetes.

Clotting

A blood clot can occur in the umbilical cord, blocking blood and nutrients reaching the baby, although this is rare. A thrombophilia test looks for anticoagulant deficiencies that might cause a blood clot. There are many types of thrombophilia. Some types run in families and others can develop during pregnancy. Often a thrombophilia test is only given if there is a family history of clotting or if you had a previous miscarriage.

If the thrombophilia test is positive, heparin (enoxaparin) is given to women with a family history of thrombophilia [65]. Those without a family history of thrombophilia but maybe still at risk are often prescribed aspirin (acetylsalicylic acid) to thin the blood and reduce the risk of a blood clot forming. Acupuncture has been shown to increase blood flow to the uterus without any side effects [66].

Blood Pressure

Your blood pressure will be taken at most antenatal visits. A rise in blood pressure during pregnancy can be a sign of pregnancy-induced hypertension. If you have high blood pressure, or hypertension, your heart has to work harder to pump blood around your body. This can affect the heart muscle.

Hypertension affects around 3–5 per cent of pregnancies, but is commonly seen in new mums [3]. There are three main types of hypertension in pregnancy:

1. Pregnancy-related high blood pressure (gestational hypertension).
2. Pre-eclampsia [57].
3. Chronic hypertension (where the high blood pressure was present before pregnancy).

Gestational hypertension is when blood pressure increases after the twentieth week of pregnancy. It affects between 5 and 10 per cent of pregnancies [3] [4]. Around 25 per cent of women with gestational hypertension will develop pre-eclampsia or eclampsia (see page 46).

Chronic hypertension is when there is hypertension before pregnancy or before the twentieth week of pregnancy [4]. Chronic hypertension can lead to pre-eclampsia or eclampsia later in pregnancy.

Chromosome Screening

All pregnant women are offered chromosomal screening for three syndromes; Down's, Edwards' and Patau's. A baby with Down's syndrome will have some level of learning disability, characteristic facial appearance and a 50 per cent chance of having congenital heart disease. Around 1 in 700 babies will have Down's syndrome [67]. This incidence increases with the mother's age. However, babies born with Down's syndrome live normal lives. Edwards' and Patau's syndromes are more commonly seen in babies born from older women and do not have a good prognosis [68].

Screening tests

The screening tests available include:

- Testing for Down's syndrome along with Edwards' syndrome and Patau's syndromes can be started from week 10 with a blood test called a Harmony test (see below). This test checks for the risk of trisomy 21, 18 and 13, and has a high rate of accuracy with a false-positive rate of less than 0.1 per cent. It is possible to check for Turner and Klinefelter syndromes too. You can also select to know the gender of your baby, again from week 10 rather than the traditional week 20.

- A reflex DNA test involves analysing cell free DNA in your blood, which contains a small amount of your baby's DNA as well as your own. In pregnancies with Down's, Edwards' or Patau's syndromes there will be a little bit more DNA from chromosomes 21, 18 or 13 [69].

- The St George's Antenatal Foetal Evaluation (SAFE) test is a non-invasive prenatal test for the screening of Down's, Edwards' and Patau's syndromes only. The test is performed by taking a small sample of the mother's blood, which is sent to the National Health Service (NHS) laboratory at St George's Hospital for assessment. The results are typically available within seven calendar days. The test is suitable from 10 weeks of pregnancy for all single and identical twins pregnancies, including IVF, egg donor or surrogate pregnancies. The test is not suitable for multiple pregnancies (greater than twins), if the mother has cancer, a chromosomal or genetic condition (including Down's syndrome). It is also unsuitable for mothers who have undergone a blood transfusion in the last 4 months, had transplant surgery, immunotherapy or stem cell therapy [70].

- A blood test plus a nuchal translucency ultrasound scan (nuchal translucency is a collection of fluid at the back of the baby's neck – the thicker it is, the higher the risk). This is called the combined test and is offered between weeks 10 and 14 of pregnancy. The blood test looks at levels of free beta hCG and PAPP-A. High levels of free beta hCG with low levels of PAPP-A are associated with Down's syndrome.

- A Down's syndrome-only blood test can be offered between weeks 14 and 20 of pregnancy if you are too far along to have the combined test. This blood test is less accurate than the combined test.

If the latter two screening tests show that you have a risk greater than 1 in 150 (that is, between 1 in 2 and 1 in 150) of having a baby with Down's, Edwards' or Patau's syndromes, you will be offered further diagnostic tests to find out for certain if your baby has the condition. The diagnostic tests are:

- chorionic villus sampling
- amniocentesis
- Harmony test

Chorionic villus sampling (CVS)

CVS involves taking a sample of the placenta for DNA analysis, cytogenetic testing and enzyme testing. However, as CVS is invasive it carries a small risk of causing a miscarriage (1–2 per cent) [8]. A Harmony test is preferred as there is no risk to the baby.

Amniocentesis

Amniocentesis involves taking a sample of the amniotic fluid that surrounds the baby. This is then used for karyotyping, DNA analysis and enzyme testing. When used between weeks 16 and 18 of pregnancy, the risk of causing a miscarriage is 1 in 270 (8). It should not be conducted earlier in the pregnancy. Again, a Harmony test is safer and more accurate and should be used instead, if possible.

Harmony test

The Harmony test is a non-invasive prenatal test (NIPT), which can also be called NIPS (non-invasive prenatal screening). Today, more and more clinics and hospitals are offering pregnant mothers the Harmony test. This is a non-invasive prenatal screening which looks at fragments of your baby's DNA in your own blood and is more accurate than measuring nuchal fold thickness and nuchal transparency. The Harmony test is more expensive than traditional testing methods. The Harmony test looks for trisomy 21 (Down syndrome), trisomy 18 and trisomy 13. The Harmony test looks for SCAs such as:

- XXY (a cause of Klinefelter syndrome)
- Monosomy X (a cause of Turner syndrome)

The Harmony test also looks for 22q11.2 microdeletion, the most common genetic cause of intellectual disability and heart defects after Down syndrome [71].

Foetal Well-Being Test

It can be reassuring to a lot of expectant mothers to check their baby's well-being and ascertain that their baby is okay. This can be tested by checking the baby's heart rate (non-stress test, NST), having an ultrasound, a contraction stress test (CST) and by the mother's observations about the baby's activity. A variety of methods can be used to check the baby's activity, for example how many times the baby moves in a day and how many kicks there are in an hour[4]. There are free apps you can download on to your smartphone to help track your baby's movements.

In some circumstances, your obstetrician may wish to perform a biophysical profile (BPP) to further check your baby's well-being. A BPP consists of five tests to assess the baby's well-being and includes a NST, foetal breathing movements, foetal movement, foetal tone and the amount of amniotic fluid present. Each test is scored from 0 (absent) to 2 (present). A score of 8–10 is considered good.

Infections

Because of the worldwide COVID-19 pandemic, we are now more acutely aware of infections from viruses and bacteria. There are several viruses that could potentially affect the pregnancy. Let's now look at what tests are available to identify them.

Cytomegalovirus (CMV) test

CMV is a member of the herpes family of viruses. It affects about 1 per cent of newborns [4] [8] [57]. Most pregnant women contract CMV from a child less than three years of age [72] [73]. CMV is a virus that can be transmitted to a developing baby before birth causing birth defects including low birth weight, deafness, blindness, learning difficulties, small head size, seizures, jaundice, brittle teeth and damage to the liver and spleen [8] [57] [73] [74].

As the virus does not show any symptoms during pregnancy (it is asymptomatic), it is generally not tested for [4]. There is currently no vaccine or treatment for CMV in Western medicine [8] [57]. Instead, increased hygiene is recommended during pregnancy [72] [73]. However, research has shown that the Chinese herbal formula Jinye Baidu can prevent and treat CMV infections in pregnancy [75] [76].

Group B streptococcus (GBS)

GBS or strep is common in pregnant women and rarely causes any problems. It is very common with up to two in five women having it living in their body, usually in the rectum or vagina [77]. Most pregnant women who carry GBS bacteria have healthy babies. It is not routinely tested for, but may be found during tests carried out for another reason, such as a urine test. If you have GBS while you are pregnant:

- your baby will usually be healthy
- there is a small risk that it could spread to your baby during labour and make them ill – this happens in 1 in 1,750 pregnancies [77]

If you have a test and it is positive for GBS, or you have had a baby who was affected, you may need extra care and treatment during labour. You may be advised to:

- give birth in hospital
- have antibiotics given to you via a vein during labour
- stay in hospital for longer after giving birth

Scarlet fever

Scarlet fever is a contagious bacterial infection that causes a blotchy rash that feels like sandpaper. Scarlet fever is most common in children aged between two and eight, although anyone can catch it. It is caused by bacteria from the streptococcus (strep) group, which is the same group of bacteria that causes sore throats. There is no evidence to suggest that getting scarlet fever during pregnancy will harm your baby [78]. However, it can make you feel unwell, so it is best to avoid close contact with anyone who has it. Tell your midwife, obstetrician or doctor if you think you have scarlet fever. The antibiotics used for scarlet fever are usually safe to take during pregnancy. Both acupuncture and Chinese herbs can be used to reduce symptoms [79].

Chickenpox

Chickenpox is a highly contagious infection that causes an itchy, spotty rash. It is common in children, but adults can get it too. It is caused by the herpes varicella-zoster virus (VZV). It is rare to get chickenpox while pregnant. In the UK, it is estimated that 3 in 1,000 women (0.3 per cent) catch chickenpox during pregnancy [80]. Most pregnant women who get chickenpox recover, with no harmful effects on the baby. However, in some rare instances it may cause complications for both the pregnant woman and the baby. Seek advice from your midwife, obstetrician or doctor if:

- you think you may have chickenpox
- you have been near someone who has it (even if you have no rash or other symptoms)
- you get chickenpox within seven days of giving birth

You may be offered aciclovir, an antiviral medicine, which should be given within 24 hours of the chickenpox rash appearing. Aciclovir does not cure chickenpox, but it can make the symptoms, such as fever, less severe and help prevent complications. However, aciclovir is usually only recommended if you are more than 20 weeks pregnant, as it carries some risks [81]. Chinese herbs can be given to help relieve the symptoms of chickenpox and can be more effective than pharmaceutical medicines with fewer risks [82].

Shingles

Shingles is a painful, blotchy rash on one side of the body. It mainly affects the skin, but can sometimes affect the eyes too. You can only get shingles if you have already had chickenpox. Both illnesses are caused by the same virus: VZV. After you recover from chickenpox, the virus stays in your body and can become active again later in the form of shingles. You cannot catch shingles from someone else. Anyone can get it, but it is most common in older people. If you develop shingles when you are pregnant, it is usually mild and there is no risk to you or your baby[83]. However, you should contact your midwife, obstetrician or doctor for advice as you may need antiviral treatment. Chinese herbs can be used to treat the pain[84].

COVID-19 test

Early research has shown that COVID-19 can affect placenta blood flow but does not cross the placenta[85][86]. Women who are overweight during pregnancy are more likely to be hospitalised and are more likely to have a preterm birth[87]. However, the latest research at time of writing states that the rate of infection from mother to baby is low and is not increased by having a vaginal birth, breastfeeding or when the baby is kept close (rooming in)[88][89]. Fortunately, breast milk can protect a baby from the coronavirus[90].

If you think you may have been in contact with someone who showed symptoms of COVID-19 or you think you may have had the virus, I would recommend getting yourself tested. This helps your obstetrician or midwife to monitor blood flow to your placenta.

For most women, the risk of getting an infection is low, especially with the world's new awareness of infections and the additional precautions in place to prevent them. Let's now look at ways you can make your pregnancy even safer for you and your baby.

Chapter 5

Pregnancy Disorders

During pregnancy some women may experience problems ranging from minor to more problematic. It is difficult to predict what you will experience. As a general rule, your pregnancy symptoms and any problems may be similar to those that your mother experienced, but not always. You may just want to dip into this chapter as and when you need, so as to not cause you unnecessary anxiety. I have included the more serious problems in this chapter so the small minority of women experiencing these have the information readily at hand.

Bleeding in Pregnancy

Some women will bleed during early pregnancy. This is every woman's worst fear as they think they are miscarrying. However, this is not always the case, so try not to panic. As the pregnancy takes hold, changes taking place within the uterus can cause pockets of blood (often polyps or cysts) to become dislodged, which then rupture causing bleeding. The bloody discharge is either red or dark red in colour. Sometimes there will be pain too as these pockets of blood push on surrounding body parts. This is actually a good thing as the pregnancy is helping to clean up and heal the uterus. Some women will bleed only in early pregnancy while others will bleed throughout their whole pregnancy, although this is rare. In such cases, make sure you take an additional iron supplement and ask your midwife, obstetrician or doctor to regularly check your blood and iron levels.

Anxiety and Stress

Being anxious is common during pregnancy. Worrying about the pregnancy is normal. Women can also feel a great sense of responsibility once pregnant, as they are the ones 'carrying the baby' and are responsible for its growth and health. The pressure to do and eat the right things can cause anxiety, pressure and stress.

Stressful situations should be avoided in pregnancy as they can affect levels of stress hormones in your body, which can then affect the developmental growth of your baby. Studies have shown that there are long-term side effects to a child who has been exposed to stress while in the womb, for example attention deficit hyperactivity disorder (ADHD) [91]. Stress can also delay the onset of a natural labour. Acupuncture is very good at reducing anxiety, improving sleep and energy levels, and reducing depression in pregnancy [39] [41] [42] [43] [44]. Pregnancy yoga, meditation, calming music, walks in Nature and hypnobirthing can also be used to reduce anxiety and stress. A foot bath with lavender is useful to have during pregnancy as it helps to reduce anxiety, stress and depression [92].

Morning Sickness and Nausea

Morning sickness does not necessarily just take place in the morning; it can last throughout the day or occur in the evening time. However, as most women experience it in the morning, it is referred to as morning sickness. Around 70 per cent of pregnant women will experience morning sickness [8]. The severity of morning sickness can be divided into three groups (see the table below). Odours such as cooking smells, especially fried foods, seafood, coffee, cigarette smoke, cleaning products and artificial odours such as perfume and air fresheners, can trigger feelings of nausea and vomiting [93]. For most women, it will usually subside between weeks 12 and 16.

Level	Symptoms
Mild NVP	Nausea and occasional morning vomiting
Moderate NVP	More persistent vomiting
Severe NVP	Hyperemesis gravidarum

Table 9. The levels of nausea and vomiting in pregnancy (NVP) [57]

The ways you can relieve nausea include:

- Drinking fizzy (carbonated) drinks that do not contain sugar, caffeine or artificial sweeteners, such as fizzy water.

- Drinking ginger tea or eating ginger biscuits. If you have heartburn (acid reflux), substitute ginger for mint or peppermint.

- Eating every two hours.

- Eating little and often as soon as you wake up in the morning.

- Eating plain food, such as crackers, dried biscuits or toast.

- Having acupuncture regularly. This is very effective in dealing with nausea [94]. As the effects of each acupuncture session last three to four days, it is best to have treatment twice a week.

- Trying not to eat big meals or rich foods.

- Wearing travel sickness bands on your wrist. These push on to the acupuncture point acupuncturists use to treat nausea (Neiguan, PC6). Research has confirmed that applying pressure to this point reduces morning sickness [95] [96] [97] [98].

Around 0.5–2 per cent of women may experience hyperemesis gravidarum (HG), which is a serious condition that requires intravenous fluids, electrolyte replacements and sometimes nutritional support. Severe nausea and vomiting during pregnancy can cause hyperthyroidism. Hyperemesis gravidarum usually resolves itself by week 18 [4].

The treatment in Western medicine is to use antihistamine H1-receptor blockers such as promethazine, or in more severe cases prochlorperazine, cyclizine or metoclopramide, with the latter causing temporary neurological side effects [99]. Vitamin B_1 (thiamine) is often given alongside medications to prevent neurological problems [57].

Heartburn

Heartburn (acid reflux) usually occurs further into the pregnancy when the baby grows and pushes the stomach up, compressing it, causing heartburn, although some women may experience heartburn earlier. There are various antacids on the market that effectively treat heartburn and are popular with pregnant women.

Foods that are acidic or eating large meals can aggravate heartburn [4], while sitting upright can help to reduce it [57]. Most over-the-counter antacids are safe to take in pregnancy. However, some contain sweeteners, which I would avoid taking while pregnant.

Prescription antacid medications such as H2-receptor antagonists (H2RAs) and proton pump inhibitors (PPIs) are the main treatment for women who suffer from severe indigestion (dyspepsia) and heartburn (gastroesophageal reflux) in pregnancy [100]. Research has shown that use of these medications during pregnancy can increase the risk of the child developing asthma [101]. Acupuncture can be used to treat heartburn and indigestion in pregnancy without any side effects [102] [103] [104].

Hypertension

Hypertension is when a pregnant woman has high blood pressure during pregnancy. There are two different levels of hypertension in pregnancy:

1. Mild hypertension: systolic pressure between 140 and 180mmHg or a diastolic pressure between 90 and 100mmHg or both.

2. Severe hypertension: systolic pressure greater than 180mmHg or a diastolic pressure greater than 100mmHg or both [4].

There are four drugs that can be prescribed to treat hypertension, all of which are given orally:

1. Methyldopa. Side effects include: stomach upset, dry and inflamed mouth, slow heart rate, hypotension, swelling, drowsiness, headaches, dizziness, lack of energy, muscle pain, joint pain, pins and needles, nightmares, psychosis, depression, impaired mental thinking, Parkinson's-like symptoms, Bell's palsy, inflamed liver and pancreas, jaundice, anaemia, reduced blood production, abnormal blood, rashes and nasal congestion. This drug should not be taken if the mother suffers from depression. It is not known to be harmful to the baby, although the side effects can weaken the mother [99].

2. Labetalol. Side effects include: hypotension, tiredness, weakness, headaches, rashes, scalp tingling, difficulty urinating, stomach pain, nausea, vomiting and liver damage. It can affect the growth of the baby and reduce their heart rate. It should not be taken in the first trimester. It can also affect the baby if the mother is breastfeeding [99].

3. Hydralazine. Side effects include: rapid heart rate, palpitations, flushing, hypotension, fluid retention, stomach upset, headaches, dizziness, fever, inflamed nerves in hands, pins and needles, joint pain, muscle pain, difficult breathing, nasal congestion, agitation, anxiety, anorexia, blood disorders, abnormal liver function, jaundice, protein and blood in the urine. It can reduce the platelet count in the baby. It should not be used in the first or second trimester. It can still be present in breast milk but is not known to be harmful [99].

4. Nifedipine. Side effects include: stomach upset, hypotension, swelling, palpitations, dizziness, headaches and tiredness. It

should not be taken before week 20 of pregnancy or when breastfeeding. It can prevent labour starting[99].

Acupuncture is good at helping to reduce hypertension without any side effects[105][106][107][108][109].

Low blood pressure

Some women may have low rather than high blood pressure during pregnancy, especially in the middle of the pregnancy, than at other times. Low blood pressure is a sign of a blood deficiency in Chinese medicine, brought on by the mother being drained. Taking iron supplements throughout pregnancy helps to ensure adequate levels of blood and can reduce the risk of developing low blood pressure. Having low blood pressure and a lack of blood can reduce the baby's growth rate[110].

Pre-eclampsia

Pre-eclampsia is a combination of hypertension with protein in the urine (proteinuria). It affects 3–5 per cent of pregnancies[3]. The symptoms of pre-eclampsia include:

- headaches
- high blood pressure (>140/90mmHg) together with protein in the urine (>0.3g)

- seizures
- stomach pain
- swelling
- visual disturbances

Classification of pre-eclampsia can vary, but is generally divided into three degrees of severity, as shown in the table on the next page.

Level	Symptoms
Mild	Protein in the urine with blood pressure greater than 140/90mmHg
Moderate	Protein in the urine with blood pressure greater than 160/110mmHg
Severe	Protein in the urine with blood pressure greater than 140/90mmHg after 34 weeks

Table 10. The classification of pre-eclampsia [57]

Predisposing factors for developing pre-eclampsia include:

- diabetes
- family history (mother or sister)
- first pregnancy
- more than 10 years since previous pregnancy
- multiple pregnancies
- obesity
- older age
- pre-existing hypertension
- previous pre-eclampsia
- renal disease [57]

There is no cure in Western medicine for pre-eclampsia, only management until the baby is born. Aspirin (acetylsalicylic acid) is often recommended by obstetricians, as it can reduce the incidence of pre-eclampsia by 15 per cent [3]. However, aspirin has an impact on the male baby's testosterone development if taken during pregnancy and can increase bleeding during labour and afterwards [111] [112] [113] [114]. Adequate calcium intake during pregnancy (1000mg) has been shown to reduce the risk of developing pre-eclampsia [115]. Magnesium sulphate can be used to prevent seizures and reduces the rate by 50 per cent [116]. New research has shown that a compound found in vitamin B3 (nicotinamide) can reduce blood pressure and prolong pregnancies in women with pre-eclampsia [117]. Acupuncture can also reduce high blood pressure in pregnant women and prevent pre-eclampsia [118] [119].

Urinary Tract Infection (UTI)

Some women may experience a UTI while pregnant. Symptoms include:

- blood in the urine
- needing to urinate suddenly or more often than usual
- pain or a burning sensation when urinating
- smelly or cloudy urine [120]

When asked to supply a urine sample by your midwife, obstetrician or doctor, you will need to clean your vulva first and then catch a portion of your urine during the middle of uninterrupted flow, known as 'clean-catch midstream'[4]. If you have a UTI, antibiotics such as ciprofloxacin or levofloxacin (avoid while breastfeeding) will be prescribed [4] [99]. The following antibiotics should be avoided in pregnancy, if possible:

- gatifloxacin
- trimethoprim
- sulfamethoxazole [99]

You can also use natural ways to clear the infection, such as:

- Drinking plenty of water and cranberry juice.
- Using a condom during sexual intercourse.
- Taking probiotics.
- Wiping from front to back.

Constipation and Haemorrhoids

Constipation is common during pregnancy affecting around 20 per cent of women [57]. It is often caused by constriction of the intestines by the baby, increased transit time, increased water absorption, decreased bulk, increased levels of progesterone and iron supplements [121]. Women will often change their diet when pregnant, which can be another cause of sluggish bowel movements as the body readjusts.

Drinking more water and eating more fruit as well as nuts and seeds can help to better regulate bowel movements. Acupuncture can help regulate the digestive system and promote regular bowel movements [122] [123]. Otherwise, mild laxatives such as docusate can be used for a short time to help relieve constipation [124] [125] [126]. However, laxatives should be used only as a last resort as they can stimulate the uterus lining, which can cause problems [3] [127] [128]. Women are also often advised to take supplemental dietary fibres such as psyllium hydrophilic mucilloid [4].

Haemorrhoids are commonly seen during pregnancy and postnatally. They are an enlargement of the haemorrhoidal vein caused by constipation, the weight of the uterus and the process of giving birth [3] [129]. The treatment of haemorrhoids involves relieving constipation and the use of creams and ointments [130]. A sitz bath can also be used during pregnancy when the mother has haemorrhoids, and it is an effective form of treatment [131]. Haemorrhoids usually reduce after delivery, although some women will have them but less pronounced. In such cases acupuncture and Chinese herbs can help to reduce them [132].

Headaches

Some women will experience headaches during pregnancy. The reasons for this are unknown in Western medicine. In Chinese medicine, additional heat caused by the growing baby and being physically drained during pregnancy can lead to headaches. In such cases, I do not recommend taking painkillers of any type as they may harm the baby (see page 82). Instead, use cold compresses, drink plenty of water, have acupuncture or a massage, apply Tiger balm to your head, and eat, sleep and rest [133] [134] [135] [136].

Back Pain

It is common to experience backache and even sciatica during pregnancy. Ligaments relaxing and the weight of the baby are usually the cause. If you have pain, try not to take any painkillers as they may harm the baby (see page 82). If you have pain anywhere other than the abdomen, you can use a hot water bottle or a heat pad on the painful area, which should help. Ointments such as Tiger balm can also be used to relieve muscle tension and pain. Avoid wearing shoes with high heels as they can cause back pain. A back brace and a firm mattress may also help. Alternatively, ask your partner for a back massage or see a professional who can give you a pregnancy massage. If the pain is acute, you can use acupuncture to relieve the pain. Acupuncture is safe and very effective for the relief of back pain [137] [138] [139] [140] [141] [142] [143]. If you do not like needles, then osteopathy is also an effective treatment for back pain in pregnancy.

Pelvic Girdle Pain (PGP)

Pregnancy-related PGP (or symphysis pubis dysfunction, SPD) affects one in three pregnant women. Different women can have different symptoms and PGP is worse for some than others. Symptoms include:

- Pain across one or both sides of your lower back.
- Pain in the area between your vagina and anus (perineum).
- Pain over the pubic bone at the front around the centre.

Pain can also radiate to your thighs and some women feel or hear a clicking or grinding in the pelvic area. The pain can be most noticeable when you are:

- Getting out of a car or bed.
- Going upstairs or walking uphill.
- Turning over in bed.
- Walking.

Research has shown that acupuncture can help reduce PGP and is safe to use in pregnancy [139] [140]. Alternatively, a chiropractor or osteopath that specialises in treating pregnant women can help to relieve the pain. Pregnancy yoga can also help to reduce PGP. I would recommend sleeping with a pillow in between your legs, keeping your legs together when turning your body, for example getting out of a car or bed, and avoiding lifting anything heavy.

Carpal Tunnel Syndrome

Carpal tunnel syndrome is when the carpal tunnel inside your wrist swells and squeezes a nerve leading to pins and needles (paraesthesia) of the fingers and numbness [3]. Hands can appear swollen and are painful. Often it is worse at night. Night splints (braces) can be used for night-time relief. Sometimes, the numbness causes a substantial lack of sensation in the hands that leads to some pregnant women accidentally harming their hands, i.e. burns.

As there is a lack of energy to the hands, they lose sensation (numbness) and can tingle. Acupuncture can give some temporarily relief of these symptoms [144] [145] [146] [147]. Putting the hands in cold water can also offer temporary relief. This condition will normally resolve itself after giving birth.

Leg Cramps

Leg cramps affect around one in three pregnant women [3]. Often cramps are felt in the calf muscles. Keeping the legs elevated and making sure you are taking enough calcium can help to relieve symptoms. Alternatively, massage, osteopathy and acupuncture can give temporary relief [148].

Swollen Ankles

Swollen ankles are a common problem in pregnancy, especially in the warmer months. By itself this is not abnormal and is caused by impaired blood flow. However, swollen ankles (oedema) can be associated with hypertension. Ankles as well as feet can swell up and are often worse towards the end of pregnancy. I have seen women in my clinic increase two shoe sizes during pregnancy. The swelling reduces once the baby is born. Keeping the legs elevated and wearing support stockings or tights can help. Acupuncture can also help to increase blood flow and reduce swelling [149].

Small Baby

A small baby means that the baby is growing slower than normal and the baby's weight is lower than it should be. Small babies can be described in several ways; intrauterine growth restriction (IUGR), small for dates (SFD), small for gestational age (SGA) and foetal growth restriction (FGR). Constitutional factors, such as being a first-time mum, small parents, mothers who are Asian or those who are carrying a girl, can naturally lead to a smaller baby, which is normal [57].

A baby's growth is measured using a percentile system (see graph below). Generally, a 'normal' growth pattern would match that of a 50 percentile line. Those that follow a 10 percentile line are classified as suffering from IUGR, while those babies that follow the 90 percentile line are classified as large for gestational age. The use of gestational percentiles remains limited [4]. They are primarily used to highlight high-risk babies rather than as a definitive guide to monitor the growth of the baby through pregnancy. Factors that can lead to a small baby include:

- anticonvulsant medications [4]
- chromosomal issues
- mothers being physically weak
- older mums (over 35)
- placenta factors
- pre-eclampsia
- smoking during pregnancy [3]
- viral infection
- warfarin
- young mums (under 16)

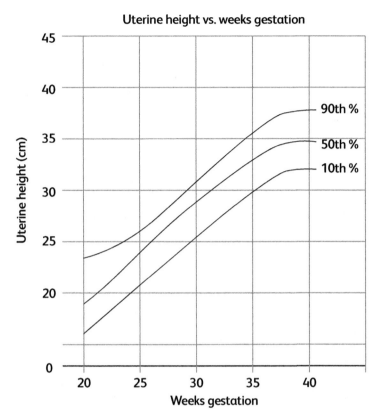

Graph 1. The different percentiles that gauge baby growth

Ultrasound scans are used to accurately check the size of the baby [3], while Doppler ultrasounds can be used to measure blood flow to the placenta (see page 30). During your antenatal check-ups, your bump may be measured using a tape measure to check how well your baby is growing. In my opinion, using a tape measure is an inaccurate method for measuring the size of your baby and should not be used, as bumps come in all shapes and sizes. Inaccurate measurements taken using a tape measure can cause unnecessary stress to the mother, which can in turn affect the baby.

The treatment for a small baby is the use of steroids before week 34 [57]. Acupuncture, Chinese herbs and iron supplements can help if the cause of the poor growth is physical exhaustion of the mother [150]

[151] [152] [153]. Eating more protein, essential fatty acids and iron-rich foods can all help to improve the mother's energy levels, which are then passed on to the baby, aiding their growth (see Chapter Twelve for dietary recommendations during pregnancy).

Gestational Diabetes

Gestational diabetes mellitus (GDM) only occurs during pregnancy. Around 2–5 per cent of expectant mothers will develop this condition [4] [8]. GDM can occur at any stage of pregnancy, but is more common in the second or third trimester [154]. It occurs when the mother's body cannot produce enough insulin to meet the demands of pregnancy. For most mothers, GDM ceases after giving birth, but some may develop type 2 diabetes in later life.

In mothers with GDM, their baby may grow larger than normal (macrosomia) due to the continuous supply of glucose [8]. This can increase the need for a caesarean delivery. The mother will also be in a higher risk category of developing pre-eclampsia and polyhydramnios (an excessive amount of amniotic fluid) or having a preterm labour, while the baby has a higher risk of congenital abnormalities, developing diabetes or jaundice or having poor health in early life [3] [8] [154]. It is therefore important to manage glucose (sugar) levels during pregnancy.

Those at a higher risk of developing GDM include those with a family history of diabetes, those from an Asian, Black, African-Caribbean or Middle Eastern origin, those with a BMI over 30 or those who previously had GDM or have given birth to a baby heavier than 4.5kg/10lb [154].

Women who are at risk of developing GDM will have their glucose levels checked between weeks 16 and 28, depending upon where they live and the obstetrician. Glucose levels are checked by taking a blood sample before and after drinking a sugary drink. This test is called an oral glucose tolerance test (OGTT), a glucose challenge test (GCT) or a glucose loading test (GLT). A GLT is a non-fasting test, whereas an OGTT and a GCT involve fasting. Fasting can be difficult for some women who need to eat if they are feeling nauseous or tired. A blood sample is taken in the morning when you have not had any food or drink for 8–10 hours (you can usually still drink water). You are then given a glucose drink. After resting for one to two hours, another blood sample is taken to see how your body is processing the glucose. GDM is diagnosed if glucose levels are >5.1mmol/L and/or after two hours at a level >8.5mmol/L [3]. Treatment for GDM includes eating a diabetic diet, which involves:

- Avoiding foods that contain sucrose, glucose, dextrose, fructose, lactose, maltose, honey, invert sugar, sugar, syrup, corn sweetener and molasses.
- Avoiding sugary drinks such as fizzy drinks, fruit juices and smoothies.
- Avoiding sugary foods such as cakes, biscuits, ice cream and chocolate.
- Eating some fruits and vegetables.
- Eating regularly and avoiding skipping meals.
- Eating more protein.
- Eating starchy and low-glycaemic index (GI) foods that release sugar slowly, such as wholewheat pasta, brown rice, whole oats, buckwheat, granary bread, all-bran cereals, pulses, chickpeas, beans, lentils, muesli and plain porridge.
- Taking myo-inositol supplements [155] [156] [157] [158].

If changes to your diet do not reduce glucose levels, metformin and insulin therapy may be prescribed by your obstetrician [3]. Acupuncture can be used either before or alongside metformin to control insulin levels [159] [160] [161] [162].

Bleeding Gums

Some women may experience bleeding gums during pregnancy, which is known as pregnancy gingivitis. Bleeding of the gums may be caused by a build-up of plaque on the teeth. Hormonal changes during pregnancy can make the gums more vulnerable to plaque, leading to inflammation and bleeding. It does not mean that you have a lack of calcium or necessarily gum disease. Bleeding gums can be caused by excessive heat in Chinese medicine, which causes inflammation and bleeding or being run-down and tired. Make sure you floss twice daily to ensure good gum health and eat cooling foods and tonics (see Chapter Twelve).

Depression

Some women may experience depression during pregnancy, which is normal. This may be caused by a combination of factors, such as feeling overwhelmed about being pregnant and the future, together with the physical changes, lack of energy and nausea. For women who are tired, their social and lifestyle activities may be sacrificed in favour of rest and sleep, which can lead to feelings of depression, although this is often mild.

It is important to talk to your partner, friends and family or a healthcare professional and ask for help. It is a big job growing another human being! Try not to feel guilty about needing extra help with things. Being pregnant is a big change, even before the baby is born. Feeling tired, experiencing discomfort, nausea and an inability to do much except the minimum can be normal. Remember that it will not last forever and will pass with time. It is not ideal to take antidepressants in pregnancy unless absolutely necessary (see page 86). Research has shown that acupuncture can be an alternative to antidepressants as it is able to reduce depression rates in pregnant women and is safe to use without any side effects [44] [163] [164] [165] [166] [167].

Placenta Disorders

There are several disorders of the placenta.

Placenta previa

Placenta previa is where the placenta grows over the cervix, blocking the baby's exit and natural delivery route. There are four classifications of placenta previa:

1. low-lying
2. marginal
3. partial
4. complete [4]

Placenta previa occurs in around 1 in 200 pregnancies [8] and causes include:

- older mothers (over 40) [168]
- pregnant with more than one baby
- previous caesarean delivery
- previous placenta previa
- smoking

A transvaginal ultrasound is used to locate the placenta and see if it is blocking the cervix. Most women with placenta previa will experience some bleeding without pain, usually at around weeks 29–30, which is normal. If the placenta previa is low-lying or partial, the problem may resolve itself by weeks 32–35, allowing for a natural vaginal delivery [4]. In other instances where the placenta previa is complete, a caesarean delivery will be used, often around weeks 36–38 once the baby's lungs are mature.

Placental abruption

Placental abruption is when the placenta separates from the uterus wall before birth. There are three classifications of placental abruption:

1. marginal abruption
2. partial abruption
3. complete abruption [4]

Placental abruption occurs in around 1 in 120 pregnancies [8]. It is a potentially serious condition for both mother and baby. Increased risks of developing placental abruption stem from:

- a high number of previous pregnancies
- pre-eclampsia [57]
- pre-existing hypertension
- a deficiency of folic acid and vitamin B_{12} [169]
- thrombophilia (inherited blood-clotting) [169]
- smoking while pregnant [169] [170]
- cocaine and amphetamine use while pregnant [171]
- IUGR [57]
- the use of in vitro fertilisation (IVF) and intracytoplasmic sperm injection (ICSI) to achieve pregnancy [172] [173] [174]
- twin pregnancies [169]
- women over 40 years of age [175]

Often a Doppler ultrasonography is used to determine placental abruption. However, magnetic resonance imaging (MRI) is a more precise examination [176]. If placental abruption occurs before week 34, is minor and the baby is not distressed, steroids are often prescribed to the mother alongside close monitoring of the placenta and baby [57]. From week 37 onwards, the baby will often be medically induced for delivery [57] and, in some instances, a caesarean delivery will be performed [3].

Placenta accreta

Placenta accreta is a serious pregnancy condition that occurs when the placenta grows too deeply into the uterine wall. There are three classifications of placenta accreta:

1. placenta accrete (superficial intrusion)
2. placenta increta (moderate intrusion)
3. placenta percreta (complete intrusion) [4]

Fortunately, this is a rare condition and is only seen in around 1 in 7,000 pregnancies [8]. The risk is higher, however, if you had a previous caesarean delivery [4]. Normally, the placenta detaches from the uterine wall after childbirth. With placenta accreta, part or the entire placenta remains attached. This can cause severe blood loss after delivery.

Vasa previa

Vasa previa is when there is bleeding from the umbilical vessels. It is a rare condition that occurs in around 1 in 5,000 pregnancies [57]. Unfortunately, it is not usually detected using an ultrasound. Instead, a colour flow Doppler ultrasound can detect vasa previa [3]. The only form of treatment is to perform an emergency caesarean delivery [8] [57].

Oligohydramnios

Oligohydramnios is an abnormally small amount of amniotic fluid surrounding the baby in the uterus. It occurs in 5–8 per cent of pregnancies. Oligohydramnios is diagnosed by ultrasound when the total amniotic fluid volume is less than 300ml (10½oz) or when the amniotic fluid index (AFI) is less than 5cm (2in) [8]. Causes of polyhydramnios include:

- non-steroidal anti-inflammatory drugs (NSAIDs) [8]
- insufficient blood flow [177]

Oligohydramnios can lead to a prolonged pregnancy and FGR [3]. Oligohydramnios can be treated naturally by increasing water and iron intake and by using Chinese herbal medicine. The Chinese herb Dan Shen *(salvia miltiorrhiza)* has been shown in research to be an effective treatment for oligohydramnios [177]. Consult a qualified and accredited Chinese herbalist before taking Dan Shen *(salvia miltiorrhiza)* in pregnancy. Other treatments include:

- acupuncture [178]
- amnio-infusion during labour through an intrauterine catheter

- injection of fluid prior to delivery
- intravenous (IV) fluids

Polyhydramnios

Polyhydramnios is an excessive accumulation of amniotic fluid surrounding the baby in the uterus. It is a rare condition and is seen in 0.5–1.5 per cent of pregnancies. Causes of polyhydramnios include:

- diabetes [4]
- NSAIDs [8]

Polyhydramnios is diagnosed by ultrasound when the total amniotic fluid volume is greater than 2 litres (68oz) or when the AFI is higher than 25cm (9½in). Polyhydramnios can cause pregnancy complications such as laboured breathing (dyspnoea), water retention (oedema), breech baby, a difficult labour and excessive blood loss [8].

Treatment for polyhydramnios usually involves either draining the excessive amniotic fluid or the administration of pharmaceutical drugs such as indomethacin [8]. Indomethacin is generally contraindicated during pregnancy as it can increase the risk of closure of the blood vessel connecting the pulmonary artery to the proximal descending aorta (foetal ductus arteriosus) and can cause high blood pressure (pulmonary hypertension) in the baby and can bring on labour [8] [99]. Natural alternative treatments for polyhydramnios include the use of Chinese herbal medicines, which do not have side effects [179].

Deep Vein Thrombosis (DVT)

A DVT (venous thromboembolism) is when a clot forms in a deep vein within the calf muscle of the lower leg. The majority of DVTs are in the left leg [3]. The lower leg (below the knee) can feel heavy or painful and may be swollen and tender. A Doppler ultrasound is often used to diagnose a DVT [8]. It is often caused by poor blood flow returning from the legs to the heart and increased blood-clotting during pregnancy. DVT occurs in around 1 per cent of pregnancies[57]. Risk factors include:

- a BMI greater than 30
- a family history of thrombophilia or DVT
- being sedentary for more than four days
- mothers older than 35 years
- pre-eclampsia
- smoking
- the use of IVF to conceive
- underlying illnesses such as heart or lung disease
- varicose veins [3]

Do not massage the area or apply heat to the calf muscle as this may cause the blood clot to break off causing more serious problems [180]. Anticoagulant drugs are often given to thin the blood, such as heparin (LMWH).

Part Two

Chinese Medicine's View of Pregnancy

China has the largest population in the world and therefore has the most successful rates of pregnancy. This is largely thanks to the traditional form of medicine practised in China, known as Chinese medicine. It may therefore be useful for your pregnancy if you know how some background theory of Chinese medicine.

Chapter 6

The Five Essentials of Chinese Medicine

Within Chinese medicine, there are five main substances involved in pregnancy:

1. yin
2. yang
3. qi (energy)
4. blood
5. jing (essence)

Making sure that you have adequate levels of all these substances will help to ensure the healthy growth and development of your baby.

Yin and Yang

Yin and yang is the most important concept in Chinese medicine. Most people have heard of yin and yang and know the famous symbol, as shown below, but perhaps do not know how they relate to pregnancy.

Women are predominantly yin, while men are predominantly yang. Oestrogens are yin, while testosterone is yang. Yin and yang should be in balance. When they fall out of balance, dis-ease occurs. Yin and yang are rooted in Nature. They come from observing the world around us. If we fight against the laws of Nature, our health can suffer.

If there is too much testosterone (yang) being given to the baby, they will be more masculine. If there is too much oestrogen (yin) being given to the baby, they will be more feminine.

Figure 1. Yin and yang symbol

Qi

Qi (pronounced 'chee') is the same as energy. However, in East Asia, energy has more functions than just giving us energy and power [181]. It holds our organs in place, including the baby, and helps to prevent a miscarriage. Qi also protects the body from viruses and bacteria by maintaining the immune system. It keeps the body warm, including the uterus, thereby making it a suitable environment for your baby to call home for nine months. For these reasons, qi is yang in Nature.

Western medicine can measure a person's energy expenditure and energy intake, but it cannot measure their current energy level. Chinese medicine can measure a person's current energy level through pulse diagnosis [182].

Energy levels decrease with age. You may see young people walking around in the cold wearing fewer clothes than others. This is because as they are young, they have more energy, which aids in keeping them warm (yang). In the elderly, they are often cold and need to heat their homes more than younger people, as they have less energy (yang) as they have spent it through living.

When asked, most people will say their energy levels are good. However, upon pulse diagnosis, I find that it can be weak. This is because some people have their awareness plugged into their thoughts. We are more than our thoughts; we are the awareness that sits behind our thoughts. We tend to identify with our thoughts as we are constantly plugged into them. If you can unplug your awareness from your thoughts and plug it into your body, some people will find their body is weak and wants to rest. You can unplug your awareness from your thoughts through activities such as meditation, pregnancy yoga and mindfulness.

As a pregnant mother, it is normal that you would sacrifice a part of your health for your baby, but unfortunately your body does not function like this. It is a survival organism that will only support the baby if you, the mother, have enough energy after your daily needs have been met. Energy is finite – there is only so much you have. If you spend too much of your energy working, commuting, socialising, exercising or using technology such as social media, you will have less energy left over for your baby (see figure 2 on the next page).

To improve the health of your pregnancy, I recommend doing less and conserving resources to support and grow your baby. Doing less is difficult for some people as our minds tell us that we need to work hard to get what we want or finish off those things on our 'to-do list' before the baby arrives so we can allow ourselves to relax. In terms of your pregnancy, it is the opposite: doing less will actually improve your pregnancy. Start trying to listen to your body rather than your thoughts as it is your body that will have your baby, not your mind!

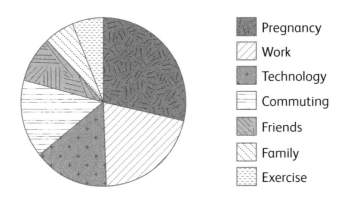

Figure 2. An estimate of energy expenditure in a typical person

Blood

Blood is similar in Chinese medicine as it is in Western medicine. It nourishes the body and the uterus and feeds your baby. Blood goes hand-in-hand with qi. Where qi goes, blood goes. A lack of qi can sometimes mean blood is not sent to the areas where it is needed, i.e. the uterus. Great demands are placed upon blood when growing the placenta and your baby.

The body lives in the now and will react to the environment it is put in. Working or commuting long hours will deplete energy and blood as the body thinks it needs to spend these resources fighting for survival. The body will move energy and blood to this fight, leaving less left over for your baby. This can affect the baby's growth rate and size.

Having cold hands and feet is a sign of a lack of blood and qi. Blood is like the water in your home's central heating system, while qi is the boiler that heats it and moves it. If you have a lack of blood, there is less of it to keep the whole body warm. The body will keep the main organs warm at the expense of the hands and feet, which are less important. Blood nourishes the whole body – the muscles, skin, the placenta and the baby. For these reasons, it is categorised as yin.

As blood is the same in Chinese medicine as it is in Western medicine, if you are anaemic in Western medicine, you will be lacking blood in Chinese medicine too. However, there are two distinct differences:

1. Chinese medicine will diagnose you as lacking in blood a lot sooner than Western medicine. This is because the Western medical range of what is a good amount of blood is narrow and relates to illnesses such as anaemia. The range in Chinese medicine is a lot broader, allowing Chinese medical practitioners to identify a lack of blood sooner and treat it in order to optimise a person's health long before it develops into a problem. I have often seen women at the start of their pregnancy and told them they are lacking in blood only for it to be confirmed months later by a blood test. It is best for the baby's health to treat it as soon as it is diagnosed.

2. In Chinese medicine, overexerting yourself can reduce levels of blood in the body. Just as when you do too much and you feel tired and have a lack of energy, you can also have a lack of blood. Levels of blood can fluctuate like energy levels and potentially affect your pregnancy. A good example of blood levels fluctuating is during a growth spurt of the baby.

Blood does more than just move oxygen around the body; it carries your hormones and immune system, it is needed to thicken the uterus lining and grow the placenta, as well as helping your baby to grow. This is why extra iron is needed during pregnancy.

Jing

Jing translates into English as essence [183]. Essence is a more concentrated form of yin. It is like concentrated moisturising cream but in a fluid form that the body uses. It is related to our genes and the baby's chromosomes. We are born with a set amount of jing that we inherit from our parents and which we in turn pass on to our children.

If we have good amounts of jing, we pass that on to our child, like passing on good genes. Having good levels of jing comes from having good levels of yin, which in turn comes from having good levels of blood.

Chapter 7

Acupuncture All the Way!

Acupuncture is one of the most popular alternative therapies for pregnant women. Acupuncture does more than just relax you; it balances the hypothalamus, thereby enhancing pregnancy hormones from the pituitary gland as well as regulating energy and blood flow to the uterus, which aids the growth of your baby. All this helps to maintain a healthy pregnancy and labour.

History of acupuncture

Acupuncture is often viewed as a strange form of therapy originating from East Asia where they are all Buddhists. This is far from the truth! There is now some proof with the discovery of the frozen Ötzi tattoo man found in the Italian Alps in 1991 that acupuncture may have been around in Europe over 5,000 years ago [184]. Therefore, acupuncture may not necessarily belong to East Asia. What is known is that its use has been well-documented in East Asia for over 2,000 years and it has a long and successful history. When people think of acupuncture, they tend to think of China. However, acupuncture has been practised all over East Asia, including Japan, Korea and Vietnam. It is therefore not the sole property of the Chinese, though they had the most influence in its development.

Acupuncture probably originated in ancient times through massage (acupressure and scraping), when people would massage a point on the body and found that it helped another part of the body that was in discomfort. People in East Asia then added their unique understanding and awareness of Nature to these points to give us the acupuncture we know today.

The technology used to make acupuncture needles, or rather pins, has evolved over the centuries from stone, to thick needles to the ultra-fine pins we use today [185]. In the West, these ultra-fine pins are just used once and then disposed of in a special container (sharps box), which is then incinerated for health and safety reasons.

A country's success is greatly influenced by the medicine it uses. Its fertility and pregnancy rate are all largely dependent upon the healthcare system practised within that country. The Chinese population are successful in all these areas of life, due to their cultural awareness of Nature, diet, lifestyle and the medicine they use. It is therefore no wonder that the Chinese have the largest population in the world. This is largely thanks to Chinese medicine.

Is acupuncture safe in pregnancy?

Research studies have found acupuncture to be very safe during pregnancy [186] [187]. However, in most Western countries, obstetricians, physiotherapists, osteopaths, chiropractors and nurses can legally perform 'acupuncture' after just a short course. It is not possible to learn over 2,000 years of medicine in a few weekends. This can have an effect upon the safety and efficacy of the acupuncture treatment. Therefore, I would recommend only having acupuncture from a qualified and accredited acupuncturist.

How does acupuncture work?

Acupuncture is made up of points on the body where the energy can be influenced. These points connect together to form the channels (meridians). These channels look like the underground (tube or metro) map, with lots of different lines crisscrossing each other. The stations are like the acupuncture points. Each point has an associated health property. By inserting a pin into the acupuncture point, it tells the body to initiate a healing response.

Generally, acupuncture is good at helping to regulate energy and blood flow throughout the body. When these two important aspects are regulated, the body is able to heal itself and return to a state of balance (known as 'homeostasis' in Western medicine). During an acupuncture session, you may go into a deep state of relaxation where you are able to switch off from your worries and stresses, allowing the body to heal itself.

Today there are currently two theories as to how acupuncture works and what makes up the acupuncture points and channels. Within Western medical thinking, it is believed acupuncture works on the nervous system, hence its ability to relieve pain. However, this theory is not recognised within the acupuncture community, or in East Asia, because acupuncture is able to do a lot more than just relieve pain. A better theory originates from Korea, where researchers believe they have found the channels anatomically within the body [188]. They believe they have observed the acupuncture channels running within the lymphatic (immune) system [189]. Other research conducted in Belgium also found the same structures [190].

How will I feel after having acupuncture?

The most noticeable effect people feel after having acupuncture treatment is a great sense of calmness, a relief of a discomfort they may have experienced and a rejuvenation in their well-being. Some even sleep during acupuncture treatment, which can restore their energy levels. Some people say they feel a bit light-headed after, which is normal. I find that the more the person relaxes during treatment while lying on the couch, the better the acupuncture works. After having acupuncture, it is safe to drive or go back to work. However, most people like to have acupuncture after work as they often feel too relaxed to want to return to work.

When should I have acupuncture during pregnancy?

It is beneficial to have acupuncture during each trimester of your pregnancy. It can be used to address many pregnancy-related problems, such as:

- back pain [139] [191] [192]
- to reduce morning sickness [94]
- to reduce fatigue
- to improve sensitivity to insulin [193]
- to increase blood flow to the uterus [66] [194] [195] [196]
- pelvic girdle pain [197]
- to reduce heartburn [198] [199]
- to reduce anxiety, stress and depression [163] [200] [201]
- to reduce labour duration and pain [202] [203] [204]
- to reduce uterine contractions [205] [206]
- to reduce weight [207]
- to regulate oestrogen levels [208] [209]
- to regulate the stress hormone cortisol [210]
- ripening the cervix before labour begins [211] [212]

How often do I need to have acupuncture?

Acupuncture is a dose like every other medical treatment. Its effects last for around three to four days and then it needs to be repeated. If you are suffering from morning sickness or other chronic pain, it is ideal to have acupuncture twice a week. Otherwise, you can have acupuncture once a week. Having acupuncture less frequently than once a week is not advisable because its effects will be minimal.

How long should I have acupuncture for?

If you fall pregnant naturally, you should continue having acupuncture until at least week 12. If you conceived using assisted reproductive technologies such as in vitro fertilisation (IVF), I would recommend having acupuncture until week 20. However, some women like to have acupuncture for longer to help with anxiety and ensure the pregnancy carries on smoothly, which is good for the mother and the baby as any problems can be picked up before they develop any further. Having acupuncture throughout the whole pregnancy is ideal.

If you are over the age of 40, I would recommend having acupuncture throughout your whole pregnancy.

Does it hurt?

Some people do not like the idea of needles and worry that acupuncture will hurt. This fear of needles normally comes from bad memories after having a blood test or a vaccination. Having acupuncture is not the same as having a blood test, as the acupuncture pin is a lot thinner – as fine as a human hair (you can fit 20 acupuncture needles into one syringe) – and is not inserted into a vein but rather a muscle.

Some people will feel the acupuncture pins more than others. This is often due to a lack of energy. The weaker the person is, the more sensitive they are and the more they will feel the pin breaking the skin, causing a tiny prick sensation. When the pin hits the acupuncture point, the sensations a person can feel are unlike anything you have normally felt and can be:

- a deep feeling of relaxation
- a dull throbbing ache
- pulling sensation
- a tingling sensation
- an electrical sensation that travels along the body

Chapter 8

The Benefits of Chinese Herbs in Pregnancy

Chinese herbs are often overlooked in pregnancy. This is because most people are unaware of their benefits. The use of herbs in pregnancy can greatly benefit both the mother and baby. With the vast amount of health benefits, I recommend and prescribe herbs to most of my patients. I take them daily myself, as does my partner who was pregnant when I first started writing this book.

History of Chinese herbs

Herbs have been used to treat various health problems all over the world, including Europe, the Americas, Africa and Asia, for tens of thousands of years. In the West, the word 'medicine' used to mean herbal medicine. It is only in the last 125 years, since aspirin was extracted from the bark of the willow tree [213], that pharmaceutical drugs have become more and more popular and the use of plants has become less so.

Pharmaceutical drugs are often the synthesised active ingredients of plants. A quarter of all pharmaceutical drugs originate from plants [214]. The active ingredient is then patented and its potency increased many times over to make it very effective and quick-working. However, as it is now just one part of the original plant, it is no longer part of

Nature and as we are still part of Nature, it causes us side effects. If the original herbs are used instead, the actions take longer to work but seldom have side effects. Herbal medicine is really the traditional medicine of the world and the use of pharmacological drugs is a newer alternative.

How can herbs help your pregnancy?

It is not often known that in China people opt for herbs first before trying acupuncture. This is because herbs are more powerful and can treat a problem a lot quicker. In the West, it is the opposite, as acupuncture gets more press so tends to be more popular than herbs. In terms of your pregnancy, it is best to have both. I would recommend trying to find a practitioner that practises both acupuncture and Chinese herbal medicine. Research-proven benefits of Chinese herbs in pregnancy include:

- inducing labour and calming the mother [215]
- preventing a miscarriage [216] [217]
- preventing and treating a cytomegalovirus (CMV) infection [75] [76]
- ripening the cervix [218]
- treating depression [219]
- treating haemorrhoids [132]
- treating intrauterine growth restriction (IUGR) [150] [151] [152]
- treating oligohydramnios [177]
- treating polyhydramnios [179]

Is it safe to take herbs?

When herbs are prescribed by a qualified and accredited herbalist, they are largely safe – often safer than pharmaceutical drugs. Some people have a negative view of Chinese herbs as they tend to get a lot of bad press. We often hear negative stories such as endangered species or steroids being found in Chinese herbs. As medicine in China was unified in the 1950s [220], both Western pharmaceuticals and Chinese herbs are used together, so a single pill will contain both types of medicine – pharmaceutical agents and herbs – to make it a lot more effective and safer. Unfortunately, some of these pills were shipped to Western countries, where the medicine is not unified, creating bad press.

The use of Chinese herbs in Western countries is now tightly controlled and all the herbs imported are monitored for quality. In rare news stories, we hear of people suffering from kidney failure or even death after taking herbs. These types of stories make headline news, while the 237 million medical mistakes made a year in the UK do not [221]. Around 62,000 people are admitted to hospital every year in the UK from adverse reactions to pharmaceutical drugs [222] and medical errors are the third biggest killer of people in the USA [223].

Side effects from herbs are not common. Minor side effects include stomach upset and/or constipation/loose bowels. Deaths from taking herbs are very rare. However, the wrong herbs in the wrong hands, those who have not been taught or licensed to prepare herbs, can potentially cause problems. Therefore, always see a qualified and accredited herbalist.

How will I feel after taking herbs?

Herbs can cure and remedy an array of bodily symptoms. For example, when people visit my clinic, they usually talk about other physical problems they might have, for example feeling tired or dizzy, or having heartburn or a sluggish digestion. After discussing their case, they often realise that all their problems are connected to each other. Once your symptoms have been diagnosed through a consultation and you are prescribed a tailor-made herbal formula and start treatment, you will start to notice an improvement in your symptoms and a change in your health. For example, once people start taking herbs, they often notice that their other symptoms, such as being dizzy or tired, have gone, making them feel better. This is because Chinese medicine sees the person as a whole and not as different segments that different specialist doctors need to treat. This departmentalisation in Western medicine often means that one department is unaware of the other department and how related they are to each other, sadly to the detriment of the patient's health.

How do you take herbs?

Traditionally herbs come in their raw form, for example bits of root, bark, seeds or flower heads that you cook in water, then drain and drink. This process takes hours, can stink out your kitchen and leaves sediment at the bottom of your cup, which can make you gag when you drink it. Thankfully, nowadays it is a lot easier. The herbs come in powder form, which means that you do not need to spend hours cooking them. Instead, you just add hot water and honey (if preferred), wait for them to cool down and then drink. They often do not taste nice, hence the honey. Herbs are generally taken twice a day, in the morning and evening, allowing the beneficial actions of the herbs to be spread out throughout the day. For some pregnant women, once nausea sets in, it can be difficult to take Chinese herbs, which is normal.

Dosages

There are two dosages in Chinese herbal medicine: the raw herbs/ powders and small black pills. The small black pills are standard off-the-shelf formulas at a very weak dose. You can no buy longer buy these in Europe. I do not recommend using these pills as they are too weak, take a long time to work and cannot be customised to a person's individual needs. A lot of people are attracted to them because they are cheap. I do not recommend self-diagnosing or self-treating using Chinese herbs. Prescribing an accurate and effective formula should only be from a qualified and accredited herbalist.

How long do I need to take herbs?

You can take Chinese herbs throughout your pregnancy. They are perfectly safe to take and will help your baby grow and ensure you have good levels of energy and blood needed for growing your baby and for breastfeeding. Taking Chinese herbs will also reduce any side effects the pregnancy may have upon your body, for example depression (baby blues), anxiety and physical depletion (see Chapter Thirteen).

Part Three

Keeping Your Baby Safe

One of the first instincts of an expectant mother is the desire to protect her unborn baby from any threats or dangers. These include the more obvious dangers, such as smoking and alcohol, but also other less obvious dangers, such as medications and factors that increase the risk of autism. In this part, I'll outline each of the dangers and how you can protect your baby from them.

Chapter 9

Protecting Your Baby

During pregnancy, your body is in a more vulnerable state than normal. It is therefore important to know the risks to you and your body in order to protect your baby. In this chapter, I will discuss what to avoid and how to protect your baby.

Medications During Pregnancy

During pregnancy, you may need to take medications to help with a health problem. However, the number of medications that you are able to take reduces considerably as some can be harmful to the baby. Always consult with your obstetrician or doctor first and read any literature that is provided with the medication before taking it.

Painkillers

Most pharmaceutical painkillers should be avoided during pregnancy as they can harm the baby, including:

- aspirin (acetylsalicylic acid)
- non-steroidal anti-inflammatory drugs (NSAIDs, ibuprofen and indomethacin)
- paracetamol (acetaminophen, Tylenol)

Paracetamol, ibuprofen and aspirin are widely used during pregnancy and are known to cross the placenta to the baby. Studies have shown that aspirin and paracetamol prevent the male baby's hormone human chorionic gonadotropin (hCG) from producing testosterone, resulting in an increased risk of the baby being born with undescended testicles (cryptorchidism), one of the most common abnormalities in newborn male babies worldwide [111] [112] [224] [225] [226] [227].

Paracetamol is still currently recommended by midwives, obstetricians and doctors to take during pregnancy for pain relief, despite numerous research studies that show that mothers who take paracetamol during pregnancy affect their male and female baby's reproductive health [113] [228]. Paracetamol can cause infertility in boys in later life as well as increase the rate of them developing asthma [229]. Further research has found a link between pregnant mothers taking paracetamol and an increase in autism in male babies [230]. Girls born from mothers who took paracetamol during pregnancy have lower follicle reserves and fertility [228]. There is also a link between use in pregnancy and babies developing attention deficit hyperactivity disorder (ADHD) and delayed development [229] [231] [232]. As paracetamol and aspirin are often found in tap water, I recommend filtering your tap water before drinking it.

NSAIDs, such as ibuprofen, aspirin, diclofenac, Advil, indomethacin, etc., can cause a congenital heart defect in babies (foetal ductus arteriosus) as well as restrict placenta transfer, thereby negatively affecting the growth of the baby leading to intrauterine growth restriction (IUGR). Indomethacin can also cause cryptorchidism [233]. I recommend trying not to take any type of painkillers during pregnancy if possible. Acupuncture is very effective at relieving all types of pain and is safe to use during pregnancy (see Chapter Seven) [186] [234]. You can also use a TENS machine at home to relieve various types of pain (see page 213).

Antacids

Some pregnant women will experience heartburn (acid reflux, gastric reflux – see page 44) during their pregnancy [235]. An antacid is a substance which neutralises stomach acidity and can be bought over the counter. They are commonly used during pregnancy when the growing baby pushes the stomach upwards, effectively squashing it, which makes the stomach acid unsettled causing heartburn. Most over-the-counter antacids are safe to take in pregnancy. However, some contain sweeteners, which I would try to avoid taking during pregnancy.

Prescription antacid medications such as H2-receptor antagonists (H2RAs) and proton pump inhibitors (PPIs) are the main treatment for women who suffer from severe indigestion (dyspepsia) and heartburn (gastroesophageal reflux) in pregnancy [100]. Research has shown that use of these medications during pregnancy can increase the risk of children developing asthma [101]. Acupuncture can be used instead to treat heartburn and indigestion in pregnancy without side effects [102] [103] [104].

Antibiotics

Certain antibiotics are generally safe to take in pregnancy. However, they should be avoided where possible in the first trimester, only used when absolutely necessary and at the lowest dose possible [236]. The following antibiotics are thought to be safe in pregnancy:

- cephalosporin
- erythromycin
- fusidic acid
- nitrofurantoin
- penicillin [237]

Antibiotics that should be used with caution in pregnancy include:

- ciprofloxacin
- clindamycin
- gentamicin
- metronidazole
- nalidixic acid
- ofloxacin
- rifampicin
- spectinomycin
- vancomycin [237]

Antibiotics that should be avoided in pregnancy include:

- aminoglycosides
- chloramphenicol
- colistin
- co-trimoxazole
- dapsone
- fosfomycin [237]
- macrolides (excluding erythromycin) [238]
- metronidazole [238]
- quinolones [238]
- sulfonamides [238]
- tetracyclines [238]

Antifungals

Antifungals (antimycotic) are a pharmaceutical fungicide or fungistatic used to treat and prevent infections such as athlete's foot, ringworm, candidiasis (vaginal thrush), fungal nail infection, etc. Antifungal agents clotrimazole, miconazole and nystatin are considered safe to use during pregnancy [239] [240]. Antifungals that should be used with caution in pregnancy include:

- amphotericin
- econazole (first trimester) [240]
- fluconazole
- flucytosine
- griseofulvin
- iodides [241]
- isavuconazole [242]
- itraconazole
- ketoconazole
- posaconazole [242]
- terbinafine [237]
- voriconazole [243]

Antihistamines

Antihistamines are drugs that treat allergic rhinitis and other allergies. These medications are available over the counter in most countries. First-generation antihistamines such as chlorpheniramine, hydroxyzine and dexchlorpheniramine are considered safe to use in pregnancy [244] [245] [246]. However, diphenhydramine should be avoided in pregnancy [239].

Antivirals

Antivirals are medications that reduce the ability of flu viruses to multiply. Aciclovir and trichloroacetic acid (TCA) are considered safe to use in pregnancy [240]. Antivirals that should be avoided in pregnancy include:

- ganciclovir [242]
- podofilox [240]
- podophyllin [237]

- ribavirin
- salicylic acid (third trimester) [240]

Antidepressants

The use of antidepressants is growing each year. Roughly one in six people take antidepressants in the UK [247]. Women are two and a half times more likely to take an antidepressant than men [248]. Around 6–10 per cent of women take antidepressants during pregnancy [249] [250]. Consult with your obstetrician or doctor if you have any concerns about your antidepressant.

Selective serotonin reuptake inhibitor (SSRI)

The antidepressant escitalopram is considered the safest to take during pregnancy [251] [252] [253]. Growing research has found the use of SSRI antidepressants in pregnancy can cause autism, low birth weight, preterm birth, birth defects, seizures, speech/language disorders, and even spontaneous miscarriages [254] [255] [256] [257] [258] [259] [260] [261] [262] [263] [264] [265] [266] [267]. There is not enough research to determine whether the antidepressants fluvoxamine or sertraline are safe to take during pregnancy or not [268] [269]. The following SSRI antidepressants should be avoided in pregnancy, if possible:

- anxiolytic [270]
- citalopram [271]
- fluoxetine [258] [260] [264]

- paroxetine [259] [263] [264] [265] [272] [273]
- venlafaxine [274]

The increased serotonin level that comes from taking SSRI medication may impact the central nervous system of the developing baby. In addition, laboratory investigations have shown that serotonin has a constrictive effect on umbilical arteries, which can reduce blood flow to the baby. The increased serotonin levels that result from the mother's ingestion of SSRIs may increase the risk of adverse outcomes that are sensitive to the placental blood flow, such as IUGR and preterm births, which have been observed consistently in various studies [267].

Tricyclic

Tricyclic antidepressants (TCAs) are a class of antidepressant medications that share a similar chemical structure and biological effects. Scientists believe that patients with depression may have an imbalance in neurotransmitters – chemicals that nerves make and use to communicate with other nerves. There is not enough research to determine whether the antidepressants imipramine, nortriptyline and trimipramine are safe to take during pregnancy. Nortriptyline is the safest to take while breastfeeding [275] [276]. However, imipramine should not be taken in high doses [277]. The following TCAs should be avoided in pregnancy, if possible:

- amitriptyline [274]
- clomipramine [275] [278] [279]
- doxepin (third trimester and caution when breastfeeding) [280] [281] [282]
- dosulepin (caution when breastfeeding) [275] [283]

Monoamine oxidase inhibitor (MAOIs)

MAOIs were the first class of antidepressants to be developed in the 1950s. They became less popular when negative interactions were discovered between certain foods and other medications. It is preferable to avoid taking MAOIs during pregnancy due to their side effects, if possible [284].

Other antidepressants

There is not enough research to determine whether the antidepressants agomelatine, bupropion, duloxetine, mirtazapine, moclobemide, reboxetine, trazodone and vortioxetine are safe to take in pregnancy [285]. Venlafaxine should be avoided in pregnancy, if possible [274].

Natural alternatives

If you find the side effects of antidepressants uncomfortable, you can opt for natural alternatives instead, such as St John's wort [286] [287] [288] [289]. Acupuncture has also been shown to reduce depression [290] [291] [292]. Chinese herbs can increase the effects of acupuncture [219]. However, in some instances, where depression is a serious condition, antidepressants may be a better option.

Anticonvulsants

Anticonvulsant (anti-seizure) medications are commonly given to people who suffer from seizures such as epilepsy or who are bipolar. Oxcarbazepine and levetiracetam appear to be the safest to take during pregnancy [293] [294] [295] [296] [297] [298] [299] [300] [301] [302] [303]. The following anticonvulsant medications should be avoided in pregnancy, if possible:

- carbamazepine [304] [305] [306] [307] [308] [309]
- lamotrigine [310] [311]
- lithium [308]
- phenobarbital [298] [312]
- pregabalin [313] [314]
- topiramate [312]
- valproate [308] [312] [315]

Vaccines

All live vaccines should be avoided in pregnancy and include:

- BCG
- cholera
- measles
- mumps
- rubella
- sabin poliomyelitis
- typhoid
- yellow fever [237]

Chinese medicine was the first to discover and use vaccinations in 1,000AD [316]. Today there are various vaccinations on offer to pregnant women, including the flu jab and whooping cough.

Flu vaccine

The flu jab helps to protect babies from the current flu, usually three strains of the flu, circulating in the parts of the world that are currently experiencing winter. Although rare, pregnant women have a higher risk to the 2009 influenza A (H1N1). Pregnant women with 2009 influenza A (H1N1) who had early antiviral treatment had fewer admissions to an intensive care unit (ICU) [317]. Flu vaccination also helps protect women during pregnancy and their babies for up to six months after they are born.

COVID-19 vaccine

The advice as to whether expecting mothers should have the COVID-19 vaccine is constantly changing. Data shows that one in five pregnant women who become unwell with COVID-19 needs to have her baby delivered early [318]. As the time of writing this book, the Joint Committee on Vaccination and Immunisation in the UK advises that pregnant women should all be offered the Pfizer-BioNTech or Moderna vaccines where available. It is not recommended to have the AstraZeneca vaccine while pregnant. The Royal College of Midwives in the UK suggest that women can be vaccinated at any time during their pregnancy although they may prefer to wait until after the first trimester or the first scan [318].

Research from the US, involving more than 90,000 pregnant people found no risk, and experts say there is no reason to think there is any increased risk of miscarriage – as the vaccine does not appear to cross from the placenta. However, data suggests that 58% of pregnant women have declined a COVID-19 vaccine [319]. More research is needed to reassure pregnant women of the risks of the various COVID-19 vaccines. Unvaccinated or partially vaccinated pregnant women should take steps to avoid infection by continuing to practice social distancing, particularly in their third trimester.

Whooping cough (pertussis)

Whooping cough is a bacterial infection of the lungs and breathing tubes that is sometimes seen in newborns. Newborn babies with whooping cough can be very unwell and most will be admitted to hospital because of their illness. Expectant mothers can help to protect their babies from the whooping cough by getting themselves vaccinated, ideally when they are between weeks 16 and 32 of pregnancy [320]. The whooping cough vaccine is considered safe to take during pregnancy [321]. The early symptoms of whooping cough in babies are often similar to those of a common cold and can include:

- mild cough
- runny nose
- pause in breathing (apnoea)
- slightly raised temperature [322]

These early symptoms of whooping cough can last for up to a week before becoming more severe. It is best to speak with your midwife, obstetrician or doctor to determine whether your baby has whooping cough or not. Severe symptoms can include:

- intense bouts of coughing, which brings up thick phlegm
- a 'whoop' sound with each sharp intake of breath after coughing
- vomiting after coughing
- tiredness and redness in the face from the effort of coughing [320]

Autism

Since the 1980s, there has been a tremendous growth in the number of autism spectrum disorders (ASDs) [323]. It has moved from a relatively rare condition (1 in 10,000) to 1 in 68 in the US [324] [325]. Autism is commonly seen more in boys than in girls [326] [327]. There is great controversy over the causes of autism.

Vaccines are a concern to many people because of stories of their link to autism, although this has now been discredited [328]. Vaccines have a history of using the metals mercury and aluminium. Mercury in the form of ethyl mercury (thiomersal) was used as a preservative in most hepatitis B, haemophilus influenza type B (HiB) and diphtheria/tetanus/pertussis (DTP or DTaP) vaccines [329] [330]. However, today most vaccines no longer contain mercury [331] [332].

Aluminium is used in vaccines such as hepatitis A, hepatitis B, diphtheria/tetanus-containing vaccines, haemophilus influenza type B and pneumococcal vaccines, as it enhances the binding ability of the vaccine to the immune system [333] [334] [335] [336]. However, it is not used in live, viral vaccines, such as measles, mumps, rubella, varicella and rotavirus [337]. Aluminium is the most abundant metal in the earth's crust, but it is never found free in Nature [338]. Studies have shown that having too much aluminium in our bodies can be a cause of autism [339]. The amount of aluminium in vaccines currently licensed in the US ranges from 0.85 to 0.125mg/dose [333]. When combined with other sources of aluminium in our day-to-day lives, such as those from underarm deodorants [340] [341], the risk is increased of pregnant mothers overdosing and the possible development of autism in their children. The dose at which aluminium may trigger autism in pregnancy or early childhood is still unknown.

There are many other causes of autism in pregnancy, including:

- a lack of maternal folic acid (folate) [342] [343] [344] [345] [346] [347] [348]

- a lack of maternal omega-3 [349] [350] [351] [352]

- a lack of maternal oxytocin [353] [354]

- a lack of maternal vitamin D [347] [348] [355] [356] [357] [358] [359] [360] [361] [362]

- a lack of maternal zinc [363] [364] [365] [366] [367] [368] [369] [370] [371]

- a viral infection during pregnancy (MIA) [355] [372] [373] [374] [375]

- air pollutants ($PM_{2.5}$) from cars and industry [325] [347] [376] [377] [378] [379] [380] [381] [382] [383] [384] [385]

- the antiepileptic medication valproate [386] [387] [388] [389] [390] [391]

- BPAs [347] [385] [392] [393] [394]

- excessive ultrasounds in the first trimester [62] [395] [396]

- exposure to herbicides [397] [398] [399] [400] [401] [402] [403]

- exposure to mercury in the womb and early childhood [347] [369] [385] [393] [404] [405] [406] [407] [408] [409]

- exposure to parabens [410] [411] [412]

- exposure to pesticides [347] [348] [385] [413]

- exposure to phthalates [347] [385] [414] [415] [416]

- exposure to plasticisers [417]

- a high-fat diet in pregnancy [54] [351]

- mothers who take paracetamol (acetaminophen, Tylenol) during pregnancy [230] [403] [418] [419] [420] [421] [422]

- smoking cannabis while pregnant [423]

- use of antidepressants (SSRIs) during pregnancy [254] [257] [348] [424] [425] [426]

You can reduce the risk of your baby developing autism by:

- avoiding eating foods high in mercury, such as tuna, swordfish, king mackerel, lobster, Spanish mackerel, marlin, grouper and shark
- avoiding using cosmetics

- eating foods high in omega-3 or taking DHA (not from cod liver oil)

- eating no more than 10 per cent of fat a day in your diet

- eating organic foods

- not taking antidepressants in pregnancy, if possible
- not taking paracetamol (acetaminophen, Tylenol) in pregnancy, if possible
- reducing the number of ultrasounds in the first trimester
- reducing your exposure to chemicals
- taking a probiotic that contains *lactobacillus reuteri* [54]
- taking folic acid (220mcg/day), vitamin D (10–15mcg/day) and zinc (15mg/day)
- using a HEPA filter at home
- wearing a N95 or N99 face mask when outside near cars or factories

You do not have to be diligent with all of this advice; just try to reduce the incidences of them occurring.

Ways to Reduce Your Chance of a Miscarriage

Advancing through pregnancy is like jumping over hurdles; the longer you go into the pregnancy, the smaller the hurdles become as the risks lower. From my experience, there are three key hurdles during pregnancy: week 8, week 12 and week 20. After week 20, the risk of having a miscarriage falls greatly.

Western medicine does not offer much advice on how to avoid a miscarriage. Sometimes heparin or aspirin are prescribed to pregnant women to help with blood flow to the uterus as they act as an anticoagulant. These medications just thin the blood to help it flow better, but with side effects. I recommend taking iron supplements throughout pregnancy, which increase the amount of blood in the mother and allow more of it to flow and nourish the baby.

Research has shown that acupuncture can reduce the risk of miscarrying [427] [428] [429]. Further research has shown that Chinese herbal formulas such as Xiong Gui Jiao Ai Tang are more effective at preventing a miscarriage than the administration of human chorionic gonadotropin (hCG) [216].

From a Chinese medicine viewpoint, there are steps that can be taken to help prevent a miscarriage from occurring. Firstly, reduce your energy expenditure once you find out that you are pregnant. Western medicine says to carry on as normal, but I disagree. Feeling very tired is a red flag. When you feel very tired, you must rest, lie down, eat and sleep. If you push through this red flag and carry on, you greatly increase the risk of having a miscarriage. This is because there is only so much energy and blood in your body. If you push your body to carry on using energy and blood, your body will divert resources to this at the detriment of the baby. The Chinese herbal formula I regularly use in my clinic to help prevent miscarriages is a simple energy and blood formula, which helps to make sure there is more for both mother and baby.

Here are my recommendations on preventing a miscarriage:

- Avoid having an invasive procedure such as a chorionic villus sampling (CVS) or an amniocentesis to test for any chromosome abnormalities. Have a Harmony test instead (see page 36).

- Avoid having hot baths as it may cause the embryo to dislodge from the uterus wall.

- Avoid placing any heat on your abdomen.

- Avoid precooked meats, cured meats, unpasteurised dairy products, soft ripened cheeses (i.e. Brie, Camembert, blue vein types) and shellfish, including sushi.

- Distract yourself from worrying and being anxious by doing things that you enjoy.

- Do not lift or carry anything heavy.

- Eat a diet rich in protein, omega-3 and iron.

- Eat little and often. Always make sure you have some food and water with you at all times.

- Go to bed early, for example around 9–10 p.m.
- Have acupuncture regularly.
- Reduce exercising or stop if you feel tired.
- Reduce your social activities.
- Reduce your time using gadgets such as smartphones and social media.
- Reduce your workload and make sure you take your lunch break.
- Take a good-quality prenatal supplement with adequate levels of vitamins and minerals, especially iron.
- Take prescribed Chinese herbs daily if you feel exhausted or are an older mother (over 38).

We have looked at ways to protect your baby. Let's now look at ways in which you can optimise your lifestyle for a healthy pregnancy and labour.

Chapter 10

Optimising Your Lifestyle

When you move into a new house, you first make sure that it can protect you from the environment outside, that it is warm, does not have damp and has water. It therefore makes sense to make your uterus a comfortable home for your baby to live and grow in for the next nine months by making sure your uterus is warm enough, has enough energy and blood, is not damp and is protected from the harshness of the surrounding environment we call Earth. Your uterus is a place for your baby to grow and acts as a transitional home, allowing your baby to acclimatise to our world.

Optimising your lifestyle is an easy way to take control of your pregnancy and take proactive steps to ensure a healthy pregnancy and labour, and improve your baby's growth and development.

Avoid heat on the abdomen

More often than not, women tend to love having hot baths. However, having a hot bath while pregnant is a no-no, as the heat around the uterus can cause a fertilised embryo to dislodge from the uterus wall. It can also cause the baby's heart rate to increase as it receives less oxygen due to the mother's body redistributing blood to the surface to cool down rather than to the uterus [430]. A warm/tepid bath is okay.

For the same reason, an electric blanket or hot water bottle should not be placed on your abdomen. If you feel cold, you can place a hot water bottle on your lower back.

Prioritise sleep

Some women will feel exhausted while pregnant, especially if they are working and/or caring for another child. For them, sleep is golden and they tend to sleep early. For other women, they can still carry on and sleep late. However, sleep can greatly affect the pregnancy. Going to sleep near midnight or afterwards damages yin as midnight is the highest point of yin. This can affect energy levels and growth rates. There is a saying: 'Two hours before midnight is worth ten after.' I couldn't agree more! Those two hours before midnight safeguard your yin for your pregnancy. To enhance your pregnancy, try not to go to sleep later than 10 p.m. It will take some practice if you are not used to it, but you will notice how much better you will feel.

Having power naps in the afternoon is a great way of boosting your energy levels and your pregnancy. You only need to nap for 20 minutes to revive your body's energy levels. Having naps is a good habit to get into, as when the baby naps in the daytime, it would be good if you napped too, as it will help restore your energy levels.

Not only is the quantity of time you sleep important but also its quality. The quality of sleep can be affected by anxiety, vivid dreams, urinating at night, noise disturbances or discomfort from the weight of your baby. Having a comfortable mattress and pillows can be very helpful in pregnancy. There are various specialised cushions and pillows you can invest in, which are designed to help make pregnant women feel more comfortable at night and assist in falling into a deep sleep. A lot of pregnant women will dream at night, which is normal. If you are sensitive to noise, use ear plugs. If you wake at night to urinate, try not to drink any fluids an hour or so before bed.

If you find it hard to sleep or you wake during the night or at

5 a.m., then your mind is most likely restless and you are thinking too much. Try to wind down before going to bed. Switch off the TV, phone, computer or tablet for at least one hour before you sleep as a lot of stimuli can keep you awake, especially blue light. Instead, read a book, listen to music or practise pregnancy yoga to stretch out the stresses of the day, or hypnobirthing. This will help you to wind down, relax and make falling asleep easier.

Exercise mindfully

Most midwives, obstetricians and doctors tend to suggest carrying on exercising in pregnancy and, for most women, this is okay. Regular exercise has been shown in research to reduce the likelihood of the child developing health problems in later life such as heart disease, stroke and type 2 diabetes [431]. However, I would recommend not exercising vigorously in the first 12 weeks of pregnancy, as there are a lot of energy demands being placed upon your body with the rapid growth of the baby and the placenta. Gentle exercising such as walking or pregnancy yoga would be better. Exercising too much during this period can put a strain upon energy and blood levels.

Some women may feel too tired to exercise during pregnancy, especially during the first trimester, which is normal. A few won't and will be happy to exercise and that's okay too. As a general rule, if you feel better after exercising, then it is having a beneficial effect upon your body, but if you feel tired after exercising, then you should rest instead. For older mothers, those over 38, I would recommend waiting until week 20 to start exercising and then only light exercising, such as swimming, walking, tai chi or pregnancy yoga. Nothing too intense or high impact, such as running or aerobics. However, if you have any of the following symptoms, then you should stop exercising:

- amniotic fluid leakage [4]
- calf muscle pain or swelling
- chest pain
- decreased baby movements
- dizziness
- headaches

- muscle weakness
- shortness of breath
- vaginal bleeding

Slow down

Today's modern pace of life can be a strain on our health. The faster we move or do things, the more energy we use up. It is like having a fast car: a car with a bigger engine and more cylinders uses more petrol (energy), while a car with a smaller engine and fewer cylinders uses less energy. By moving at a fast pace, we use up energy and blood that could otherwise be used to grow your baby. If we move at a slower pace and have more patience, we use up less energy and are able to conserve more for the baby.

Wear the right clothing and footwear

It is important to keep your uterus warm and protect it from the wind or cold. You would not leave the doors or windows open in your baby's nursery to let the cold in, so why do it with your uterus? If possible, keep your abdomen covered when the weather is cold.

If you feel too warm, then this too can be an inhospitable environment for your baby to call home for nine months. You may need to wear thinner clothing to allow the air to circulate and make changes to your diet to cool yourself down, such as drinking peppermint tea and not exposing your body to excessive heat, such as from the sun, heated car seats, spicy foods and stress.

For a lot of pregnant women, shoes can be an issue in pregnancy. The additional weight of the baby means it can be difficult to wear high heels, as it causes back pain. Other women may experience swollen or hot feet, which means they prefer open shoes such as sandals or flip-flops. However, if you have cold feet, it makes the body feel cold and can slow down blood flow around the body, including to the uterus. In wintertime, it is important to wear shoes that have thick soles to protect your feet from the cold ground.

It can also be important to keep your feet warm while indoors, especially in the winter or in cold buildings or on cold floors. Wearing socks and slippers around the home will help to regulate blood flow around the body and to your uterus. If you suffer from very cold feet, I would recommend using a warm foot spa daily to help improve blood flow and circulation.

Donating blood

Donating blood plays an important role in today's society, which helps other less fortunate people and should be applauded. Without it, many people would die. However, when pregnant, you are not allowed to give blood. You may need to wait for six months from the birth of your baby to give blood again [432].

Don't smoke

When pregnant, women should not smoke. Women who smoke tobacco or cannabis during pregnancy double their risk of having a miscarriage, a preterm birth, and a baby born with birth defects, learning difficulties and a low birth weight [433]. Pregnant women should also avoid passive smoking.

Attend antenatal classes

Your hospital or clinic may offer antenatal classes. These provide you with the basics you need to know to prepare you for motherhood. There may be additional private antenatal classes available in your area that are more in-depth. These courses run for longer and also have the added benefit of being a place where you can meet people and make friends, which can be a vital support network for later on. However, these classes often run in the evening, which may be too late for some women, who feel tired early and want to sleep. This is normal. Try to find a weekend class instead.

We have looked at ways to optimise your lifestyle. Let's now look at how you can optimise your environment for a healthy pregnancy and labour.

Chapter 11

Optimising Your Environment

In today's modern world, we are constantly being bombarded with a multitude of different types of chemicals, metals and pollutants. Some of these can cross the placenta and affect your baby's natural development. It is therefore important for the health and growth of your baby to reduce your exposure to these chemicals, metals and pollutants.

Reducing Your Exposure to Chemicals

Since the Second World War, approximately 80,000 new synthetic chemicals have been manufactured and released into the environment, with 10 new chemicals being introduced every day [434]. As technology advanced, many chemicals were created to enhance our lives by killing bacteria to keep our living and working areas clean. Others were created to help clothe us, such as in the manufacturing of the synthetic polymers nylon and polyester. Chemicals were used in the farming of animals. Even more chemicals were created for healthcare, beauty and hygiene. Suddenly chemicals that do not exist in Nature were bombarding people's bodies. Our bodies come from Nature; they are not man-made and struggle to coexist with man-made chemicals. In this short space in our history, we have not evolved to live in harmony with such chemicals [435].

We now live in what is termed a man-made 'chemical cloud'. Our bodies are constantly being surrounded by complex chemicals, from fragrances in soaps, shampoos and perfumes to nail polish, make-up and cleaning products. Unknowingly this affects our health and that of our baby [28] [436].

We are not exposed to one toxicant at a time, but rather, to hundreds if not thousands of man-made chemicals present in our environment. Collectively, they can be hazardous to human reproductive health [437].

Hormones in food

Foods derived from animals are an important source of nutrition and vitamins. Methods of production vary globally and include the use of hormones in cattle to increase growth and lean tissue with reduced fat. The hormonal compounds are naturally occurring in animals or are synthetically produced man-made chemicals that have an effect upon oestrogen and progesterone hormone activity. The use of synthetic hormones is still permitted in North American countries but is no longer allowed in Europe, which also prohibits the importation of meat and its products derived from hormone-treated cattle as it may induce free-radical damage of DNA [438]. Foods in North American countries are some of the most altered in the world.

The accumulation of endocrine-disrupting man-made chemicals (xenobiotics) in food sources, such as fish and animal meat, exposes people to increased concentrations of these compounds. Products from animal sources, such as cow's milk, can also be a source of exposure to exogenous oestrogens [437].

Contaminated food and water may contain environmental pollutants, such as pesticide residues and heavy metals, in addition to processing aids and anabolic steroids used in food production, which disrupt normal hormone regulation. Most people have traceable amounts of these substances in their blood or urine [439].

Herbicides

It was during the 1940s that modern agricultural practices were established with the use of pesticides to kill off insects that would eat and damage crops, and herbicides to kill off weeds. These were introduced at a time when people could still remember the rationing of foods in Europe during the Second World War, and they were therefore seen as necessary to feed the population. Throughout most of the 1950s, consumers and most policymakers were not concerned about the potential health risks of using pesticides. Food was cheaper because of these new chemicals and there were no documented cases of people dying or being seriously hurt by their use.

Glyphosate (Roundup) is now the most widely used herbicide on the planet [397]. Many farmers routinely use glyphosate and other herbicides to clear their fields of weeds before crops emerge in the spring. But what is more alarming is that they also use glyphosate on crops shortly before they are harvested. Glyphosate kills parts of the crop that have not ripened evenly and dries the crop. This allows combine harvesters to move more quickly and cover more ground during harvest, thereby reducing costs. But applying glyphosate so close to harvest makes the likelihood of finding residues in food even higher. Glyphosate is one of three pesticides regularly found in routine testing of British bread [440]. Around 60 per cent of all herbicides interfere with thyroid function, which affect the development of the baby while in the womb [398] [441]. Its increasing use over time in the US aligns well with increasing rates of autism [397] [442]. Research has linked an increased use of glyphosate with an increased prevalence of attention deficit hyperactivity disorder (ADHD) in people [443] and an increased prevalence of autism [323] [397] [400] [444]. Other pesticides too have been linked to an increased rate of children developing autism [392].

Pesticides

Dichlorodiphenyltrichloroethane (DDT) does not occur naturally in the environment; it is a man-made chemical. Large amounts of DDT were released into the air and on soil or water when it was sprayed on crops and forests to kill insects. Organochlorine compounds, such as DDT, dichlorodiphenyldichloroethylene (DDE), and dichlorodiphenyldichloroethane (DDD), last in the soil for a very long time, potentially for hundreds of years [445]. Many studies have been conducted to determine the concentration of environmental contaminants, especially organochlorine compounds and polychlorinated biphenyls (PCBs, found in meat, fish, poultry) and in the tissues of humans. Both DDT and DDE have been shown to reduce levels of oestrogens and progesterone leading to early pregnancy loss [446]. DDT was banned in the USA in 1972, but still lives on in our environment.

Due to its high lipid content, organochlorine chemicals accumulate in breast milk. Infants are likely to be exposed to higher concentrations of xenobiotics during nursing than at any other time. Pesticides such as DDE and hexachlorobenzene can affect the mother's thyroid function in pregnancy [447]. It is also speculated in research studies that exposure of the mother to these environmental hormones could have a potential effect on the male or female baby, while inside the womb. The development of a foetus into male or female is very different. Male foetus development is totally hormone dependent whereas female foetus development is largely hormone independent. Exposure to anti-androgens such as flutamide, vinclozolin or p,p'-DDE can interfere with masculinisation of the internal reproductive organs and the external genitalia in male babies. It is therefore best to eat organic or biodynamic fruit, vegetables and meat whenever possible. I would also recommend washing your fruit and vegetables if you bought them, or you could even grow your own. For more information on foods, see Part Four (pages 122–166).

Hormones in water

In France, studies have identified numerous compounds in surface water (before treatment), including acetaminophen (paracetamol), salicylic acid, analgesics, psychotropic drugs, antibiotics and beta blockers, as well as natural hormones (oestrogens, progesterone and androgens) and synthetic progesterone [448]. These compounds come from farming, the public (the contraceptive pill) and hospitals. The number of pharmaceuticals and hormones and their presence in the final waters indicate that most treatments fail in their total elimination [448]. Recent research found 11 pharmaceuticals in drinking waters from Germany, the UK, Italy, Canada and the USA [448]. The levels of hormones present are small, yet in conjunction with hormones in meat and beverages, as well as cosmetics and man-made products, their levels increase and can affect the level of hormones in pregnancy.

Another problem with disinfected drinking water is the by-products found in virtually all chlorinated water supplies. Research conducted in California found that women who drank more than five glasses of cold tap water a day, if it contained more than 75mcg/l of total trihalomethanes (THMs), had an increase in low birth weight babies, preterm births, birth defects and miscarriage rates [449] [450] [451] [452]. Another pollutant of water is polyfluorinated chemicals (PFCs). In developed countries and industrialised areas, PFCs were found in surface water, ground water and drinking water, which showed positive correlation with PFC contaminations in humans [453]. I would recommend drinking filtered tap water or bottled water, preferably from a glass container.

Household hormones

Environmental hormones include numerous synthetic substances used as industrial lubricants and solvents and their by-products, for example PCBs and polybrominated diphenyl ethers (PBDEs), which are used as a flame retardant.

Cleaning products

It is normal for a lot of expectant mothers to feel the sensation of wanting to prepare the home for their new baby, commonly known as 'nesting'. During this period, people like to prepare the baby's clothes, furniture and nursery, and get the home clean ready for the new baby's arrival.

Research has shown that the use of cleaning sprays, air fresheners and solvents during pregnancy may increase the risk of wheezing and infections in children [454] [455], while other research has shown that newborns need certain bacteria to help their respiratory systems and prevent the development of asthma. These four types of bacteria are *Faecalibacterium, Lachnospira, Veillonella,* and *Rothia* (Flvr) and if they are not present for the first 100 days of the baby's life, the baby is at higher risk of developing asthma at the age of three [456]. The inhalation of cleaning products during pregnancy may be a factor in the lack of these four vital types of bacteria needed for good respiratory function. Further research has shown a correlation between solvent use during pregnancy and an increased risk of children being born with birth defects such as a cleft lip and urinary and male genital deformities [457].

I recommend that you should avoid contact with all chemical-based cleaning products. If you have to use them, use ones that are less harsh (i.e. eco-friendly) and wear gloves and an N95 or N99 face mask, or ask someone else to do the cleaning for you.

Polybrominated diphenyl ethers (PBDEs)

Exposure to PBDEs during pregnancy can affect the mother's thyroid function, which can cause problems with the baby's development in the womb [458] [459] [460] [461]. PBDEs can also cross the placenta and reduce the baby's birth weight and neurodevelopment [462] [463] [464].

Organophosphate (OP)

Flame-retardant chemicals, such as OP compounds, have replaced PBDEs in recent years. OP compounds have been found in house dust, which is then digested by the occupants [465]. Children born from mothers exposed to OP chemicals can develop cognitive and behavioural deficits and neurodevelopmental disorders [466] [467] [468].

Alkylphenol ethoxylates (APEs)

APEs are detergents, emulsifiers and wetting agents used in paints, household products, toiletries, pesticides and many other industrial and agricultural products. APEs accumulate in river sediment and in the fat of exposed fish, thereby entering the food chain. Around 82 per cent of APEs contain nonylphenol (NP) ethoxylate. NP can cross the placenta and is found in breast milk [469] [470]. Mothers exposed to NP during pregnancy are at greater risk of giving birth to males with reduced reproduction development [471].

Polychlorinated biphenyls (PCBs)

PCBs are industrial chemicals that were once widely used as lubricants and coolants, and now persist in the environment despite being banned [472]. Exposure to PCBs in pregnancy can affect the mother's thyroid function [447]. Bioaccumulation of PCBs resulting from years of exposure of the mother and their potential risk in pregnancy is a special concern because they are released during pregnancy and breastfeeding [473]. Research conducted in Norway found that girls born from mothers exposed to PCBs in their diet had reduced language skills [474]. Polybrominated biphenyls (PBBs) are similar to PCBs and have been linked with poor health in children [475].

Polyfluorinated chemicals (PFCs)

PFCs are also known as perfluorinated chemicals, perfluorochemicals, perfluoroalkyls, perfluorinated alkyl acids, polyfluorinated chemicals, polyfluorinated compounds and polyfluoroalkyl substances. In recent years, PFCs have increasingly been investigated for their potential harm to humans.

PFCs are a large group of manufactured compounds that are widely used to make everyday products designed to repel soil, grease and water, including: carpet and furniture treatments; food wraps; sprays for leather, shoes and other clothing; paints and cleaning products; and even shampoo and floor wax. PFCs may be used to keep food from sticking to cookware (non-stick frying pans), to make sofas and carpets resistant to stains, to make clothes and mattresses more waterproof and may also be used in some food packaging (such as fast-food containers or microwave popcorn bags), as well as in some firefighting materials [476].

The most well-known PFCs are perfluorooctane sulfonic acid (PFOS), perfluorooctanoic acid (PFOA) and their derivatives belonging to the group of perfluoroalkylated substances. PFCs are very persistent in the environment and some of them have been discovered as global pollutants of air, water, soil and wildlife. Bioaccumulation occurs in humans and everybody in our society has traces of these PFCs in their blood and internal organs such as the liver, kidneys, spleen and gall bladder [476]. Most westernised countries have now banned their use. However, hundreds of related chemicals are not regulated. PFCs still exist in the environment and therefore the food chain. Research conducted in Vancouver found PFCs in pork-based foods, raw fish and shellfish, microwave and movie theatre popcorn, from time spent in cars and airplanes, mattress age, stain repellent use on carpets, spot remover use on carpets, rugs and furniture, and in dust [477].

PFCs can affect the pregnant mother's thyroid function, which can have an effect on their unborn child [477]. PFCs can cross the placenta and can cause a low birth weight [478] [479] [480]. Babies and toddlers may be more exposed to house dust while playing on the floor and will then collect these contaminated dusts on their fingers and put them in their mouth and ingest them [481]. Relative to body weight, children have a 5–10 times larger intake of indoor PFCs than adults [476]. Around 1 per cent of a mother's PFC level can be passed on to her baby through her breast milk [482]. PFCs have been linked to ADHD in teenagers [483].

International awareness and concern is increasing. In 2000 the main producer, the 3M Company, voluntarily stopped the production of one of the chemicals (PFOS) and a ban of some fluorotelomers was introduced in Canada in 2006 [476]. In Europe, PFOS and its derivatives were banned in 2008, while in the USA they were banned in 2000 [476]. However, in China, PFOS levels have increased exponentially since 2003. Levels of PFOS in Shenyang, China in 2004 were approximately seven times higher than those found in the US general population at that time [484]. PFOS are only a small part of the problem. The family of PFCs consists of several hundred other unrestricted chemicals.

Hormones in cosmetics

Man-made chemicals are commonly used in cosmetics too. Unlike soaps or shampoos, which are rinsed off, other cosmetics remain on the body for considerably longer. These man-made chemicals, such as parabens (in most make-up, moisturisers, haircare products and shaving products), antiperspirant aluminium salts, cyclosiloxanes (silicones, in combination or alone in personal care products and as carriers, lubricants and solvents), triclosan (TCS, found in antibacterial soaps and body washes, toothpastes and some cosmetics), ultraviolet (UV) screens and phthalates, have an oestrogenic potency and react like oestrogens, which can disrupt the normal balance of hormones in mother and baby [485].

TCS is an antibacterial and antifungal agent present in some consumer products, including toothpaste, soaps, detergents, toys and surgical cleaning treatments. Exposure to TCSs can affect the mother's thyroid, which can reduce the baby's birth weight and gestational age [486] [487] [488] [489].

Phthalates and parabens are found in nail polish, cosmetics, lotions and perfumes [490]. Women who use four or more personal care products – perfume, deodorant, lipstick, nail polish and hand/face cream, for example – have more than four times higher concentrations of phthalates than in women using only two or three products [491]. Parabens can affect the mother's thyroid function [487]. Pregnant women should avoid using any cosmetics that contain phthalates as they can cross the placenta and disrupt the baby's hormones and increase the risk of the child developing autism [414]. Exposure to phthalates in pregnancy has also been linked with an increased rate of asthma in children [492].

If you are unsure what is in your cosmetics and whether they are safe to use while pregnant, you can download an app on to your smartphone that will tell you. I would recommend minimising the number of cosmetics you use in pregnancy and avoid using perfume.

Protecting your baby

It is better for your baby if you limit the amount of chemicals in your home (including your garden) and in your body. I recommend avoiding these chemicals:

- bisphenol A (BPA)
- bisphenol S (BPS)
- glyphosate (Roundup weed killer)
- parabens
- phenols
- phthalates
- polybrominated diphenyl ethers (PBDEs)
- polychlorinated biphenyls (PCBs)
- polyfluorinated chemicals (PFCs)
- triclosan
- trihalomethanes (THMs)

Fossil fuels

Other environmental pollutants include those from air pollution and the burning of wood. Air pollution can actually cross the placenta [493] [494]. The burning of wood releases a number of pollutants including polychlorinated dibenzodioxins and dibenzofurans, polychlorinated biphenyls, particulate matter and polycyclic aromatic hydrocarbons (PAHs). Pregnant women exposed to PAHs are at greater risk of their baby developing intrauterine growth restriction (IUGR) or being born with a low birth weight [495]. Other air pollutants, such as those from diesel car engines, have been linked to an increased rate of autism amongst children [392]. I would recommend wearing a N99 face mask when outside as this will filter any pollution before you breathe it in. While indoors, I would recommend using a HEPA air purifier to clean the air of any pollution.

Reducing Your Exposure to Heavy Metals

Exposure to heavy metals can damage the baby causing birth defects. The most important heavy metals are listed below.

Cadmium (Cd)

Cadmium is a pollutant commonly seen in modern industrial processes, for example the burning of fossil fuels and the manufacture of nickel–cadmium batteries. Cadmium is absorbed in significant quantities from cigarette smoke and shellfish, i.e. oysters [496]. A single cigarette contains 2.8µg of cadmium [497].

Women who smoke during pregnancy have double the levels of cadmium, half the level of progesterone and reduced iron in their placenta. Concentrations of cadmium in the ovaries increase with age and have been associated with implantation failure, early pregnancy loss and birth defects.

Lead (Pb)

Lead can be found in all parts of our environment – the air, soil, water and even inside our homes in a wide variety of different products, including paint, ceramics, pipes and plumbing materials, toys, batteries, ammunition and even cosmetics. Much of our exposure comes from human activities including the burning of fossil fuels and past use of leaded petrol and some types of industrial facilities.

Lead is a well-known toxic metal that can damage human health. Studies have shown that it can cause birth defects. In women, exposure to lead can increase the risk of miscarrying [498]. Lead can accumulate in our bodies over time, where it is stored in bones along with calcium. During pregnancy, the baby takes half the mother's calcium to help it form its own bones and is then exposed to this stored lead [498]. Lead can cross the placenta exposing the baby, resulting in reduced growth and preterm birth.

Mercury (Hg)

Low doses of mercury have been shown to affect the baby. Mercury is found in fish high up the food chain, for example tuna, swordfish, king mackerel, lobster, Spanish mackerel, marlin, grouper and shark. High levels of mercury are also found in the air from coal smoke and acid rain.

Mercury can pass through the placenta and into breast milk causing a slowing of physical and emotional reactions, deficit in language (late talking), memory deficit in attention, autism and late walking in children [404].

Carbon monoxide (CO) poisoning

It is impossible to detect CO using human senses because it is colourless, tasteless, odourless and non-irritating. When inhaled, CO is readily absorbed from the lungs into the bloodstream, where it forms with haemoglobin (Hb), known as carboxyhemoglobin (COHb). The presence of COHb in the blood decreases its oxygen-carrying capacity, reducing the availability of oxygen to the mother and baby, causing developmental disorders, chronic cerebral lesions and possible death [499]. Despite the sensitivity of the baby to CO-induced hypoxia (lack of oxygen), these effects may not become apparent for months or years.

The early symptoms of CO poisoning include headaches, dizziness, weakness, nausea, confusion, disorientation and visual disturbances. Often, women suffering from CO poisoning are unaware of their exposure because the symptoms are similar to those associated with pregnancy. Exposure to carbon monoxide comes from:

- air pollution from industry
- burning of gas, coal, kerosene and wood stoves
- incorrectly installed/maintained or poorly ventilated household appliances, such as cookers, heaters and central heating boilers
- car exhaust fumes
- cigarette smoke
- outdoors; concentrations of CO are highest near traffic intersections, in congested traffic, near exhaust gases from internal combustion engines and from industrial combustion sources and in poorly ventilated areas, such as parking garages and tunnels [499]

Ways of preventing CO poisoning include:

- Not smoking when pregnant or not breathing in second-hand cigarette smoke. Cigarette smoke is particularly damaging to the baby's brain in the third trimester.

- Not using unvented combustion sources indoors, such as space heaters or cooking devices (e.g., charcoal grills and hibachis).

- Wearing an N95 or N99 face mask when walking next to roads.

- Installing CO alarms in the home, especially in the kitchen.

- Using an air purification system with a HEPA filter or installing a HEPA filter in your vehicle.

- Not allowing automobiles to run idle in closed or open garages.

- Avoiding heavy traffic, intersections and journeys in long tunnels.

- Frequently inspecting and routinely maintaining vented combustion appliances and fireplaces.

Reducing Your Exposure to Electromagnetic Waves

Most people today own and use a portable device of some kind, from a mobile phone to a tablet or laptop. Mobile phones and Wi-Fi emit electromagnetic fields known as electromagnetic radiation, which includes microwave radiation and radio waves. Electromagnetic fields can change the atomic energy level and the direction of electron spin, thereby increasing the number of free radicals causing free radical damage (reactive oxygen species, ROS). In addition, a reduction in the number of antioxidants in our defence system can lead to cell death and tissue injury [500]. Mobile devices and their base stations both emit ultra-high frequency–electromagnetic fields (UHF–EMF). Research has shown that UHF–EMFs can damage a growing baby's genetic information within their blood [501].

Avoid using your mobile phone excessively or resting any laptops or tablets on your belly as the radiation they omit can pass through your abdomen to your baby causing free radical damage to the kidneys, brain and testes [502] [503]. Research has shown that children can develop hyperactivity/inattention problems if exposed to radio frequency radiation [504].

In today's modern world we are constantly being bombarded with electromagnetic waves (EMWs), from radio, phone masts, wireless devices, etc., and they can shorten a pregnancy and increase preterm birth [505]. You can protect yourself from EMWs by either reducing your use of gadgets that emit EMWs or from buying items that neutralise them, i.e. semi-precious stones such as tourmaline [506]. You can now buy maternity clothes that block EMWs and help to protect your baby, for example blankets, aprons, maternity belts and underwear [507].

Reducing Your Exposure to Plastics

There are many food-related products that contain man-made oestrogens, which can unbalance your baby's own hormones. It is beneficial to reduce your exposure to man-made oestrogens in your day-to-day life.

Hormones in food packaging

There is growing concern around hormones found in food packaging. An example is bisphenol A (BPA). BPA was first synthesised in 1891, as a synthetic oestrogen. It is now used to make plastic hard, coat paper (till receipts) and to line tins and lids of foods and drinks [508]. Exposure to BPAs during pregnancy can affect the baby's health and cause respiratory problems such as asthma [509] [510] as well as genital abnormalities in boys and early sexual maturation in girls [508]. BPAs can cross the placenta – studies have found concentrations in both mother and baby[508]. It has also been linked to autism[392].

Products that may contain BPAs include:

- baby food jar lids, liquid baby formula, dummies (pacifiers), sippy cups, straws
- plastic cups, cooking utensils and dishes
- plastic dishes, knives, forks and chopsticks
- toys, especially ones that can become warm, i.e. in the bath tub
- water bottles, cups and food storage containers
- food processors and blenders (with plastic containers and lids)
- tinned foods (BPA is in the liners in nearly every tin)
- takeaway hot beverage cups, i.e. coffee (BPA is in the lining)

Recent studies have concluded that plastic packaging is an important source of endocrine disruptors in the average human diet. Repeated exposure of food-contact materials to UV light, heat and acidic/alkaline contents may cause the polymers contained within the packaging to break down into monomers as phthalates and BPA, which then leach into food and beverages that are then consumed[439].

There is chronic intake of endocrine disruptors even from bottled water. Some of these endocrine disruptors are being replaced by other equally bad substances: many 'BPA-free' water containers contain bisphenol S (BPS) instead, which also exerts both genomic and non-genomic endocrine-disruptive effects upon the body[439]. I would recommend minimising eating food that contains plastic packaging where possible and reducing your use of plastic in the kitchen.

Know your plastics

Plastics are categorised according to their content and recyclability. The recycling symbol number is the code that shows what type of plastic was used to make the product. Plastics with recycling symbols

2, 4 and 5 are generally considered okay to use (see below). Avoid plastics with recycling symbols 3 and 6. Plastics with recycling symbol 7 are okay to use as long as they also say 'PLA' or have a leaf symbol on them. Recycling symbol 1 is okay to use, but should not be used more than once (do not refill plastic water bottles for example). Keep all plastic containers out of the heat and sun as these can cause the chemicals within them to be released into your food and fluids. Always try to buy foods that are not prepacked in plastic and use paper bags to pack loose fruit and vegetables.

Plastic codes

1. Polyethylene terephthalate (PETE or PET): includes clear plastic water and soft drink bottles. Generally considered okay to use, but do not reuse them.

2. High-density polyethylene (HDPE): includes opaque milk jugs, detergent bottles, juice bottles, butter tubs and toiletry bottles. Generally considered okay to use.

3. Polyvinyl chloride (PVC): includes cling film (food wrap) and cooking oil bottles. Do not cook food in these plastics and try to minimise using them around any type of food (use wax paper, kitchen foil or glass containers instead of cling film). Avoid where possible!

4. Low-density polyethylene (LDPE): includes grocery bags, some cling films, squeezable bottles and bread bags. Generally considered okay to use.

5. Polypropylene (PP): includes most yoghurt pots, tea bags, water bottles with a cloudy finish, medicine bottles, and sauce and syrup bottles. Generally considered okay to use.

6. Polystyrene/Styrofoam: includes disposable foam plates, cups and packing materials. Do not cook food or put hot food onto these plastics. Avoid where possible!

7. All other plastics not included in the other categories and with mixes of plastics 1 to 6 are labelled with a 7. Polylactic acid (PLA) is a plastic made from plants that is also labelled with a 7. PLA plastics do not contain BPA, which are bad (see page 116). No safety concerns have been raised about using PLA plastic with food. It is often difficult to tell the difference between a PLA number 7 plastic and a BPA-containing number 7 plastic. Do not cook food in plastics that are not PLA and avoid using these plastics around any type of food. Office water coolers tend to use reusable plastic bottles made from polycarbonate, number 7, which contain BPAs. Avoid where possible!

How to avoid exposing yourself to BPAs

- Avoid any plastics with recycling numbers 3, 6 or 7.

- Avoid plastic water bottles. Use filtered tap water and refill metal or glass reusable water bottles.

- Check that baby formula does not come in a container made out of 3, 6 or 7 plastic and is not lined with plastic BPA.

- Cover food with parchment paper rather than cling film (plastic wrap) or kitchen foil[511].

- Do not drink a hot beverage from a takeaway cup.

- Do not heat baby formula or breast milk in plastic.

- Do not microwave or heat anything plastic.

- Do not put hot food into plastic containers.

- Reduce your use of tinned foods.

- Use baby bottles that are glass or 'BPA free'.

- Use glass, porcelain or stainless steel to store food.

Hormones and Sexuality

Research today is showing how changes to hormone levels within the womb can affect and change a child's sexual identity. The baby's brain develops in the presence of testosterone in boys or the lack of testosterone in girls [512]. Our gender identity (the conviction of belonging to the male or female gender) and sexual orientation are programmed or organised into our brain structures when we are still in the womb [513]. Therefore, gender identity may be determined by prenatal hormonal influences [514].

The baby's testicles and ovaries develop in the sixth week of pregnancy [513]. Once the differentiation of the sexual organs into male or female is settled, the next thing that is differentiated is the brain, under the influence, mainly, of sex hormones such as testosterone, oestrogens and progesterone on the developing brain cells. The changes brought about in this stage are permanent. Later, during puberty, the brain circuits that were organised in the womb are activated by sex hormones [513].

The brain structure differences that result from the interaction between hormones, genes and developing brain cells are thought to be the basis of sex differences in a wide spectrum of behaviours, such as gender role (behaving as a man or a woman in society), gender identity (the conviction of belonging to the male or female gender), sexual orientation (heterosexuality, homosexuality or bisexuality), and sex differences regarding cognition, aggressive behaviour and language organisation [513]. Factors that interfere with the interactions between hormones and the developing brain systems during development in the womb may permanently influence later behaviour [514].

Girls who are exposed to high levels of testosterone in the womb, tend to choose boys as playmates, play preferentially with boys' toys, have increased interest in rough-and-tumble play, present less interest in infants than other girls and are called tomboys [514] [515]. Boys with higher than normal levels of testosterone can be more aggressive and autistic [514]. Exposure to man-made chemicals outside the womb may further antagonise these hormone imbalances.

Part Four

Dietary Advice

Eating healthily is not always straightforward while pregnant. Some women will go off certain types of foods, while others will crave different foods. Eating well is a difficult balancing act between eating good foods and following your cravings. In my view, the body has an intuitive knowledge of what it needs to help grow your baby and will express this through cravings. I therefore feel that cravings are important and should be listened to, but not overindulged to excess, and should be balanced with awareness of why you are having them (for example, craving sugar usually means you are tired and need to rest).

Chapter 12

Optimising Your Diet

For centuries Chinese people have added certain foods to their cooking to improve their health. Food is healthcare. Medicine is not healthcare – it is sick care. The Chinese believe that a happy stomach leads to a healthy body, because if the stomach is happy, it will produce abundant amounts of energy and blood for the body's needs and to grow your baby. Chinese people avoid cold foods that can damage the stomach, such as ice, ice cream, salads, smoothies and other raw foods. This is why you never see salad on a menu in a Chinese restaurant. These foods are cold and uncooked, which makes the stomach work harder to process them, thereby weakening it. The opposite is also true: if the stomach becomes too hot it will spit stomach juices upwards like an erupting volcano causing heartburn (acid reflux). In such cases, the stomach should be cooled down by eating fewer hot, spicy, greasy foods and eating cooling foods such as mint and yoghurt.

The stomach needs to be balanced at the right temperature for optimal digestion. For this reason, there is an old Chinese saying that, 'You should chew your fluids and swallow your foods', which means that by chewing your fluids they become the same temperature as your body before they hit the stomach, to avoid damage from the cold; and if you swallow your food then it has been chewed enough so that the stomach can spend less energy processing it. A happy stomach is a happy body, and a happy body is a happy baby!

Foods can be grouped into different natures: 'hot', 'cold', 'damp' or 'tonics'. Plants that take longer to grow, such as carrots, parsnips and cabbage, are more warming than those that grow quickly, such as lettuce, squash, radish and cucumber, which are cooling [516]. Tonics are foods that increase energy (qi) to promote general health and well-being. Damp foods include dairy, cheese, cream, gluten and rich foods, which make the digestive system work harder and use up energy that could have been used to grow your baby.

If a person has an imbalance, they can remedy this by eating the opposite food, for example cold foods for too much heat or hot foods for too much cold. If a person has excessive fluid retention or is weak, tonic foods should be eaten. The aim of a good diet is to balance your yin and yang and boost your energy and blood levels. When they are all balanced, your body will be in an optimal position to maintain a healthy pregnancy.

Most women can use dietary therapy together with an optimised lifestyle and supplements to support the growth of their baby. For those expectant mothers who are older or weaker, rectifying health with these measures can take longer. In such circumstances, Chinese herbs can be used to speed up the process of balancing yin and yang and boosting energy and blood levels.

The Ideal Diet

The ideal diet during pregnancy is a combination of protein, essential fatty acids, complex carbohydrates, vegetables high in iron and fruits rich in antioxidants. However, it is well known that a woman's dietary habits can change in pregnancy. A lot of women will try to eat healthier, but may not be able to resist foods they crave. It is common for some pregnant women to go off their favourite foods in favour of other food groups. The body instinctively knows what it needs. Try not to resist any food cravings. Eat what you crave and do not worry if you cannot eat fruit, vegetables or meats in the short term.

Pregnant women often crave carbohydrates in the early weeks of pregnancy. Carbohydrates are an important fuel source that the body needs to help sustain an early pregnancy and grow the placenta. Your cravings may change and you may be able to eat fruit, vegetables and meats later in your pregnancy. Some pregnant women will often crave salty foods in the first trimester. Salt relates to the kidneys in Chinese medicine and means the baby is draining your kidney energy, which is normal.

Ideally, you should consume 1,800 calories a day in the first trimester, rising to 2,200 calories a day in the second trimester and 2,400 calories a day in the third trimester [2]. If you have nausea, eat simple, plain food such as crackers, dried biscuits, toast and mints, and try fizzy drinks that do not contain sugar, caffeine or artificial sweeteners. Nausea usually comes when you are feeling hungry. You can fend off those hunger pangs by eating little and often, for example every two hours. It is important to carry something to snack on and a bottle of water with you at all times.

If you do not feel like eating too much, try to keep drinking plenty of water, ideally not from the tap – filtered or bottled water is best as it has fewer impurities in it. It is ideal to drink around two litres (half a gallon) of water a day. Dehydration in pregnancy can cause a lack of amniotic fluid in the womb (oligohydramnios), which can cause complications to the growing baby [517]. Try to follow these simple rules during pregnancy. Everything counts and is important in supporting your baby's growth:

- Avoid pre-made processed foods.

- Do not freeze meats or foods – cook and eat fresh.

- Do not microwave foods or drinks as they will have little energy left in them and can also irritate the digestive tract (see page 141).

- Eat foods that are organic or biodynamic, where possible.

All types of food are graded according to their quality. The quality of our food can affect your pregnancy and the baby's growth. Some people may choose the cheapest foods, thinking they look the same so they must be the same, but they are only the same skin-deep. Upon closer inspection, food varies greatly. For example, meat in one store can be very different to meat in another store. Non-organic meat contains a multitude of impurities that can damage the baby's health (see page 103). You often get what you pay for, so paying a bit extra for better-quality food will greatly improve your pregnancy and the health of your baby.

A typical Western diet tends to be high in sugar and gluten, which are hard on the digestive system, making it weak and sluggish. These foods reduce the amount of energy and blood produced, making the body weaker, which means fewer resources are available to grow your baby. The ideal diet is a Paleo diet, one which we have evolved over millions of years to eat. A Paleo diet includes all foods in their natural form, as Nature intended, with nothing man-made – for example, bread, pasta, refined sugar, etc. Instead, we should eat fresh meat, fish, grains, fruit, vegetables and low-glycaemic index (GI) carbohydrates like quinoa, oats, brown rice and sweet potatoes.

Most people eat with their eyes and their mouths rather than with their stomachs. Any food that takes too long to digest, such as gluten, is bad for the digestion. Research has shown that people sensitive to gluten are more likely to be deficient in iron, which can affect their pregnancy[518]. In Chinese medicine, this is due to a weakened spleen not producing enough blood. For a healthy pregnancy you should eat with both your mouth and your stomach. That way, the food you eat will be the best for your body and will not weaken it.

Foods to avoid

There are many foods to avoid while pregnant. However, this varies from culture to culture and country to country. The foods I would recommend avoiding during pregnancy include:

- alcohol
- blue cheeses
- fizzy drinks with added caffeine or sweeteners
- fortified cereals, foods and flour with vitamin A
- game such as pheasant, deer and grouse
- liver and pâté
- natural or manufactured laxatives
- no more than two portions of oily fish a week
- predator fish: shark, swordfish, king mackerel and tilefish (golden or white snapper)
- processed meats, such as hot dogs, etc.
- raw or partially cooked eggs from outside the UK [519]
- raw sprouts, such as alfalfa, clover, mung bean and radish
- salads
- shellfish, such as oysters and clams
- soya
- sushi
- uncooked deli meats
- unpasteurised dairy products, including milk and soft cheese

---

Food Groups

There are ten main food groups:

1. carbohydrates
2. cold foods
3. fats
4. fibre
5. hot foods
6. proteins
7. sugars
8. tonics
9. vitamins and minerals
10. water

Eating a balanced diet incorporating all these food groups is important for your health and that of your baby. However, as I shall now discuss, some are more important than others during pregnancy.

Fats

We have all been told that fats are bad for our health, but, in fact, we all need some fats, just not too much and none of the bad ones. Bad fats are the trans-fatty acids (hydrogenated oils) found in processed foods and too much fat from red meat, all of which contain cholesterol. Our bodies need cholesterol to maintain good health; it helps to convert vitamin D in the skin, which reduces the risk of rickets and autism [356]. We just do not want too much of it – no more than 200mg/dL a day. Ideally our diet should contain no more than 10 per cent saturated fat in each day.

Saturated fats are found in everyday food items such as:

- butter, ghee, lard, coconut oil and palm oil
- cakes and biscuits
- cheese
- chocolate and chocolate spreads
- coconut cream and coconut milk
- cream, crème fraîche and sour cream
- cured meats like salami, chorizo and pancetta
- fatty cuts of meat
- ice cream and milkshakes
- pastries, such as pies, quiches, sausage rolls and croissants
- sausages and bacon [520]

Eating too much saturated fat in pregnancy can increase the risk of the mother developing gestational diabetes (see page 54) as well as the baby developing autism and reduced cardiovascular function [54] [521]. To reduce the effects of fats in your body, you can increase your consumption of lipotropics. Lipotropics increase the liver's production of lecithin, which keeps cholesterol levels down. Lipotropics include methionine, choline, inositol and betaine and are found in a wide range of foods, such as Brazil nuts, turkey, chicken, eggs, yoghurt, etc. Be careful when selecting foods that proclaim they are either low in fat or fat-free as often manufacturers have replaced the tasty fats with something even worse – refined sugar!

Sugar

Naturally-occurring sugars, for example those found in fruit, are actually good for the body and help to fuel muscles, nerves and the brain. It is the refined form of sugar that is the problem. A lot of people crave refined sugars, which are found in foods such as cakes, biscuits, sweets (candy) and fizzy drinks. Craving sugar is like an addiction and acts on the brain in the same way as cocaine [522]. Refined sugar passes quickly into the bloodstream in large amounts, giving the stomach and pancreas a shock. The digestive system is then weakened and food cannot be digested properly. This leads to a blood sugar imbalance and further cravings for sugar.

If you crave refined sugar, your body is most likely tired and deficient and wants quick energy. Instead of giving your body more sugar, have a nap, reduce your energy expenditure and eat more protein and iron-rich foods. The body would rather have more blood than more sugar. Eating a diet that is high in refined, processed sugar can affect insulin levels. High levels of insulin can cause gestational diabetes (see page 54).

Avoid artificial sweeteners too, which can cause weight gain in pregnant women and lead to preterm births [523]. Artificial sweeteners taken during pregnancy have also been shown to double the risk of babies being overweight at the age of one year and increase the risk of them developing asthma [524] [525] [526]. Artificial sweeteners can be found in soft drinks and other beverages, baked goods, sweets, puddings, tinned foods, jams and jellies, dairy products and even in heartburn medications.

Essential fatty acids

Essential fatty acids (EFAs) are a group of oils known as long-chain polyunsaturated fatty acids (PUFAs). They come in two types: omega-3 (linolenic acid) and omega-6 (linoleic acid). Omega-9 is not considered an essential fatty acid as our bodies can make it from omega-3 or -6. Our bodies cannot produce omega-3 or -6, which means that we have to get them through our diet. During pregnancy, the recommended dietary intake of omega-3 fatty acids a week is 650mg, of which 300mg is docosahexaenoic acid (DHA) [527]. The US Food and Drug Administration (FDA) and the NHS recommends eating two to three servings of lower-mercury fish per week (225–340g, 8–12oz) [528].

DHA is an omega-3 fatty acid that is important for the baby's brain and eyes. DHA is commonly found in pregnancy supplements. Eicosapentaenoic acid (EPA) is also an omega-3 fatty acid and is important for improving childhood development [529]. It is found in cold-water fatty fish, such as salmon, and in fish oil supplements, along with DHA. Pregnancy supplements often contain DHA but not EPA (see page 146).

Modern Western diets tend to overdose on omega-6 (sunflower, corn and cottonseed oil) and under-consume omega-3 [527]. Only 19 per cent of American adults consume the recommended two servings of fish each week [527]. In the UK, people consume on average only one serving of fish a week [530]. Based on consuming two fish servings a week, the average intake per day of omega-3 fatty acids is 100–250mg omega-3 fatty acids and 50–100mg DHA [527]. It is advised not to eat more than two portions of fish a week while pregnant due to pollutants (toxins) in the fish [531]. An additional supplement may be needed to top up the omega-3 level to 650mg a week. Research has shown that expectant mothers who ate a diet including omega-3 had a lower risk of their child being born autistic [532] [533] [534]. The highest amount of omega-3 can be found in certain types of fish, seeds and dark greens, such as:

- anchovies
- butterfish
- catfish
- cereal grasses (rice, rye, oats, maize, buckwheat, millet)
- chard
- chia seeds
- flaxseeds
- hempseeds
- herring
- kale
- parsley
- pilchards
- pollock
- pumpkin seeds
- rainbow trout
- rapeseed
- salmon
- sardines
- scallops
- shrimp
- walnuts

Prolonged stress, such as anxiety or dieting, can put the body into a state of resistance – level two of the body's stress response – causing a reduction in lipid reserves [6]. Lipids are an organic compound made up of fats and oils that are important for bodily functions and for pregnancy. As most people are stressed for more than two hours, which is the time needed to put the body into the resistance phase, most people are deficient in lipids and EFAs (omega-3). Additionally, poor lifestyle habits can also affect the metabolism of omega-3 in the body, worsening omega-3 levels. These include:

- a deficiency of vitamin B_6, zinc and magnesium
- dieting
- excessive consumption of
- trans-fatty acids, sugar or animal fat
- exposure to pollutants
- smoking [535]

EFAs are particularly important during pregnancy, as they are required for the development of the baby's brain and eyes [527]. During pregnancy, mothers put on 11–16kg (25–35lb) of weight. EFAs can be stored within fat reserves and later released during breastfeeding to help support eye and brain development during the first four to six months of the baby's life [535].

Pregnancy requires high levels of EFAs. As most people's diets are low in omega-3s, stores can often be depleted in a woman's first pregnancy, especially if she is carrying more than one baby. Stores of EFAs can then remain low, which can influence the second child's intelligence level [535]. Research has found that maternal blood levels of DHA were significantly lower in women who had previously given birth compared to those pregnant with their first child [535].

Mothers who maintain good levels of omega-3s during their pregnancy are less likely to have a preterm delivery and their babies are born with a better birth weight [527] [536] [537]. Eating polyunsaturated fats while pregnant can also reduce the risk of developing gestational diabetes [538]. During the last trimester, the baby accrues about 50–70mg a day of omega-3 fatty acid, DHA [527].

Vegetarian and vegan mothers may be deficient in omega-3 because of the exclusion of fish in their diet. Vegetarians and vegans can take one tablespoon of flaxseed oil a day, for example, which has a total EFA of 8.9g. However, plant-based omega-3 fatty acids, like flaxseed oil, are poorly converted to the biologically active omega-3 fatty acid EPA and convert even less to DHA. Unfortunately, it is impossible for pregnant women to meet their omega-3 fatty acid requirements from omega-3-rich vegetable oils [527]. Therefore, in order to make up the omega-3 fatty acid deficit in their diet, vegetarian or vegan pregnant women are left with essentially two choices: fish oil supplements supplying EPA and DHA, or algae-derived DHA.

Protein

Proteins are made up of amino acid chains, forming the structural material of muscles, tissues and organs [180]. They are important in the growth and development of your baby. Dietary protein can be divided into two groups: first-class proteins, which contain significant quantities of all the essential amino acids and are derived from animal meat, fish, eggs and dairy products, and second-class proteins, which contain some essential amino acids but not all and are derived from vegetables, rice, beans and nuts [535]. Second-class proteins need to be mixed and matched by eating as wide a variety of foods as possible.

Below is a list of meat and non-meat foods that contain high levels of protein – more than 15g of protein per 100g serving:

- beef jerky (organic) 30–40g
- Parmesan 32g
- tuna steak (light) 32g
- chicken (organic) 31g
- pumpkin seeds 30g
- turkey (organic) 30g
- peanuts 25–28g
- Edam cheese 27g
- tilapia 26g
- tinned tuna (light) 25g
- Cheddar cheese 25g
- seitan 25g
- beef (organic) 20–24g
- salmon 24g
- halibut 23g
- almonds 21g
- sardines 21g
- cod 20g
- lamb (organic) 20g
- mackerel 20g
- pistachios 20g
- tempeh 20g
- pork loin (organic) 17–20g
- pollock 19g
- cashew nuts 18g
- mozzarella 18g
- chia seeds 17g
- walnuts 15–17g

Factors that can deplete protein include:

- poor diet, refined sugars and coffee
- stress, worry, overwork and trauma

Nuts are a rich source of protein and are commonly eaten by vegetarians and vegans. New research has overturned the old belief that women should avoid eating nuts while pregnant [539]. Today, it is believed that eating nuts while pregnant can actually make your child less allergic to nuts in later life. Current advice is to eat nuts while pregnant, if you yourself are not allergic to them [531]. Brazil nuts are a rich source of selenium, which if eaten during pregnancy has been shown to improve the child's cognitive function [540].

Salt

Some women will crave salty foods in early pregnancy, which is normal. However, eating too much salt later in the pregnancy can lead to hypertension, pre-eclampsia and swollen legs. Salt is often hidden in processed foods such as tinned products, nuts, ready-prepared meals, biscuits, cakes and breakfast cereals. When reading food labels, those that list salt as sodium need to be multiplied by 2.5 to give the table salt content, for example 0.4g of sodium contains 1g of salt [535].

Red meat

Red meat is good for you and your baby. It is a rich source of protein, iron, zinc and vitamin B_{12}, all of which are important for a healthy pregnancy. We need to have some of it in our diet, but not too much. Excessive red meat consumption can be bad for health. In the US, anabolic sex steroid hormones are administered to cattle and other animals for growth promotion 60–90 days before slaughter [541] [542]. This practice was banned in Europe in the 1980s. Processed red meats have previously been shown to have higher concentrations of hormone residues compared with other meats, raising concerns regarding the potential reproductive health consequences of consuming these foods.

The best red meat to eat is organic lean red meat that has not been frozen or processed; as close to Nature as it can be and only one serving a week. Some pregnant women will no longer want to eat meat and may not like the smell, which is normal. In such cases, it's important to find alternative sources of protein that you can eat (see list on page 134).

Carbohydrates

There are two main types of carbohydrates: simple and complex. Simple carbohydrates include white and brown sugar, glucose, corn syrups and fruit juices, etc., which are bad. Complex carbohydrates include whole grains, yams, brown rice, potatoes, carrots, broccoli and green beans, etc., which are good to eat during pregnancy. Some women will crave carbohydrates in pregnancy, especially in the first trimester, which is normal. After week 12, it is best to try to avoid eating simple carbohydrates and stick to complex ones instead as this will help to reduce the risk of developing gestational diabetes.

Vegetarianism

More and more people are choosing to become vegetarian, especially with animal welfare being so poor and the inclusion of antibiotics and steroids in meat. However, being a vegetarian is not easy. It requires a varied diet to ensure all minerals, vitamins and amino acids are included as well as taking DHA, EPA or algae supplements during pregnancy. If a varied diet is not eaten, women can become deficient in iron, protein and omega-3, which can affect the baby's growth and development.

If you are vegetarian, you need to be very diligent with your diet and eat a wide range of good-quality foods to maintain high levels of energy and blood as well as eat enough protein and omega-3 from non-animal sources. With today's hectic lifestyle this is a challenge and can lead to a lack of blood. Half of women in India, where a high percentage of the population is vegetarian, are anaemic [543].

Veganism is also on the rise, with concerns around climate change, animal welfare and health compelling more and more people to follow a plant-based way of life. However, vegans can have more exaggerated deficiencies than vegetarians. Vegetarians and vegans tend to be deficient in iodine [45], which is needed for both the mother and baby's thyroid gland. On the plus side, vegetarians and vegans tend to have lower levels of mercury because they do not eat fish.

Caffeine

Caffeine is the world's most widely consumed psychoactive substance [544]. Caffeine is a stimulant, similar to sugar; it gives us a false sense of having more energy. Caffeine is found in some foods and drinks, such as tea, coffee, chocolate, energy drinks, cold and flu remedies and some soft drinks, such as cola.

Pregnant women should minimise their caffeine consumption to a maximum of 200mg a day [545]. Excessive caffeine consumption during pregnancy can reduce the absorption of calcium as well as affect the baby [546] [547] [548]. Caffeine can be found in varying quantities, for example:

- 1 mug of instant coffee: 40–140mg
- 1 mug of filter coffee: 60–200mg
- 1 mug of decaffeinated coffee: 4–9mg [549]
- 1 mug of tea: 20–75mg
- 1 can of cola (330ml): 12–60mg
- 1 can of energy drink (250ml): up to 80mg – larger cans may contain up to 160mg

- 1 bar of plain chocolate (50g): most products on the UK market contain less than 5–35mg
- 1 bar of milk chocolate (50g): most products on the UK market contain less than 10mg [549] [550]

Caffeine can enter breast milk and expose the baby during its period of neurodevelopment [551]. Other possible side effects of caffeine use upon the baby while breastfeeding include irritability, jitteriness, restlessness, overstimulation, wakefulness, poor feeding and a mild iron deficiency caused by decreased iron content in breast milk [552].

Alcohol

When pregnant, a woman should stop drinking any type of alcohol for the duration of her pregnancy as alcohol is known to cause reduced birth weight and birth defects [553] [554] [555] [556].

Water

Being adequately hydrated during pregnancy is important. Water makes up 55–60 per cent of the body. A good amount of water ensures blood moves smoothly and tissues are nourished. I recommend drinking two litres (half a gallon) of water a day. It sounds like a lot, and drinking this much water a day can take practice and time. If you work at a desk, put a two-litre (half a gallon) glass or metal bottle on it and sip from it throughout the day. You will then achieve your daily quota. Do not drink water straight from the tap; filter it first to remove any traces of chemicals and medications. Drink water from a glass or porcelain cup rather than from plastic.

Hot foods

Hot foods can be divided into two types: warm or hot. Warm foods include onion, garlic, ginger, wasabi, paprika and turmeric. These foods are often good for the digestion as they help to keep the stomach warm. The stomach needs to be warm to facilitate the breakdown of foods and digestion. Ginger is known to help with nausea and morning sickness as it warms the stomach, making it feel more balanced. However, for some women who suffer from heartburn (acid reflux), even these warm foods will be too much for their stomach. In such cases, omit these warm foods and replace them with cooling foods such as mint and yoghurt.

Hot foods include chilli. Eating chilli can create internal heat in the body, which can make the baby restless as well as cause heartburn. I would try to avoid eating chilli while pregnant. Some women will feel warm and even hot while pregnant and will naturally not want to eat spicy foods such as chilli.

Cold foods

Cold foods include salads, ice, ice cream and chilled water and foods. Salads are seen in the West as being healthy and good for you as they are natural and low in calories. However, salads are cold and raw which makes the stomach work harder to process them. They also do not contain many calories, which you need in pregnancy to help the baby grow. Cold foods make the stomach weaker, which affects digestion and reduces the amount of energy and blood produced, which again the body needs to support the growth of your baby. Ice and ice cream do the same thing – they make the stomach cold and inefficient.

Another food trend at the moment is the drinking of raw juices. Raw juices are cold and can stress the stomach in the same way as salads, weakening it and causing a reduction in the production of energy and blood. Having a warm liquid ginger drink in the morning would be better for your digestion and pregnancy.

Tonics

Tonics are foods that can boost your digestive system and the health of you and your baby. When your digestive system is working more efficiently, your body produces more energy and blood for you and your baby. A good example of a tonic is probiotics. Probiotics are considered safe to take in pregnancy [557] [558]. Probiotics increase good bacteria in the stomach, which improves stomach function, digestion and cognitive function [559]. Research has shown that taking the probiotic *lactobacillus reuteri* during pregnancy can increase oxytocin levels, reduce the risk of autism, reduce pregnancy gingivitis and group B streptococcus, aid the baby's immune system and reduce the risk of your baby developing eczema after birth [54] [560] [561] [562] [563] [564] [565] [566].

Foods that affect progesterone levels

Progesterone is important during pregnancy, especially in the first trimester. Foods that contain apigenin can increase levels of progesterone [567] [568], which can help to maintain the uterus lining and support the pregnancy. Apigenin is found in higher levels in foods such as chamomile tea, celery, yarrow, tarragon, liquorice, flax, passionflower, spearmint, basil and oregano [569].

Controlling Weight During Pregnancy

Being pregnant will mean gaining around 11–16kg (25–35lb) in weight, which is normal. However, it can be a balancing act between putting on weight but not too much, as unfortunately being overweight can cause problems in pregnancy.

Research has shown a link between being obese in pregnancy caused by eating a high-fat diet and children subsequently developing autism [54]. Mothers with obesity were one and a half times more likely to have a child with autism. The risk of children developing autism increased two-fold when mothers had both obesity and gestational diabetes together [54]. Further research has shown that mothers who are obese during pregnancy have children with a greater risk of developing asthma [570] [571].

Dieting and excessive exercising are not recommended ways to lose weight while pregnant. Dieting just starves the body at a time when it needs additional calories, proteins and vitamins to support the baby's healthy growth. Exercising too much in pregnancy is similar to dieting, in that it uses up important calories and nutrients that could otherwise be used to help the baby's growth. I recommend not to diet at all during pregnancy and to exercise after week 20, and then only gentle exercising, i.e. pregnancy yoga, pregnancy Pilates, swimming, etc. (see page 98).

The ideal way to control weight in pregnancy is by:

- Eating a low-glycaemic index (GI) diet and cutting out simple carbohydrates, such as white and brown sugar, glucose, corn syrups and fruit juices. Carbohydrates like quinoa, oats, brown rice and sweet potatoes should be eaten instead.

- Eating foods rich in copper as it is important in fat metabolism [572]. Foods high in copper include whole grains, beans, nuts, potatoes, dark leafy greens and dried prunes.

- Trying acupuncture, which has been shown in research to help with controlling weight [131].

- Cutting out gluten will help you to control weight gain as gluten can impair the spleen's function, weakening it, which causes weight gain.

- Cutting out refined sugar from your diet. Refined sugar is found in fizzy drinks, biscuits, chocolate and even bread.

Microwaves

Microwaves have become the norm for most people in today's world because they are quick and convenient. However, research has shown that foods heated in plastic packaging in microwaves can contain harmful chemicals which have leached into the food from the plastic container [573] [574].

I believe that food which has been heated using a microwave offers little energetic value. Its energy has been zapped and it lacks vitality. Essentially, it is dead food. Eating microwaved food regularly can lead to a lack of energy, tiredness and a weakened stomach as the heat from the microwaved food can irritate and damage the digestive tract [575] [576].

Microwaves work by making the atoms in the food rub together to generate heat, which cooks the food. However, as you then eat the food while the atoms are still vibrating, it can affect the cells in the body that they come into contact with. You can normally tell when food has been heated in a microwave, as your stomach is unusually hot afterwards. I recommend avoiding microwaved food or fluids whenever possible and always cook from fresh.

Eating Soya in Pregnancy

Naturally-occurring oestrogens come from plants and are called phytoestrogens. When we eat these plants, we introduce oestrogen into our bodies. Phytoestrogens can cross the placenta and affect the baby's hormone levels [577] [578] [579].

Genistein is found exclusively in soya foods, such as soya milk, tofu, miso and tempeh [580]. Unknown to a lot of people, soya is also found in meat substitute products, energy bars, sports drinks, imitation dairy products, some cereals, bread, biscuits, chocolate spreads, ice cream, cheeses and infant products [581]. In Japan, where they eat the most amount of soya in the world, large-scale studies have shown that eating too much soya in pregnancy can cause genital defects in boys [582] [583]. I therefore recommend reading food labels and avoiding a high consumption of soya.

Although diet is important during pregnancy, it cannot always provide enough vitamins and minerals for optimal pregnancy health. Let's now look at additional supplements that are important during pregnancy for both you and your baby.

Chapter 13

Supplements

During pregnancy, it is important for you to take supplements for the health of you and your baby. I would recommend taking a good-quality vitamin and mineral supplement that has omega-3 in the form of docosahexaenoic acid (DHA) and eicosapentaenoic acid (EPA), but not from cod liver oil as that contains vitamin A [527]. Overdosing on vitamin A, which is rare, can be harmful to your baby [584] [585] [586]. Beware of fortified products, such as cereals and flour, as they can sometimes contain vitamin A.

All minerals and vitamins are important for health; however, the most important ones for your baby are listed below. The dose of these supplements may not be enough in your pregnancy supplement, so you may need to take extra.

The daily dosage is the total daily amount, which includes sources from both food and supplements. Please check the dosage carefully as different supplements have greatly different dose ranges. A milligram (mg) is one thousandth of 1 gram (g), while a microgram (mcg) is one millionth of 1g. Therefore, 1g equals 1000mg or 1,000,000mcg, while 1mg equals 1000mcg.

Baby's Health

There are several specific supplements that are important to the health and development of your baby:

Beta-carotene

Beta-carotene is converted into vitamin A only when the body needs it [580]. It is safer to take beta-carotene than vitamin A. However, do not take it if you have hypothyroidism (underactive thyroid) as levels may already be high [587]. Beta-carotene can be found in apricots, sweet potatoes, broccoli, pumpkin, carrots, mangoes and peaches. The recommended daily dose during pregnancy is 3–6mg.

Biotin

Biotin is essential during pregnancy as deficiencies have been linked to birth defects [588] [589]. Biotin is found in meat, oily fish (salmon), whole grains, rice, nuts, sunflower seeds, cauliflower and egg yolks. The recommended daily dose during pregnancy is 30mcg [590].

Calcium

Calcium is essential for developing your baby's bone structure and teeth. Women who do not consume enough calcium (less than 500mg/day) may be at risk of increased bone loss during pregnancy and an increased risk of developing pre-eclampsia and having a preterm delivery [115]. The recommended daily dose in pregnancy is 1,000mg [591]. Calcium remains important during breastfeeding too. Baby girls need more calcium in breast milk than boys, who need more fat [592].

Calcium is depleted by caffeine (including tea, coffee and soft drinks that list caffeine on the label), carbonated drinks and simple (refined) carbohydrates. Try to avoid dairy sources of calcium, such as milk, as too much dairy can weaken the digestive system leading to a weakened body. Have you ever wondered why a glass of milk at night helps you to sleep? It is because the spleen finds it hard to process milk as it is damp, making it weak. If the spleen becomes weakened, we feel tired, making it easier to sleep[593]. There is more absorbable calcium in vegetables such as broccoli than there is in milk[535].

Good sources of calcium include:

- Brazil nuts
- broccoli
- cabbage
- Cheddar cheese
- hazelnuts
- kale
- mozzarella
- nori seaweed
- parsley
- peanuts
- pilchards
- salmon
- sardines
- sunflower seeds
- walnuts
- yoghurt

Choline

Choline is vital for the development of your baby's memory in future life. It becomes depleted during pregnancy and lactation. Egg yolks and green leafy vegetables are a good source of choline. The recommended daily dose in pregnancy is 450mg, increasing to 550mg while breastfeeding[594].

Copper

Copper is an essential trace element that is found to be deficient in most people. It helps with oxygen and iron transportation as well as breaking down fat cells into energy[572]. Copper is important in the development of the baby and can prevent a low birth weight[595]. A deficiency of copper can cause anaemia[572]. Copper is found in nuts, wholegrain cereals, dried prunes, avocados, artichokes, radishes, garlic, mushrooms and green vegetables. The recommended daily dose during pregnancy is 1,300mcg[596].

DHA

DHA is an omega-3 essential fatty acid (see page 131). DHA is essential in brain development and growth, ultimately affecting learning abilities [597]. Around 50 per cent of the baby's brain is formed during the foetal stage, while the remaining 50 per cent is formed in the first year of birth. Vegans tend to be deficient in DHA [598]. Good sources of omega-3 are oily fish, walnuts and flaxseeds. The recommended daily dose during pregnancy is 650mg. Pregnancy supplements often contain DHA but not EPA. As only 4–11 per cent of DHA is converted to EPA, pregnant women who just take DHA supplements, without any dietary EPA, may limit the amount that reaches the baby [527].

Folic acid (vitamin B₉, folate)

A woman's requirement for folic acid increases dramatically during pregnancy. Studies have linked folic acid to the prevention of neural tube defects such as spina bifida [599] [600] [601]. Other studies have shown that women who continue to take folic acid into pregnancy, for at least eight weeks, have children with fewer language development delays at the age of three years [602]. The recommended daily dose during pregnancy is 400mcg plus sources from foods [603], which include:

- asparagus
- avocados
- black-eyed peas
- broccoli
- Brussels sprouts
- green peas
- kidney beans
- mustard greens
- rice
- spaghetti
- spinach [604]

Iodine

Pregnant women need about 50 per cent more iodine to provide enough for their baby [605]. Iodine is an essential trace element that is vital for the production of two thyroid hormones: thyroxin (T_4) and triiodothyronine (T_3). A deficiency of iodine may lead to an underactive thyroid and in newborns a condition called cretinism [535]. As well as having an underactive thyroid, the child's brain cannot develop properly, leading to learning difficulties.

The recommended daily dose during pregnancy is 220mcg. Iodine is found in fish, seaweeds such as kelp, onions and unrefined sea salt. Most salts (sodium) are refined and have been stripped of nearly all their 60 trace elements and replaced with fortified iodine. Try to use salt that has not been refined or altered.

Sources of iodine include:

- dairy products, such as yoghurt and cheese (in small quantities)
- fish (such as cod) and other seafood
- fruits and vegetables, although the amount depends on the iodine in the soil where they grew and if any fertiliser was used
- grains
- seaweeds, such as kelp, dulse and wakame
- unrefined sea salt

Iron (ferrous fumarate, ferrous gluconate, ferrous sulphate)

Iron is an essential mineral needed for the production of haemoglobin, the red blood pigment which transports oxygen and carbon dioxide around the body. Iron requirements increase during pregnancy as a mother's red blood cell and haemoglobin count increases by 30–35 per cent [4]. It is estimated that half of pregnant women globally are deficient in iron [606]. Iron in pregnancy is important as a deficiency can lead to anaemia. The recommended daily dose during pregnancy is 27mg. If your blood test comes back as iron deficient (ferritin ug/ litre <30), I recommended a daily dose of 100mg.

Iron is in high demand at different times throughout pregnancy, initially as the woman's blood volume expands, then when the placenta is grown and subsequently when the baby needs to lay down its own iron stores. It is recommended to take iron supplements during pregnancy as research has shown that expectant mothers who took iron supplements resulted in their baby being on average 41.2g heavier at birth with a reduced risk of low birthweight by 19 per cent [110] [607].

To absorb iron efficiently certain nutrients are required, namely folic acid, vitamins C, B_6 and B_{12}, calcium and copper. If you take high doses of iron, your stools may be dark in colour, which is normal. If constipation occurs, try taking a 'gentle' iron supplement. Rich sources of iron include:

- beef
- cashew nuts [608]
- chickpeas
- dark chocolate (over 85 per cent cacao)
- kidney beans
- lentils
- potatoes (with skin)
- sardines
- spinach
- tomatoes
- white beans

Iron is depleted by:

- antacids (which pregnant women often take for heartburn)
- caffeine
- excessive phosphates (found in commercially produced food such as preserved meats, soft drinks and ice cream)
- smoking
- tea

Probiotics

Probiotics are useful in reversing damage caused by antibiotics and can improve cognitive function. Probiotics that contain *lactobacillus reuteri* have been shown to increase levels of oxytocin, which contribute to breast milk production and reduced autistic traits [54]. I recommend a daily dose of 5–10 billion CFUs. Always buy probiotics that have a long shelf life.

Pyrroloquinoline quinone (PQQ)

PQQ is a vitamin-like substance that is a powerful antioxidant. Preliminary research has shown that it can improve the growth of the baby [609] [610]. The recommended daily dose during pregnancy is 20mg.

Spirulina

Spirulina is a superfood and is known as blue-green algae (*arthrospira platensis*). It is packed full of protein with more than 60 per cent per 100g. It contains high levels of iron and vitamin B_{12}, all the essential amino acids as well as essential minerals and vitamins. It contains 180 per cent more calcium than whole milk, 670 per cent more protein than tofu, 3,100 per cent more beta-carotene than carrots and 5,100 per cent more iron than spinach [611]. Spirulina has omega-3 fatty acids in the form of alpha lipoic acid (ALA), EPA and DHA. It is great for vegetarians and vegans looking to get adequate amounts of DHA and EPA into their diet during pregnancy. The recommended daily dose during pregnancy is 1g.

Vitamin A (retinol)

Vitamin A is important in the growth of the baby's skeletal system and internal organs [612]. During pregnancy, it is important not to exceed the daily dose, especially during the first seven weeks [535]. Taking more than the recommended dose can increase the risk of birth defects. A daily dose should not exceed 10,000 IU (3,000 RE) and a weekly dose should not exceed 25,000 IU (7,500 RE) [586]. Your baby will start to accumulate vitamin A during the third trimester of pregnancy and will need several months of sufficient intake after birth to build up adequate levels [586]. Colostrum and early milk are extremely rich in vitamin A. Young children with a lack of vitamin A can have poor health [586].

Foods that contain high levels of vitamin A include fish oils (cod liver oil), liver, pâtés and fortified foods such as cereals and flour. I recommend a daily dose of 600mcg (800 RE). It is safer to take beta-carotene (page 145) instead as it can be converted into vitamin A when the body needs it, thereby reducing the chances of overdosing (535) (580).

Vitamin D (calciferol, viosterol, ergosterol)

Vitamin D is found in five different forms (1, 2, 3, 4 and 5). Very few foods in nature contain vitamin D. The flesh of fatty fish such as salmon, tuna and mackerel are amongst the best sources. Small amounts of vitamin D are found in cheese and egg yolks. Vitamin D in these foods is primarily in the form of vitamin D_3 [613]. The recommended daily dose during pregnancy is 10–15mcg (400–600 IU).

Some vitamin D_3 is made from sunlight when the UV index is higher than three and when not using sunscreen [535] [614]. Due to the risk of skin cancer caused by too much sun exposure, it is recommended to expose the skin to 10–15 minutes of sunlight before applying sunscreen. Most people living in cloudy countries, such as the UK, Ireland, New Zealand and the east coast of America, will have low levels of vitamin D [615]. Even low sunscreens such as factor 8 reduce vitamin D production by 95 per cent [535] [614]. Vitamin D regulates the absorption of zinc, calcium and iron and low levels have been linked to anaemia. A lack of vitamin D can cause rickets and autism in children [355] [358] [359] [360] [362] [361] [535] [616].

Vitamin D is found in:

- Cheddar cheese
- chicken breast
- eggs
- portobello mushrooms
- rainbow trout
- salmon
- sardines
- tuna (light)

Vitamin K (phylloquinone, menaquinones, menadione)

Vitamin K is found in three different forms: K_1, phylloquinone; K_2, menaquinones; and K_3, menadione [535]. Ninety per cent of our dietary intake is in the form of vitamin K_1. It is necessary for the formation of prothrombin in the liver, which is essential for efficient blood clotting to occur. Vitamin K is found in certain foods but more importantly is synthesised by bacteria in the large intestine. Newborn babies are reliant on their mother's vitamin K production as their intestines are initially sterile [180]. For this reason, vitamin K is often given to the baby at birth by injection or orally. Without adequate levels of vitamin K, women are predisposed to haemorrhaging and newborn infants to haemorrhagic disease. The recommended daily dose during pregnancy is 90mcg [617].

Sources of vitamin K include:

- acidophilus
- alfalfa
- broccoli
- carrot juice
- cauliflower
- collards
- egg yolks
- kelp
- meat
- nattō
- okra (ladies' fingers)
- olive oils
- pine nuts
- pomegranate juice
- potatoes
- pulses
- pumpkins
- rapeseed
- safflower oil
- spinach
- tomatoes
- turnip greens [617]

Vitamin K is depleted by:

- air pollution
- antibiotics (cephalosporins)
- anticonvulsants (phenytoin) [580]
- aspirin
- freezing foods [580]

Zinc

Zinc is an important mineral during pregnancy as it supports the growth of your baby and can increase birth weight [595] [618]. During fertilisation, zinc is released which causes a 'zinc spark': a flash of light at the moment of conception [619]. Zinc can be found in red meat, pumpkin seeds, whole grains, ground mustard, eggs and cheese. The recommended daily dose during pregnancy is 15mg [620].

Mother's Health

There are many supplements and herbs that can help support your health during pregnancy.

Alpha lipoic acid (ALA)

ALA is also known as thioctic acid. It is present in the body in small quantities where it reacts with B group vitamins to speed up metabolic reactions needed for energy production. ALA is a powerful antioxidant that enhances other antioxidants such as vitamins C and E [621]. The recommended daily dose during pregnancy is 50–100mg.

Bee pollen

Bee pollen consists of approximately 250 chemical compounds, especially vitamins A, B, C, D and E, proteins, amino acids and fatty acids, as well as flavonoids, sterols, simple and complex sugars, and micro and macronutrients such as potassium, calcium, magnesium, phosphorus and iron [535] [622]. In Chinese medicine, it is used to enhance yin and blood levels. Various research studies suggest not to take bee pollen in high doses or if you are allergic to bee products or bee stings [623]. If you wish to take this supplement, I recommend taking it in low doses, starting with a few granules daily and if you have no allergic symptoms (runny nose, bumps on the skin, hives, itchy throat, rash, sneezing, swelling, watery eyes), increase the dose to 250mg–2g daily [535].

Biotin

Biotin is essential in the synthesis and metabolism of glucose, fatty acids, amino acids and stress hormones. As biotin has the potential to improve glucose metabolism by stimulating insulin secretion, it can be of benefit to women with gestational diabetes, who are often insulin-resistant. Biotin is found in meat, oily fish, whole grains, rice, nuts, cauliflower and egg yolks. The recommended daily dose during pregnancy is 30mcg, increasing to 35mcg while breastfeeding [590].

Chlorella

Chlorella is also known as blue algae (chlorellaceae) and is similar to spirulina (see page 150). It contains vitamins B, C and E as well as zinc and iron. The recommended daily dose during pregnancy is 1g.

Chromium

Chromium deficiency is thought to be common and linked to glucose intolerance, weight gain and depression. Chromium is found in broccoli, grape juice, potatoes, garlic, basil, egg yolks, beef, turkey, cheese, fruit, whole grains, honey, vegetables, black pepper and thyme. The recommended daily dose during pregnancy is 30mcg, increasing to 45mcg while breastfeeding [624].

L-arginine

L-arginine forms the basis of nitric oxide. L-arginine helps to prevent gestational hypertension, pre-eclampsia, uterus contractions and helps to maintain the health of the uterus lining [625] [626] [627] [628]. L-arginine is found in nuts, seeds, pulses, beetroot, onions, grapes, rice, egg yolks and red meat. Do not take once you are breastfeeding. The recommended daily dose during pregnancy is 2–3g.

Magnesium

Magnesium is the fourth most common mineral found in the body and yet deficiencies are common. It is needed for the function of over 300 enzymes. Amongst its uses is its ability to regulate the interaction of hormones to their receptors and reduce the risk of birth defects [629] [630]. Dark chocolate (70 per cent cocoa solids) contains high levels of magnesium. Magnesium is also found in almonds, spinach, cashews, peanuts, black beans, kidney beans, potatoes and rice. The recommended daily dose during pregnancy is 360mg [631].

Manganese

Manganese is an essential mineral that has several roles. A deficiency can cause poor memory, weak nails and hair loss [535]. Manganese is found in hazelnuts, pecans, peanuts, brown rice, chickpeas, spinach, oatmeal and lentils. The recommended daily dose during pregnancy is 2mg, increasing to 2.6mg while breastfeeding [632].

Myo- inositol

Myo-inositol is a B-complex vitamin. It is found in both meat and plants. Fresh meat, vegetables and fruits contain more myo-inositol than frozen, tinned or salt-free products. I recommend a daily dose of 250mg from 12 weeks of pregnancy if you are at risk of developing gestational diabetes.

Stinging nettle *(urtica dioica)*

Stinging nettle leaves are rich in chlorophyll, protein, vitamins A, C, D and K, phosphorus, iron and sulphur, as well as some B vitamins and magnesium. Up to 20 per cent of the leaf constituents are mineral salts, mainly calcium, potassium, silicon and nitrates. Nettle extract contains all of the essential amino acids [633]. Stinging nettle leaves are considered safe to take during pregnancy [218]. This herb can also be used as a therapy for anaemia [633]. Nettle tea works well in conjunction with red raspberry and lemon balm to support optimal health during pregnancy [215]. The recommended daily dose during pregnancy is 250–500mg [580].

Vitamin B₁ (thiamin)

Vitamin B_1 is needed for the production of energy and red blood cells. The body can only store it for one month. It is present in lots of foods, however food preparation drastically decreases levels of vitamin B_1 (for example, meat that has been frozen loses 50 per cent of its vitamin B_1) [535]. Vitamin B_1 can be found in rice, egg noodles, pork chops, trout, black beans, tuna (light), macaroni and acorn squash. This vitamin is destroyed by drinking large amounts of tea or coffee. The recommended daily dose during pregnancy is 1.4mg [634].

Vitamin B₁₂ (cobalamin)

Vitamin B_{12} can be stored in the liver for several years. However, vegetarians, and especially vegans, tend to be deficient in it [535]. In conjunction with folic acid, it is needed when new genetic material is made during cell division, which helps to prevent birth defects such as spina bifida [535]. Vitamin B_{12} can be found in trout, tuna (light), salmon, haddock, beef and dairy products. The recommended daily dose during pregnancy is 2.6mcg, increasing to 2.8mcg while breastfeeding [635].

Vitamin B₂ (riboflavin)

Vitamin B_2 is important in the production of energy and the metabolism of proteins, fats and carbohydrates. It is needed to convert vitamin B_6 into its active form [535]. Vitamin B_2 can be found in whole grains, eggs, dairy products, mushrooms, almonds, cheese, salmon and quinoa. This is the vitamin that turns urine into a bright yellow colour [535]. The recommended daily dose during pregnancy is 1.4mg, increasing to 1.6mg while breastfeeding [636].

Vitamin B₃ (niacin)

Vitamin B_3 is important in the production of energy and the use of oxygen in cells. Vitamin B_3 can be found in rice, peanuts, beef, pork, poultry, tuna (light), eggs, potatoes and sunflower seeds. The recommended daily dose during pregnancy is 18mg [637].

Vitamin B₅ (pantothenic acid)

Vitamin B$_5$ is important in the production of energy and adrenal gland hormones during stressful times. Vitamin B$_5$ can be found in shitake mushrooms, sunflower seeds, peanuts, beef, chicken, tuna (light), avocados, potatoes, eggs, yoghurt and broccoli. The recommended daily dose during pregnancy is 6mg, increasing to 7mg while breastfeeding [638].

Vitamin B₆ (pyridoxine)

Vitamin B$_6$ is essential for the action of over 60 enzymes [535]. Vitamin B$_6$ can be found in chickpeas, tuna (light), salmon, beef, chicken breast, potatoes, turkey and bananas. The recommended daily dose during pregnancy is 1.9mg, increasing to 2mg while breastfeeding [639].

Vitamin C (ascorbic acid)

Vitamin C cannot be stored in the body, therefore regular intake is necessary. It is needed for over 300 metabolic reactions [535]. It helps with the absorption of iron. Vitamin C is found in most fruit and vegetables, including green leafy vegetables. The recommended daily dose during pregnancy is 85mg, increasing to 120mg while breastfeeding [640].

Vitamin E (tocopherols/tocotrienols)

Vitamin E is an antioxidant that protects the embryo from free radical damage and is important in antibody production. Vitamin E can be found in wheat germ oil, sunflower seeds, almonds, sunflower oil, safflower oil, hazelnuts, peanuts, corn oil and spinach. The recommended daily dose during pregnancy is 15mg, increasing to 19mg while breastfeeding [641].

Other herbs generally regarded as safe in pregnancy

These herbs are regarded as safe to use in pregnancy. I would recommend consulting with a qualified and accredited herbalist before taking any herbs during pregnancy.

- arnica (external only)
- astragalus (not in the 3rd trimester)
- bilberry
- black haw
- burdock
- catnip
- chamomile
- corn silk
- echinacea
- evening primrose oil
- feverfew (after 1st trimester)
- garlic
- ginger
- horse chestnut
- lemon balm
- marshmallow
- mullein
- oatstraw
- passionflower (not while breastfeeding)
- peppermint (not while breastfeeding)
- red raspberry (after 1st trimester)
- skullcap
- slippery elm
- wild yam
- yellow dock [218]

Preventing a Miscarriage

There are several herbs and supplements that can help to prevent a miscarriage. Only take them if you have a history of miscarriage or know that your pregnancy is threatened. I would recommend consulting with a qualified and accredited herbalist before taking any herbs during pregnancy.

Black haw *(viburnum prunifolium)*

Black haw is native to North America and has a long history of use to prevent miscarriage [633] [642]. Black haw is considered safe to take during pregnancy [218]. Black haw contains salicin and scopoletin, both of which relax and sedate uterine muscle and is an effective uterine antispasmodic. However, it should not be used when a woman is suffering from hypotension. The recommended daily dose during pregnancy is 2–3ml taken two to three times per day.

Chinese herbs

Chinese herbal medicines have been used in East Asia for thousands of years to reduce the risk of miscarriage [217]. They are safe to take when prescribed by a qualified and accredited herbalist. I use Chinese herbs effectively in my clinic to support a pregnancy and reduce the risks of miscarriage. Always consult with a qualified and accredited Chinese herbalist before taking Chinese herbs.

Coenzyme Q10

Coenzyme Q10 is also known as ubiquinone. It is a vitamin-like substance that processes oxygen in cells and generates energy-rich molecules. Coenzyme Q10 can reduce the risk of miscarriage and pre-eclampsia [643] [644] [645]. Coenzyme Q10 is found in meat, fish, eggs, whole grains, nuts and green vegetables. The recommended daily dose during pregnancy is 200mg.

False unicorn *(chamaelirium luteum)*

False unicorn can be used by women who have experienced repeated miscarriages. It is used to correct a uterine prolapse and tighten a loose cervix. It is also a remedy for spotting and contractions that indicate a threatened miscarriage. False unicorn is considered safe to take during pregnancy [633]. The recommended daily dose during pregnancy is 2–3ml taken two to three times per day. If you take too much, it may cause nausea. If you feel this is happening, reduce the dose by half.

Selenium

Selenium is considered the most important trace element in our diet. Low levels have been linked with miscarriage and pre-eclampsia [535]. Selenium is found in Brazil nuts, tuna (light), halibut, sardines, macaroni, beef, turkey, chicken, rice, oatmeal and eggs. The recommended daily dose during pregnancy is 60mcg, increasing to 70mcg while breastfeeding [646].

There are several natural herbs and oils that can be used to help bring on labour (see page 186).

Supplements and Herbs to Avoid

I would recommend avoiding the following supplements and herbs while pregnant.

Blue cohosh *(caulophyllum thalictroides)*

Blue cohosh has a long history of use amongst Native Americans [633]. However, research has shown that blue cohosh (not to be confused with black cohosh above) can cause harmful effects upon the baby and should be avoided in pregnancy [211] [647] [648] [649] [650].

Bromelain

Bromelain is found in the stem of pineapples and in mango and papaya. It reduces levels of cervical prostaglandins rather than have any effect on initiating labour [211]. The eating of pineapple in India amongst traditional tribes is forbidden during pregnancy as it is believed to induce a miscarriage [651]. Bromelain acts to decrease levels of prostaglandin E_2, which are necessary for implantation [652] [653]. I recommend avoiding taking bromelain supplements during pregnancy. However, it is still okay to eat small quantities of pineapple, mango and papaya.

Cod liver oil

Cod liver oil contains important omega-3s and vitamin A. However, as the level of vitamin A within cod liver oil is difficult to determine, it may be possible to overdose, which can lead to birth defects [654]. I would recommend avoiding cod liver oil supplements when pregnant and take beta-carotene instead (see page 145).

Green tea

Green, white and black teas all come from the same shrub: *camellia sinensis*. Black tea is fermented green tea. The antioxidants in green tea extracts are 100 times more powerful than vitamin C and 25 times more powerful than vitamin E [535]. However, green tea still contains caffeine, which can affect the absorption of calcium. Tea also contains tannin, which can affect the absorption of iron and contains the polyphenols flavonoids and catechins, which, when consumed in high quantities, can reduce levels of folic acid and affect the baby [655] [656]. I would therefore limit drinking tea to 1–2 cups a day and having decaf if possible.

Liquorice *(glycyrrhiza)*

There are 20 known species of liquorice (licorice). The two most commonly consumed species are European *(glycyrrhiza glabra)* and Chinese *(glycyrrhiza uralensis)*. Research has shown that eating large quantities of both European and Chinese species during pregnancy can affect the baby [657] [658]. I would recommend avoiding eating large quantities of both species. The Chinese species is often used in Chinese herbal medicine, but in very low doses that make it safe to use.

Other herbs to avoid in pregnancy

These herbs should be avoided in pregnancy. I would recommend consulting with a qualified and accredited herbalist before taking any herbs during pregnancy.

- birthwort
- bladderwrack
- calendula
- cascara
- chapparal
- damiana
- dandelion
- elderberry
- ephedra pennyroyal
- fenugreek
- gentian
- goldenseal
- hawthorn
- horehound
- juniper
- lobelia
- mandrake
- meadowsweet
- milk thistle
- pleurisy root
- rue
- sage
- saw palmetto
- tansy
- uva ursi
- vitex
- yarrow [218]

Preparing and Using Herbs

Most herbs can be taken in several ways, with the most common being: teas, decoctions, tinctures, syrups, capsules, compresses, infused oils, salves, herbal baths, essential oils and inhalation.

Teas (infusions)

Teas are the traditional way of taking herbs. Add 1–2 teaspoons of fresh or dried herbs in 150–250ml (6–8oz) of hot water for 5–10 minutes. The herb is strained and the tea can be sweetened with honey. Organic plants are preferred, as herbs can contain pesticide and herbicide residue.

Decoctions

Decoctions are often used in Chinese herbal medicine. A tea is made from the herbs. Boil the dried herbs in water for 20–30 minutes to extract the medicinal qualities. Strain and add honey.

Tinctures

Tinctures are a common way of preparing and storing botanical medicines. Fresh or dried plant material is soaked in an alcohol or non-alcohol base for two weeks. The formula for preparation is creating a ratio of 1:4 plant to liquid: 1 part plant material, 1 part distilled water, 3 parts 80 proof vodka. A 'part' can be 1 tablespoon, ½ cup or any desired amount. Tinctures will maintain their potency for two to three years. The medicinal dose of a tincture is 20–30 drops, in water or juice, 2–3 times daily. Non-alcoholic forms of tinctures are available. These tinctures are prepared with glycerine or vinegar.

Syrups

Syrups are heat-prepared infusions or decoctions with added honey to thicken and for taste.

Capsules

Plant material is dried or flash frozen, ground into a fine powder and placed in gelatine or vegetarian capsules. However, capsules can be heavy on a pregnant woman's stomach and may cause nausea and indigestion.

Compresses (poultice)

A compress uses dried or moistened herbs that are placed in a gauze pad, cheese cloth or a soft porous fabric, folded into a 'packet' and placed directly on to the affected area for 10–20 minutes, 3–4 times daily. Compresses may also be gauze or fabric soaked in an infusion and placed directly on the affected area, for example for pain relief.

Infused oil

Plant-infused oils extract the plant's medicinal quality in an oil-based form. Apply infused oil to the affected area two to three times daily.

Salves (ointment)

Ointment is the most commonly used product. Apply a small amount to the affected area two to four times daily.

Herbal baths

For a herbal bath, do not use very hot water or submerge your bump as this can make the baby restless and increase their heart rate. For a warm bath, foot bath or sitz bath, add 1–2 cups of prepared infusion or 1–2 tablespoons of fresh or dried herbs in a cotton tea bag. Soak the affected area for 20–30 minutes, 2–3 times daily.

Essential oils

The following essential oils are regarded as safe to use in pregnancy. I would recommend consulting with a qualified and accredited aromatherapist before using any essential oils during pregnancy.

- bergamot
- cedarwood
- chamomile
- citrus (in small amounts)
- clary sage
- cypress
- eucalyptus
- jasmine
- lavender
- marjoram
- neroli
- patchouli
- rose
- rose geranium
- rosemary
- sandalwood
- tea tree
- ylang [218]

Essential oils can be used in three ways: inhalation, topical (on the skin) or in a bath (hydrotherapy).

Inhalation

You can burn the oil and inhale it by using an electric, battery or candle diffuser. Alternatively, you can place a small amount on a small piece of fabric or cotton ball. This is good for relaxation and calming.

Topical

To use an essential oil on your skin, dilute with a base oil (olive, sweet almond, jojoba, apricot kernel, or any cold-pressed oil) or distilled water.

Hydrotherapy

To use in water, add a few drops to a warm bath, foot bath or sitz bath. Pregnant women should use the 2 per cent or lower range of 4 per cent dilutions. Avoid submerging your bump in hot water.

Essential oils to avoid in pregnancy

These essential oils should be avoided in pregnancy. I would recommend consulting with a qualified and accredited aromatherapist before using any essential oils during pregnancy.

- ginger
  (not in the first trimester)
- juniper
- mugwort
- nutmeg

- pennyroyal
- tansy
- thuja
- thyme
- wormwood [218]

Pregnancy safety guidelines

Try to follow these simple guidelines when using herbs or essential oils in pregnancy:

- Use smaller doses.
- Use only herbs and essential oils regarded as safe for pregnancy (consult a qualified and accredited expert beforehand).

- Use organic herbs.
- Use a 2 per cent or low range of 4 per cent dilution of essential oils.
- Avoid labour induction herbs before week 37.
- Teas/infusions cause less indigestion than capsules.
- Discontinue essential oils if you get a headache or feel nauseous.
- Discontinue herbs if you feel nauseous/vomit, have a rash or headache.

Part Five

Your Baby's Development

During your pregnancy, the cells of your baby migrate into your bloodstream and then circulate back into the baby, in a process called foetal-maternal microchimerism. The cells circulate and merge backwards and forwards and after your baby is born, many of these cells stay in your body, leaving an imprint that can last for decades. If a mother's health is injured, foetal cells will rush to the site of injury and change into different types of cells that specialise in repairing the injury. The baby helps repair the mother, while the mother grows the baby. A true miracle of Nature. Let's now look at how your baby is growing week by week inside you.

Chapter 14

Week by Week

Your baby will grow and change dramatically week by week, forming rapidly into a little person. I have listed the various stages so you can track the changes and see what's going on inside you and how you are creating another human being – a miracle of Nature. What happens week by week will vary slightly between each pregnancy. Let's start at the beginning with how your baby was conceived.

Conception

A man's semen meets your egg in the fallopian tube during a natural conception, where dozens of sperm attack the egg, eroding down the outer layer allowing one sperm to enter. Conception happens and a flash of white light occurs called the 'zinc spark'[619]. The egg is now an embryo and travels down the fallopian tube over five days to the uterus (see figure 3 on the next page).

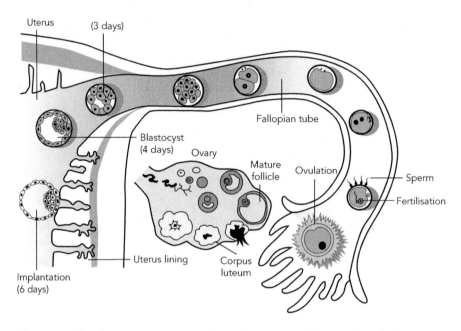

Uterus (3 days)

Fallopian tube

Blastocyst (4 days)

Ovary

Mature follicle

Ovulation

Sperm

Fertilisation

Corpus luteum

Uterus lining

Implantation (6 days)

Figure 3. Fertilisation, journey and implantation of the embryo [593]

First Trimester

Week 1

The embryo (blastocyst) loosely attaches to the uterus wall around six days after fertilisation. On day seven the embryo releases enzymes that allow it to burrow more firmly into the outer layer of the uterus called the endometrium. Once the embryo has burrowed into the outer layer of the uterus wall, the endometrium is then referred to as the decidua. The decidua separates from the uterus during labour, much like during menstruation [7].

Week 2

The outer layer of the embryo (trophoblast) forms into two layers (syncytiotrophoblast and cytotrophoblast), providing the embryo with nutrients and creating the outer sac and the placenta. The embryo releases human chorionic gonadotropin (hCG), which a pregnancy test picks up and tells you that you are pregnant. Levels of hCG peak around week 9 (see table 2, page 21) and maintains the sac that once held the egg *(corpus luteum)*, allowing it to continue releasing progesterone until the placenta takes over at around week 8–12.

A small cavity appears which enlarges to become the amniotic cavity. The amniotic cavity fills with amniotic fluid, which comes from your blood. Later the baby will contribute to the amniotic fluid from its urine. The amniotic fluid acts like a shock absorber for your baby and helps to regulate the baby's body temperature and prevents him or her from drying out or from getting stuck to surrounding parts. The amniotic fluid ruptures before birth and is known as waters breaking (bag of waters) [7].

Around eight days after fertilisation, the yolk sac forms, which supplies nutrients during the second and third week of development and is the source of blood cells that will form into the reproductive organs and part of the gut. Around 12 days after fertilisation, the chorion forms, which surrounds your baby. It protects the baby and becomes part of the placenta. It also protects the baby from your immune system by blocking antibody production and promotes the production of T cells that suppress normal immune responses. By the end of the second week, chorionic villi begin to develop. They are finger-like and connect the embryo to the uterus wall. Blood capillaries within the chorionic villi will connect to the heart via the connecting stalk, which will be the future umbilical cord.

Week 3

The third week sees the start of rapid development with the three primary germ layers that lay the groundwork for future organ development in weeks four to eight. The three primary germ layers form the endoderm, mesoderm and ectoderm. Each of these layers will grow to be different parts of the baby's body. The inner layer, called the endoderm, will form the digestive tract, urinary bladder, gall bladder, liver, pharynx, hearing, tonsils, larynx, lungs, thyroid gland, pancreas, thymus, prostate, vagina, urethra, sperm and eggs. The middle layer, called the mesoderm, becomes the heart, spleen, kidneys, blood and lymphatic vessels, reproductive organs, part of the eyes and skin, muscles, cartilage and bones. While the outer layer, called the ectoderm, becomes the brain and nervous system, the eye lenses, tooth enamel, mouth and nose, hair, skin, nails, pituitary and pineal gland and the nervous system.

During the third week of development, small spaces appear that merge to form a larger cavity that will divide the embryo into two parts called the splanchnic mesoderm and the somatic mesoderm. The splanchnic mesoderm forms the heart, pericardium, blood vessels and the muscles of the respiratory and digestive organs. The somatic mesoderm forms the bones, ligaments, blood vessels and the connective tissue of the arms and legs.

Week 4

Your baby is now the size of a pinhead. During the fourth week of development, the embryo undergoes very dramatic changes in shape and size, moving from two-dimensional to three-dimensional and tripling in size. During this process, a head fold and a tail fold form. The head fold develops into the heart and mouth, while the tail fold forms the anus. The head end of the neural tube develops into the primary brain vessels. The skeletal muscles of the neck, trunk and limb form together with the connective tissue including the dermis of the skin, vertebrae and ribs.

The foetal pole forms, where the heart will start to beat. The placenta formation begins and will take over the role of progesterone manufacture from the *corpus luteum* from around weeks 8–12. The limb buds develop. Eyes and ears begin to develop, as does the tail and body systems. Your cervical plug forms from cervical fluid and seals the head of the cervix creating a protective barrier that prevents any foreign substances from entering the womb that could cause an infection and harm the baby.

Week 5 (2mm/0.1in)

Your baby has gone from a circular celled embryo to looking like a tadpole with a tiny tail. There is rapid development of the brain, which makes the head look disproportionally bigger than the rest of the body. The baby's nervous system is developing and the foundations for its major organs are in place. As the ectoderm develops, a groove forms and the layer of cells folds to form a hollow tube called the neural tube. This will become the baby's brain and spinal cord. At the same time, the heart forms as a simple tube-like structure. Your baby already has some of its own blood vessels and blood begins to circulate.

Week 6 (4mm/0.2in)

Your baby is now the size of a pea. By week six, the head continues to grow even larger and the limbs develop substantially more. Their heart now has four chambers and starts beating at 110 beats per minute (bpm). The neck and trunk begin to straighten. Your baby still looks like a tadpole. The head is called the crown and its bottom called the rump. Measurements of the baby's growth are taken from the top of the crown to the bottom of the rump (head to bottom), as the legs grow later. The heart can sometimes be seen beating on a vaginal ultrasound scan at this stage, although not always. It depends on the location of the embryo and the equipment used, so try not to worry if you go for an early scan and they cannot find it, that can happen. The developing arms and legs become visible as small swellings called limb buds. Little dimples on the side of the head will become the ears, while small black dots on the face will become the eyes and a small bump on the head will form into the nose.

Week 7 (1cm/0.4in)

Your baby's brain is growing rapidly at an amazing rate of 100 cells a minute. This rapid growth rate requires a lot of energy from the mother, hence why a lot of pregnant women can feel tired at this time. During this period, it is important to eat, sleep and rest as much as possible. Their eyes and ears continue to develop. Your baby's mouth and tongue are being formed, as are its kidneys. The limb buds start to form cartilage, which will develop into the bones of the legs and arms. The arm buds become longer and the ends flatten out with digits forming that will become fingers. The heart beats faster at 120bpm. Nerve cells continue to multiply and develop as the nervous system (the brain and spinal cord) starts to take shape.

Week 8 (1.6cm/0.6in)

This week is the final week of the embryonic period. By the end of this week, your baby will start to look more human and less like a tadpole. During this week, the fingers grow and change from being webbed to singular, the tail becomes shorter and disappears, the eyes develop, eyelids come together and the external genitals begin to form. Your baby has grown a lot and is now the size of a bean.

Week 9 (2.3cm/0.9in)

Your baby is now called a foetus, which is Latin for 'offspring'. This is the first hurdle reached. Well done! Their heart is now beating at 170bpm. The legs are lengthening and forming cartilage. Your baby starts to look more human-like and their nose, eyes and spine develop further. Your baby is still inside its amniotic sac and the placenta is continuing to develop. At this stage, your baby still gets their nourishment from the yolk sac.

Their face is slowly forming and their eyes are bigger and more obvious and have some colour in them. The mouth and tongue are more formed and the tongue starts to form tiny taste buds. Their hands and feet are developing – ridges identify where the fingers and toes will be. The major internal organs (such as the heart, brain, lungs, kidneys and intestines) continue developing. From weeks 8–10, you may see your midwife for the first time. During that meeting they will ask you lots of questions relating to the pregnancy and check when your last period was and give you your expected due date.

Week 10 (3.2cm/1.2in)

Your baby's bones and cartilage are forming and small crevasses on the legs and arms will form into the knee and elbow joints. Fingerprints are being formed. Their ears are starting to develop on the sides of your baby's head and inside the head their ear canals are forming. The jawbones are developing and already contain all the future milk teeth. Their heart is now fully formed and beats at 180bpm, much faster than yours. You may hear this on a Doppler machine. Do not be alarmed by the rapid heartbeat as it is perfectly normal. Your baby is making small, jerky movements, which may be seen on an ultrasound scan. Your baby is already producing urine from their operational kidneys, which is excreted into the amniotic fluid. If your baby is a boy, his testosterone levels will surge from now until week 18. A Harmony test (see page 36) can identify the gender of the baby from this time.

Week 11 (4.2cm/1.6in)

Your baby is growing quickly and the placenta is rapidly developing (it will be fully formed at around week 12). The bones of the face are now formed. Hair follicles start to form. Their ear buds look more like ears as they grow. Your baby is starting to have breathing movements. They can open their mouth and swallow. The baby's head makes up one-third of its length, but the body is growing fast. The fingers and toes are separating and nail beds are starting to form.

Week 12 (5.3cm/2.1in)

This is the second major hurdle reached. Well done! All your baby's major organs, muscles, limbs and bones are in place and begin working together. The immune system, hormones and digestion start functioning. Your baby starts to make random movements. Your baby begins to concentrate iodine in its thyroid and produce thyroid hormones at about this time. The pancreas is beginning to make insulin and the kidneys are producing urine. The skeleton is made up of tissue called cartilage and starts to develop into hard bone. At this time you may have your first hospital scan, which will check the heartbeat, size, spine, organs, etc. and make sure everything is okay. You can stop your acupuncture sessions now if you want to. However, if you are still anxious or have a history of repeated miscarriages, are over 40 or used a donor egg, then I would recommend carrying on (see Chapter Seven).

Your breasts have probably increased in size and may feel uncomfortable in your usual bras. Breasts can enlarge by 25–50 per cent [4]. Have your breasts measured for a new maternity bra and find one that does not contain a wire, for comfort and support.

Week 13 (7.5cm/2.9in)

Your baby's ovaries or testes are fully developed inside their body and the genitals are forming outside their body. Where there was a swelling between the legs, there will now be a penis or clitoris growing, although usually you will not be able to find out the sex of your baby using an ultrasound scan at this stage. Your baby's vocal cords begin to form.

Second Trimester

Week 14 (8.7cm/3.4in)

Your baby's neck becomes longer and they begin to swallow little bits of amniotic fluid, which pass into the stomach and out as urine. Body hair starts to grow. Eyes and ears move to their final places. Toenails start to appear.

Week 15 (10.1cm/4in)

Your baby will start to hear its first sounds, which will be your heartbeat and voice as well as muted sounds from the outside world. Even though your baby's eyes are closed, they may register a bright light outside your body as their eyes start to become sensitive to light. Your baby moves more and may be sensed, called quickening, although most mothers do not feel their baby moving until later, which is normal.

Week 16 (11.6cm/4.6in)

The muscles of your baby's face can now move and the beginnings of facial expressions appear. Eyes begin moving but remain closed. Eyebrow hair and eyelashes are formed. Your baby's nervous system continues to develop, allowing the muscles in their limbs to flex. Your baby's lungs continue to develop and hearing improves.

Week 17 (13cm/5.1in)

During this week, your baby grows quickly. The body grows bigger, with the head and body becoming more in proportion. The face begins to look much more human. Your baby's mouth can open and close. The lines on the skin of the fingers are now formed and your baby already has his or her own individual fingerprints. Fingernails and toenails are growing. Your baby practises sucking and swallowing in readiness for your breast milk.

Week 18 (14.2cm/5.6in)

Your baby can move around quite a bit and may respond to loud noises from the outside world, such as low-frequency music (bass). You may not feel these movements yet, especially if this is your first pregnancy. If you do, they may feel like a soft fluttering sensation. Your baby may start to yawn when sleepy and hiccup as their digestive system develops. You might feel these hiccups too. Around this time, your baby becomes covered in a very fine, soft hair called lanugo. The purpose of this is thought to keep the baby warm. The lanugo hair usually disappears before birth and forms their first poo as they will eat and digest it.

Week 19 (15.5cm/6.1in)

Your baby's ears, nose and lips are now recognisable. Your baby carries on swallowing parts of the amniotic fluid that they are suspended in and gets a taste for what you have been eating that day. This helps your baby's digestive system practise for when they are born.

Week 20 (25.5cm/9.9in)

This week sees a big jump in size of your baby. At this time you may have your second hospital scan, where they will perform a thorough check of your baby's organs, size and make sure everything is okay. You should now be able to tell the sex of your baby from an ultrasound scan, if they are in the correct position on the day of the scan. The baby is covered in a substance called vernix caseosa, a greasy white protective layer that protects them from the amniotic fluid. This coating is shed before birth at around week 40, although some babies are born with it. Your baby has some scalp hair and is capable of producing its own antibodies.

Week 21 (27.2cm/10.6in)

Your baby is now able to suck and grasp and may have bouts of hiccups. Your baby is beginning to get into a pattern of sleeping and waking, which will not be the same as yours. These patterns of waking will often remain the same when they are born and wake to feed. When you are in bed at night, feeling relaxed and trying to sleep, your baby may wake up and move about. This is because when you are still, the baby notices this and wakes up. When you are active and moving around the baby finds this relaxing and sleeps, hence why new parents often put their baby in a buggy, sling or car to get them to sleep, as movement helps them to relax.

Your baby will now weigh more than the placenta. The placenta will keep growing throughout pregnancy, but not as fast as your baby. Your baby's arms and legs are now in proportion and they will be moving them around, which you may feel.

Week 22 (28.8cm/11.2in)

Your baby carries on growing and developing. Their internal organs and brain develop more. They have a better sense of the outside world and might react to loud noises. Going to the cinema or places that play loud music may wake them up and get them moving.

Week 23 (30.4cm/11.9in)

Your baby starts putting on weight and begins to fill the skin they are in. You may notice more and more movements and get a better idea of their sleep patterns. Your baby will begin to have rapid eye movements during sleep at around this time.

Week 24 (32cm/12.5in)

Due to advances in Western medicine, your baby is now viable and can survive if they are born at this time. Your baby is putting on more weight from growing bones, organs and body fat.

Week 25 (33.6cm/13.1in)

Your baby's eyelids open for the first time and they will soon start blinking. However, it is not until some weeks after birth that your baby's eyes take on their natural colour.

Week 26 (35.1cm/13.7in)

By now your baby's heart rate will have slowed to around 140bpm. Your baby's brain, lungs and digestive system carry on maturing and their nostrils start to open.

Week 27 (36.5cm/14.2in)

Your baby carries on developing and becomes more reactive to the outside world with noises, lights and the foods that you eat.

Third Trimester

Week 28 (37.9cm/14.8in)

Your baby's lungs are almost mature and operational. Your baby carries on practising sucking, swallowing and digesting until they are born. During this week, you may see your midwife to check your blood pressure, urine for protein, the size of your bump and to give you vaccinations, such as the whooping cough. Your baby has eyelashes and its skin is red in colour.

Week 29 (39.3cm/15.3in)

Your baby continues to be very active at this stage and you may be aware of lots of little movements. There is no set number of movements you should feel each day and every pregnancy is different. The sucking reflex is developing by now and your baby may start to suck their thumb or fingers. Your baby is growing plumper and their skin begins to look less wrinkled and much smoother.

Week 30 (40.6cm/15.8in)

Your baby's brain develops and starts to control and take over from things such as regulating its body temperature. The white, greasy vernix and the soft, furry lanugo (fine hair) that has covered your baby's skin begin to disappear. Your baby's eyes can now focus.

Week 31 (41.9cm/16.4in)

Your baby's brain continues to grow and develop. They carry on putting on weight and practising moving their arms and legs. Their wake and sleep patterns become more regulated. Make a note of these as they will often be the times they wake and need feeding once they are born.

Week 32 (43.2cm/16.8in)

By around now, your baby is usually lying with their head pointing downwards, ready for birth. This is known as a cephalic presentation. If your baby is not lying head down at this stage, it is not a problem as some babies move later. The amount of amniotic fluid in your uterus is increasing and your baby is still swallowing fluid and passing it out as urine. Your baby is forming muscle and storing body fat. If your baby is a boy, his testicles are descending.

Week 33 (44.4cm/17.3in)

Your baby's brain and nervous system are fully developed. Your baby's bones are also continuing to harden, apart from the skull bones. These will stay soft and separated until after the birth, to make the journey through the birth canal easier as they can overlap each other allowing the head to reduce in size. Your baby is curled up in your uterus, with their legs bent up towards their chest. They are starting to rapidly gain weight and you may feel this extra weight. This will mean less space in your uterus for them and you may see them kick or poke on the surface of your belly. Your stomach and bladder may have less space as a result of your baby's rapid growth.

Week 34 (45.6cm/17.8in)

Your baby's toenails and fingers are fully formed. If your baby is a boy, his testicles have now descended from his abdomen into his scrotum. Your baby's brain grows and matures. Your baby has around 8 per cent body fat.

Week 35 (46.7cm/18.2in)

From around now, you may be aware of your uterus tightening from time to time. These are known as practice contractions (Braxton Hicks) and are a normal part of pregnancy (see page 14). Your baby may now be head down (engaged) and getting ready for delivery. When this happens, you may notice that your bump has moved down a little and you feel more pressure on your pelvis, which might make it more uncomfortable to walk. This is normal. Sometimes the head does not engage until later or when labour starts. If your baby is breech then you can start moxibustion treatment from now. Otherwise, an external cephalic version (ECV) can be performed at around 36–37 weeks to turn a breech baby (see page 197).

Week 36 (47.8cm/18.6in)

By now, your baby's lungs are fully formed and ready to take their first breath when they are born. Their digestive system is now fully functional and ready to receive your breast milk. You can restart acupuncture treatment now if you stopped at week 12. Research has shown that having acupuncture treatment as part of your pre-birth preparation can help to normalise labour by needing less pain relief medication, less chance of being induced and less time spent in hospital [659].

Week 37 (48.9cm/19.1in)

Your pregnancy is now termed early term. Your baby's digestive system now contains meconium – the sticky, green substance that will form your baby's first poo after birth. It may include bits of the lanugo (fine hair) that covered your baby earlier in pregnancy. The lanugo that covered your baby's body is now almost all gone, although some babies may have small patches of it when they are born. Mothers older than 40 or who are at high risk, for example those that conceived using in vitro fertilisation (IVF), may be medically induced around now, although it depends on your personal circumstances, obstetrician and hospital.

Week 38 (49.9cm/19.5in)

Your baby carries on shedding their protect layer called vernix and the lanugo hair. Fat levels carry on increasing as your baby gets ready for the outside world. Your baby now has around 16 per cent body fat. The baby's skin changes from red to its natural colour.

Week 39 (50.9cm/19.8in)

Your pregnancy is now at full term (280 days). Your baby's growth has slowed down now and if its head was not engaged before it should now be. At this point, most mothers feel uncomfortable day and night due to the size of their bump and feel more pressure on their pelvis. You should now feel regular practice contractions (Braxton Hicks, see page 14).

Week 40 (51.2cm/20.2in)

Your baby is now full-sized and is the size of a small pumpkin. Although newborn sizes can vary, the average baby weighs 3.2kg (7lb). Your baby's hair and fingernails will be getting longer. Some babies with long fingernails can pierce the membrane they are in causing your waters to break. Let's now look at what happens if you go over 40 weeks.

Chapter 15

Going Over 40 Weeks

Only around 3–5 per cent of women will give birth on their due date
[8]. Most women go into labour a week either side of their due date,
but some women can go over. Giving birth just before or just after
week 40 is normal, as there is some flexibility to the 40-week due
date as there are two measurements of pregnancy: gestational weeks
and fertilisation weeks. Gestational weeks refers to when your last
period started, whereas fertilisation weeks refers to when conception
occurred, usually two weeks after your last period, which gives you two
weeks extra, until week 42.

If you conceived using assisted reproductive medicine such as
in vitro fertilisation (IVF), then your due date is the same as if you
conceived naturally and is still calculated from your last period or
when you had your down regulating bleed if you underwent a long
IVF protocol. This calculation uses gestational weeks.

Around 20 per cent of pregnancies will have their due date
changed after their first trimester scan, especially if IVF was used.
Accurate measuring of your baby at this point is important as it will
then determine if medical intervention is required to bring on labour.

If you are over 35 years old, your midwife or obstetrician may recommend procedures to help bring on labour at weeks 38–40 [660] [661] [662] [663] [664]. This reasoning comes from research which has shown inducing delivery at week 40 resulted in:

- A 48 per cent lower risk of meconium aspiration syndrome (trouble breathing).
- A 67 per cent lower risk of death of the baby.
- A 75 per cent lower risk of stillbirth [664].

Being medically induced does carry an increased risk of deliveries requiring the assistance of a surgical instrument, such as forceps, or an emergency caesarean section, and can affect the baby's respiratory system [664] [665] [666]. However, research found that being induced at week 41 resulted in:

- A 43 per cent lower risk of meconium aspiration syndrome.
- A 6 per cent lower risk of emergency caesarean section.
- A 76 per cent lower risk of death of the baby.
- A 82 per cent lower risk of stillbirth [664] [667].

If you feel that you want to carry your pregnancy past week 40, then you should discuss this with your midwife, doula or obstetrician. There are several factors that need to be taken into account when deciding whether to carry on past week 40, for example:

- Is baby facing head-down or are they breeched?
- Is this your first pregnancy?
- The position of the placenta.
- The size of your baby.
- The amount of amniotic fluid in your uterus.
- Your age.
- Your health, for example any gestational diabetes, hypertension or pre-eclampsia.

When carrying on past week 40, it is important to monitor both the baby and your placenta. You may be able to request antenatal foetal testing, which involves a non-stress test (NST, see page 37) or a biophysical profile. If you are under 35 years old, have no health issues, the baby is not too big and is not distressed and your placenta is intact, then you may be able to carry on past week 40 without any problems.

Labour Induction

A labour induction is used to bring on a vaginal delivery. It can be started either naturally via acupuncture or the taking of natural herbs or it can be medically induced. Every year, one in five labours are medically induced in the UK, the US and Canada [668]. Labour can be induced if your baby is past term, there is any potential risk to the mother or baby, if the mother is older than 35 or if you conceived using IVF. Health conditions such as high blood pressure, gestational diabetes, pre-eclampsia, intrauterine growth restriction (IUGR) or if your waters have broken but labour has not started, can result in being medically induced. Often labour is induced before there is any apparent risk to the baby as a preventative measure.

Natural induction

A natural induction is gentler and can result in fewer complications. It helps to bring on labour if the baby is ready. Remember that even though your baby is inside you, they are a little person and will only come if they are ready to take their first breath. Forcing them to come out early can cause complications for you and them. Therefore, trying naturally can be a better course of action to begin with. There are several natural ways to help bring on labour. Let's look at each of them.

Natural herbs

There are several natural herbs and oils that can be used to help bring on labour. I would recommend consulting with a qualified and accredited herbalist before taking any herbs during pregnancy.

Bethroot *(trillium erectum)*: Bethroot has a long history of being used to induce labour amongst Native Americans and early settlers in North America. It is commonly used to stimulate uterine contractions to induce labour and encourage a stalled labour [633]. The recommended daily dose during pregnancy is 2–3ml taken two to three times per day.

Black cohosh *(rhizoma cimicifugae)*: Black cohosh has a long history of being used to induce labour amongst Native Americans and is recommended by some midwives [535] [580] [633] [669] [670]. It is believed that black cohosh has an effect on oestrogens by helping to regulate and lower levels of oestrogens, thereby allowing oxytocin to initiate labour contractions [671]. The recommended dose to bring on labour is two dropperfuls sublingual plus one dropperful every four hours until contractions start [671].

Castor oil *(ricinus communis)*: Castor oil has been used to induce labour since the ancient Egyptian times [672]. It is often recommended by midwives to help bring on labour [673]. It may work on prostaglandins, helping to bring on labour and ripen the cervix and is considered safe to use [672] [674]. As castor oil is a laxative, it may cause stomach upset and loose bowels. The recommended daily dose to induce labour is 1–2 tablespoons with meals.

Cottonroot *(gossypium thurberi)*: Cottonroot bark is good at inducing labour as it makes tissues that respond to oxytocin more sensitive to the hormone, thereby aiding contractions. The recommended daily dose to induce labour is 30–60 drops under the tongue up to every half hour [215]. Use an organic tincture as pesticides are often sprayed on to cotton crops.

Dong quai *(radix angelica sinensis)*: Dong quai (dang gui) is native to China and Japan. It is commonly used in Chinese and Japanese herbal medicine. In late pregnancy it can help to ripen the cervix, thereby aiding labour [218]. The recommended daily dose to ripen the cervix is 200mg three times a day [535].

Clary sage *(salvia sclarea)*: Clary sage is a plant native to Italy, Syria and Southern France. It is used in aromatherapy and is considered safe to use in pregnancy from week 37 if your baby is head down and engaged. It can increase levels of oxytocin, thereby helping to bring on contractions [675]. You can either put a few drops on to a dry cloth or flannel and inhale the aroma or soak a few cotton balls in the oil and put them under your pillow at night.

Evening primrose *(oenothera biennis)*: Evening primrose oil is commonly given by midwives to trigger cervical ripening [670] [648] [672]. Evening primrose oil can be given either orally or vaginally to help ripen the cervix and is considered safe to use in late pregnancy [672]. The recommended dose of evening primrose oil to induce labour is 500mg orally three times per day for one week beginning at week 37 and then 500mg orally once per day until labour begins [672].

Motherwort *(leonorus cardiaca)*: Motherwort soothes and calms the nervous system, while balancing the hormones of the endocrine system, making it an excellent remedy to induce labour and calm the mother [215]. Motherwort is used a lot in Chinese herbal medicine under the name of Yi Mu Cao. The recommended dosage in pregnancy is 30–60 drops of tincture under the tongue per day.

Partridge berry *(mitchella repens)*: Partridge berry has a long history amongst the Native Americans to tone and nourish the uterus and help prevent a miscarriage [633]. However, modern use stipulates to use partridge berry from week 37 onwards to stimulate the uterus into labour [218].

Raspberry leaf *(rubus idaeus)*: Raspberry leaf has a long history of use in helping to bring on contractions and labour and is recommended by some midwives [215] [670]. It works on the smooth muscle of the uterus and is safe to take from week 32 onwards [211]. It can reduce the duration and pain of labour. It is advisable to stop taking raspberry leaf if you start having strong contractions or are taking metformin;

antidepressants; codeine; aminophylline; ephedrine and atropine [211]. The recommended daily dose during pregnancy is one cup or 800–1200mg from week 32.

Shepherd's purse *(capsella bursa-pastoris)*: Shepherd's purse helps increase tissue sensitivity to the labour hormone oxytocin. One teaspoon of the fresh, whole-plant tincture under the tongue or sipped in a cup of tea should help induce labour or deliver a sticky placenta. Multiple doses can be given and is considered safe to take. Shepherd's purse combines well with cottonroot bark [215].

Valerian *(valeriana officinalis L.)*: Valerian is a natural relaxant and can be used when entering labour. When starting labour, some women can become anxious and stressed, which can affect the release of oxytocin, the hormone that causes contractions, causing labour to stop. Valerian can help women to relax, allowing the hormone oxytocin to be released and contractions to continue. It is considered safe to use during labour [670] [676]. The recommended dose during labour is 120–200 mg, three times per day.

These natural herbs can be used alongside other forms of therapy to help bring on labour naturally, such as acupuncture.

Acupuncture

Acupuncture is a safe and gentle way to help bring on labour naturally. I use acupuncture for induction purposes at my clinic with good results. Acupuncture can gently nudge the baby out naturally but cannot push them out. A medical induction is more like a push.

Acupuncture can help to ripen the cervix and reduce stress and anxiety that could be reducing levels of oxytocin [677]. A review published in 2009 concluded that acupuncture is beneficial in labour induction [678]. I would recommend starting acupuncture treatment before needing to be induced, from week 35, as it helps to prepare your body by regulating hormones, reducing anxiety and stress, and ripening the cervix, which not only helps to bring on a natural labour but also helps to shorten the duration of labour and reduce pain levels.

Medical interventions

There are several medical interventions that can be used to bring on labour. Some are gentler than others.

Prostaglandin E₂ (PGE₂)

This involves taking a medication that contains prostaglandin E2. The medication can be taken either orally or inserted into the vagina. However, taking it orally can upset the stomach [8]. Therefore, the preferred method is to insert a tablet (or pessary) or gel into the vagina. This tablet or gel contains the medication dinoprostone. Dinoprostone should not be used if you suffer from asthma, glaucoma or a severe kidney, respiratory or liver disease [8] [99].

Induction of labour may take several hours as the cervix takes time to dilate and open up fully. The cervix generally dilates by around 1cm for every one hour. If you have a vaginal tablet or gel, you may be allowed to go home while you wait for it to work. You should contact your midwife or obstetrician if:

- Your contractions begin and are every three minutes, which means you are ready to deliver your baby.
- You have not had any contractions after six hours and will therefore need more medication.

If you have a controlled-release pessary inserted into your vagina, it can take around 24 hours to work. If you do not have contractions after 24 hours, you may be offered another dose.

Membrane sweep

A membrane sweep (stripping) is normally offered at around week 40. It involves the midwife or obstetrician inserting their fingers into your vagina to reach the cervix (neck of your womb), and then into your cervix to the uterus where they rotate their finger to strip off the lower segment membranes. This procedure is often uncomfortable and painful [57]. There might be some bleeding afterwards, which is normal. This action should separate the membranes of the amniotic sac surrounding your baby from your cervix. This separation releases prostaglandins, which should hopefully kick-start your labour. If labour does not start after a membrane sweep, you may be offered a medical induction.

Medical induction

A medical induction is offered to women who do not go into labour by week 41 or to those women considered high risk, although what constitutes high risk varies from country to country and from obstetrician to obstetrician.

If you have to be induced, you will go into the hospital's delivery ward, where a midwife will monitor you and your baby. Pads will be placed on your abdomen to monitor the baby's heart rate. Unfortunately, this will not allow you to move around and get comfortable, which may mean needing pain control medication.

A medical induction is the use of a drip containing the hormone oxytocin. Oxytocin is the hormone that causes your abdomen to contract, which pushes your baby out. Once the medical induction starts to work, labour should proceed normally, but in a small minority it can take 24–48 hours.

Research has shown that having acupuncture treatment at the time of labour reduces the dose of oxytocin needed to induce labour and the duration of labour [679] [680]. Probiotics that contain *lactobacillus reuteri* have been shown to increase levels of oxytocin naturally [54]. Using this alongside acupuncture can be beneficial for both you and your baby.

Medical inductions using oxytocin are usually more painful than a normal vaginal delivery as artificially high levels of oxytocin are poured into the body, which results in stronger contractions than normal that force the baby out. Women who are medically induced are therefore more likely to ask for strong pain relief medications, such as an epidural. Medical inductions may also stress the baby as they are pushed out quickly. Mothers who are medically induced can have lengthy recovery times because a medical induction allows for less time for the mother's body to adapt, which can be traumatic for her body.

Women who are induced are also more likely to need an assisted delivery, where forceps or ventouse suction is used to pull the baby out. This is probably due to the speed of delivery as it does not allow your vagina to adapt quickly enough and stretch open. You can aid your vagina's ability to stretch by training it several weeks beforehand by self-massaging or using either an Aniball or Epi-No balloon (see page 200) [681] [682] [683].

Being induced is a tough decision for most mothers who want things to be natural and have a strong maternal belief that the baby will come when they are ready. Recent research has shown that it is the baby who initiates labour by releasing a protein from their lungs [684]. This signifies that they are ready to breathe, the most important of all survival skills. Inducing before this protein is released can mean the baby having respiratory problems. Research has shown that the majority of natural births occur at 4 a.m., the time when the lung acupuncture channel is active [685]. You may be able to request a foetal lung maturity test to see if your baby's lungs are ready to breathe. This test involves taking a sample of amniotic fluid (amniocentesis) to measure the lecithin–sphingomyelin ratio (L/S ratio). Mature foetal lungs have a L/S ratio between 2.0 and 2.5, whereas immature lungs have a L/S ratio of less than 2.0 [686] [687].

Most women will follow their obstetrician and midwife's advice and be induced. The baby's lungs can carry on developing after birth and they should grow out of any initial respiratory problem should they have them. This is often a better option than facing other possible negative outcomes should the mother wait.

Part Six

Labour Care

Going through labour for the first time can be daunting for a lot of women. In this part, I will go through what will happen during labour in order for you to be mentally prepared. By being well informed, your mind can let go and allow your body to naturally deliver your baby. Remember that you have millions of years of evolution behind you and that your body is designed to give birth.

Chapter 16

Preparing for Labour

Preparing for labour beforehand can help reduce anxiety and help the process, making it smoother and less painful. Women are physically designed to have children when compared to men – they have a larger pelvic outlet, a broader, lower pelvis and higher pain thresholds.

Obstetricians and midwives will often use a woman's shoe size to determine whether her pelvic outlet is large enough to allow the baby's head to pass through. It is believed that women with a foot size greater than 3 UK (35–36 European or 5 US) have a large enough pelvic outlet to allow a normal vaginal delivery. This is a rather antiquated rule that does not take into account genetics, i.e. long legs or a large head, which the baby may have inherited and can cause problems during delivery. During an ultra sound, it can be determined if the baby is growing too large for the birth canal. If not, then a caesarean delivery can be planned for.

Non-steroidal anti-inflammatory drugs (NSAIDs) such as ibuprofen, aspirin, ibuprofen, diclofenac, Advil, indomethacin, etc. can delay the onset of labour and increase its duration. It is therefore best to avoid these medications in the late stages of pregnancy, if possible [99].

It is also important for expecting fathers to prepare for labour and use relaxation techniques to keep themselves calm as agitated fathers can affect the mother. The same techniques for mothers can also be used for expecting fathers.

Breech Babies

A breech baby is when their head is not facing downwards towards the opening of the cervix and the vaginal canal. There are three types of breech presentation, depending upon the baby's position inside the womb:

1. Frank breech. The legs are straight up in front of the body, with the feet near the head, making the buttocks the first part of the baby to be delivered.

2. Complete breech. The buttocks are down near the birth canal. The knees are bent and the feet are near the buttocks.

3. Incomplete breech (footling breech). One or both legs are stretched out below the buttocks. The leg or legs are the first part of the baby to be delivered [688].

Breech babies are quite common. Your midwife or obstetrician may offer you an external cephalic version (ECV). This is when an obstetrician tries to turn the baby into a head-down (cephalic) position by applying strong pressure on your abdomen. It is a safe procedure but can be very uncomfortable. You may be offered pain relief during this procedure. Around 50 per cent of breech babies can be turned using an ECV and will stay head-down, allowing you to have a normal vaginal birth [57].

The gentlest way of turning a breech baby is to use the Chinese medical method called moxibustion [689] [690] [691] [692] [693]. Moxibustion is the application of heat-therapy into a specific acupuncture point on the body. Traditionally, moxibustion used the burning of a specific herb called Ai Ye (mugwort), which is placed around 2cm (1in) above an acupuncture point to pour heat into it. This method has been used in East Asia for thousands of years. I treat a lot of breech babies in my clinic. Rather than using the traditional herb Ai Ye, which produces a lot of smoke, I use smokeless moxa sticks instead, which are easier for patients to use at home and should not set off a fire alarm.

To turn a breech baby, moxibustion (heat) is applied to the acupuncture point Zhiyin (UB 67). This acupuncture point is located on the outer edge of the little toe, at the corner of the toenail (see figure 4). Applying a lit moxa stick pours heat into that acupuncture point causing heat to travel up along the urinary bladder meridian, the longest meridian in the body. The heat in the urinary bladder channel rises upwards and moves the baby thereby rectifying the breech position. It works in most cases, but not all. Sometimes there is not enough space for the baby to physically move or the baby does not want to move. The success rate of moxibustion being able to correct a breech position is around 72.5 per cent [694].

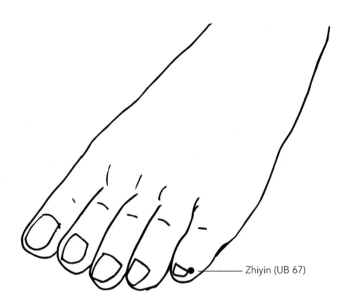

Zhiyin (UB 67)

Figure 4. Location of acupuncture point Zhiyin (UB 67)

Instructions for moxibustion home use

If your baby is breech, you can start performing moxibustion from week 35 onwards [180]. Firstly, you will need to purchase a box of smokeless moxa sticks. There are usually five in a box, which should be enough. Before using moxibustion you will need the following:

1. A lighter, preferably a BBQ or Zippo lighter as a regular lighter can break when the flame is kept lit for long periods of time.

2. A small ceramic or glass dish (or an ash tray) to place the moxa stick in.

3. A glass jar, such as a jam jar, with a lid to extinguish the moxa stick when the treatment is finished.

How to apply moxibustion for breech babies:

- Light one end of the moxa stick with the lighter. This can take a few minutes. Blow on to the end to get it nice and red hot and remove any ash that forms by tapping the stick on to the dish.

- Hold the lit end 2cm (1in) from the outer edge of your little toe, making sure there is never any direct contact with the skin. You will need a steady hand for this. I use my other hand to keep steady the hand that is holding the moxa stick.

- When the area starts to feel too hot, switch toes.

- Remember to flick any excess ash on the end of the moxa stick into the dish and blow on the end to keep it red hot.

- Apply near each little toe for approximately 20 minutes for 10 days. The best time to do this is between 3 and 5 p.m., as this is the time when the urinary bladder acupuncture channel is active.

- After 40 minutes are up, place the moxa stick in a glass jar with the lid screwed on firmly to extinguish it.

- When you feel any movement, visit your midwife and have a scan to see if the baby has moved into the correct position.

- If the baby has moved into the correct position, reduce the treatment time to 10 minutes for each toe until the tenth day.

Before performing moxibustion on yourself, I recommend visiting your acupuncturist first and watch them perform moxibustion on you. They will also be able to instruct you on how to perform moxibustion.

Pregnancy Yoga

I recommend all pregnant women try pregnancy yoga, if possible. Pregnancy yoga helps the body become more flexible and stretchier, ready for giving birth. Research has shown that pregnancy yoga increases confidence, reduces anxiety and increases pain management skills [695]. It can also help to reduce stress and is a great way to practise controlled breathing. You can either visit a yoga class in your local area, login to a class online or follow a video.

Hypnobirthing

Hypnobirthing is a method of pain management that can be used during labour. It involves using a mixture of deep breathing techniques and visualisation to relax you while giving birth. Research has shown that hypnobirthing reduces anxiety, increases pain tolerance and makes labour easier [696] [697] [698]. Hypnobirthing helps to relax your mind which can often get in the way of labour. Remember, it is your body that will give birth to your baby, not your mind! Hypnobirthing helps to get your mind out of the way, letting your body do what it has evolved to do. You can either visit a hypnobirthing class in your local area, login to a class online or follow a video.

Vagina Stretching

Some first-time mothers are likely to tear their perineum (the area between the vagina and the anus) during labour. To minimise this risk of tearing, you can stretch your vagina before entering labour. There are various ways of doing this, from self-massage to using inflatable balloons, for example an Epi-No or an Aniball balloon. Having a water birth can also help as the warm water allows the vagina to relax and expand. These techniques can reduce the risk of tearing or the need for an episiotomy (cutting of the vagina to make it bigger) during childbirth.

Positioning

There are certain practices that can be performed to encourage your baby to engage its head with your pelvis, if they are not already. These practices can be started from week 34 onwards and help your baby to lie with its back to your front, thereby allowing a normal vaginal delivery:

- Kneel on all fours allowing gravity to give the baby more space.
- Kneel on the floor leaning over a large beanbag or cushion.
- Put a cushion under your bottom when driving.
- Regularly use upright and forward leaning postures. This allows your bump to hang away from your body and gives your baby more space in the pelvis for them to turn.
- Sit astride a chair facing the back and resting your arms on back of the chair.
- Sit on a dining chair with elbows resting on the table, knees apart, leaning slightly forward.
- Sit with your knees lower than your hips, with your back as straight as possible.
- Use a stool or pregnancy comfort rocker.
- Use pillows or cushions under your bottom and in the small of your back when sitting down.

It is ideal to use forward leaning postures when having Braxton Hicks contractions, as this position can increase the effectiveness in helping to manoeuvre the baby into the optimum position. However, I would recommend avoiding the following:

- Performing squat exercises in late pregnancy, as these can force the baby's head into the pelvis before it is in the correct position.
- Relaxing in a semi-reclining position where your knees are higher than your hips.
- Sitting with crossed legs.
- Taking long trips in cars with bucket seats. If you have to, use a wedge cushion.

Preterm Labour

Preterm labour occurs before week 37 and is also known as a preterm delivery [3]. From week 37, the pregnancy is deemed as near full term, as it is around this time when your baby's lungs become functional. In 2010, it was estimated that 11.1 per cent of the 135 million births globally (14.9 million babies) were preterm [699]. There are several factors that can lead to a preterm labour, including:

- bacterial vaginosis
- cervical length
- diabetes
- extreme stress
- intra-amniotic infections
- intrauterine growth restriction (IUGR)
- maternal age
- maternal fatigue
- maternal infections and fever
- placental abruption
- placenta praevia
- polyhydramnios (excessive accumulation of amniotic fluid)
- pre-eclampsia
- urinary tract infection (UTI)
- vaginal infections [3] [4] [8] [57]

If the baby is threatened, for example by an infection, pre-eclampsia or damage to the placenta, it may trigger a 'foetal survival' response where the baby will instinctively favour its survival chances outside rather than inside the uterus. If this should happen after week 33 then the baby will most likely be fine.

New research has shown a link between preterm deliveries and air pollution (concentrations of fine particulate matter: $PM_{2.5}$). It is believed that $PM_{2.5}$ causes oxidative stress, lung and placental inflammation, problems with blood-clotting (coagulopathy), coronary artery disease (endothelial dysfunction) and blood flow to the brain (hemodynamic responses), which can cause preterm deliveries [700]. Sources of $PM_{2.5}$ include industry, car fumes, smoking and the burning of solid fuels, such as coal and wood. Countries with the highest levels of preterm deliveries – India and China – also have the worse air pollution [700].

In Chinese medicine, a preterm delivery can be caused by excessive heat (yang) or a lack of energy and blood. Growing another human being can generate a lot of heat and be very draining upon the mother, especially if she is still working, exercising and active. Research has shown that women with high-intensity jobs, which can cause fatigue, are at greater risk of preterm deliveries [701]. Towards the end of the pregnancy, stores of energy and blood can become depleted leading to poor baby growth and a preterm delivery.

Having regular acupuncture treatment with a qualified acupuncturist can reduce the risk of a preterm labour [428] [702]. Steps can then be taken to minimise any problems and herbs can be prescribed to increase levels of energy and blood, thereby reducing the risk of a preterm delivery [703]. In some circumstances, the use of medications such as vaginal progesterone in the mid-trimester can help to reduce the risks of having a preterm labour [704]. In other instances, it may be possible to strengthen the closure of the cervix with stitches.

Acupuncture for Pre-Birth

You can prepare your body for labour by having acupuncture towards the end of your pregnancy. Acupuncture treatment typically begins at week 35 and finishes when the baby is delivered. If you go over your due date, additional acupuncture points can be added to your treatment protocol to help encourage the start of a labour. Research has shown that having acupuncture before labour can:

- reduce anxiety and stress [39] [41] [42] [43] [44]
- reduce labour duration and pain [202] [203] [204]
- regulate the stress hormone cortisol [210]
- ripen the cervix [211] [212]

Using Acupressure During Labour

Using acupressure during labour can help reduce pain and shorten the duration of labour, making it an easier experience for both you and your baby. The acupressure can be administered by your partner, thereby helping them to feel included in the delivery. Acupressure is essentially applying pressure to acupuncture points on the body. The pressure should be strong and continuous in a rotating, clockwise movement for around 30 seconds each time. The point can then be left to relax for a minute or two before reapplying pressure.

Research has shown that teaching mothers how to apply pressure (acupressure) on the acupuncture point Sanyinjiao (SP 6) can help to ripen their cervix and improved dilation as well as reduce pain levels and the duration of labour [705] [706] [707] [708] [709] [710]. These studies also found that it was perfectly safe to use acupressure while pregnant. I would recommend only stimulating this point from 38 weeks onwards. Acupressure is generally applied for 20 minutes for 5 days on the acupuncture point Sanyinjiao (SP 6) – see figure 5 below. Cervical ripening was greatly enhanced after 48 hours of applying pressure. Another research study found that applying pressure to both acupuncture points Hegu (LI 4) and Sanyinjiao (SP 6) during labour shortened time in labour [711], while other studies have found that just applying pressure to the acupuncture point Hegu (LI 4) – see figure 6 below – decreased pain and labour duration [712] [713] [714]. Both these acupuncture points are quite easy to locate and can be stimulated once the cervical plug disengages from the cervix or 'the show' occurs.

Sanyinjiao (SP 6)

Both Sanyinjiao (SP 6) points are symmetrical and can be found above the ankle on the inside of the leg. Generally, it is about a hand's width from the tip of the ankle, as shown below. This is not an exact measurement as everyone's acupuncture points vary in location depending on their physical structure. Therefore, use a hand's width to then search around that area for a tender point that will be next to the bone. You can massage this point in a circular clockwise direction for around 10–15 minutes until it becomes too sore and then swap over to the other leg.

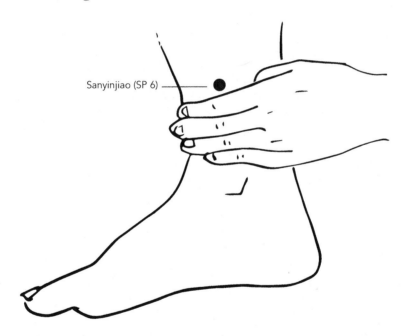

Sanyinjiao (SP 6)

Figure 5. How to locate the acupuncture point Sanyinjiao (SP 6)

Hegu (LI 4)

The acupuncture point Hegu (LI 4) is very easy to find and is one of the most popular points used in acupuncture. It is great for pain relief and can be used for headaches as well as labour pain. As with most acupuncture points, there is one on each side of the body. Hegu (LI 4) is located on each hand. You can use one hand to stimulate the other hand's point or have someone else do it for you. It is quite a sensitive point. If someone else is applying pressure, make sure they do not apply too much pressure straightaway. To locate Hegu (LI 4), place your thumb on the web between your other hand's thumb and index finger, as shown below. You should find a tender point in the centre of the web. Massage this point gently in a circular, clockwise fashion for 10–15 minutes or until it becomes too sore and then swap hands.

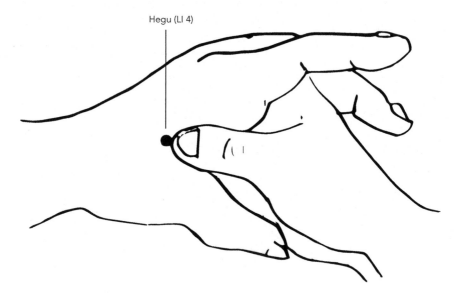

Figure 6. How to locate the acupuncture point Hegu (LI 4)

Birthing Plan

Some expectant mothers like to have a birthing plan set out before they go into labour. This can be anything from having a birth at home, a water birth, hypnobirthing or a regular hospital birth with or without pain relief. It is generally a good idea to have more than one birthing plan as things can change when labour starts.

The choice you have about where to have your baby will depend on your needs, the risks and where you live. Wherever you choose, the place should feel right and comfortable for you.

If you are healthy and considered to be 'low risk' you will be offered a choice of birthing locations. If you choose to give birth at home or in a birthing unit run by midwives, you will be given information by your midwife or obstetrician about what would happen if you have to be transferred to hospital during labour and how long this would take.

For women with medical conditions, it is often safer to give birth in a hospital as specialists are available if you need extra help during labour. Sometimes the maternity unit you choose may not be available if many women are in labour at the same time and the unit is full. Ask your midwife or obstetrician what to expect if this happens to you.

Home Birth

If you have a straightforward pregnancy and both you and the baby are well, you may choose to give birth at home. In the UK, 2.3 per cent of pregnant women (just over 1 in 50) give birth at home [715]. Women who choose to give birth at home have less complications and need less medical intervention [716] [717]. If you choose to give birth at home, you will be supported by a midwife who will be with you during your labour. If you need any help or your labour is not progressing as well as it should, your midwife will make arrangements for you to be transferred to hospital. There are many advantages of giving birth at home, including:

- Being in familiar surroundings where you may feel more relaxed, which helps the labour hormone oxytocin to flow better, which leads to better contractions.
- You will not need to leave your other children, if you have any.
- You will not be separated from your partner after the birth.

- You are more likely to be looked after by a midwife you have got to know during your pregnancy.
- You are less likely to need an epidural analgesia.
- You are less likely to have intervention such as forceps or ventouse than women giving birth in a hospital.
- You are less likely to need an episiotomy or caesarean delivery.
- You are less likely to suffer a 3rd or 4th degree perineal tear.

There are some considerations that you should be aware of if you are considering a home birth, such as:

- You may need to be transferred to a hospital if there are any complications. The Birthplace Study found that 45 out of 100 women having their first baby were transferred to hospital, compared with only 12 out of 100 women having their second or subsequent baby [718].
- Epidurals are not available at home.
- Your obstetrician or midwife may recommend that you give birth in a hospital, for example, if you are expecting twins, if your baby is breech, you used in vitro fertilisation (IVF) to conceive or are an older mum. Your midwife or obstetrician will explain why they think a hospital birth is safer for you and your baby.
- There will be a lot of bodily fluids to clean up after giving birth.

Ask your midwife whether or not a home birth is suitable for you and your baby or is available to you. If it is, your midwife will arrange for members of the midwifery team to support and help you. Below are some questions you might want to ask:

- How do I obtain a birthing pool?
- Which hospital would I be transferred to?
- How long would it take if I needed to be transferred to hospital?

- What pain relief medication can I have?
- Would a midwife be with me all the time?

Doulas

A doula is a trained companion who is not a healthcare professional but who supports you through childbirth. I would recommend hiring a doula if possible. A doula provides emotional, practical and informational support. The doula is able to offer help and suggestions about breathing, relaxation, movement and positioning. The doula's most important role is to provide nurturing, continuous support and reassurance before, during and after labour [719] [720].

Chapter 17

Pain Relief During Labour

There are several pain relief options available to you during labour. The type of pain relief needed can depend upon the type of birth you will have and your preferred option. Pain relief is often a personal choice. Some women plan to deliver their baby in a certain way and select the pain relief option that fits their planned delivery, for example acupressure during a home water birth. Other women may need to be induced or have a caesarean which requires a stronger form of pain relief. In all instances, if a woman feels in control of her pain experience, she has a more satisfying labour [721]. Let's now look at the different types of pain relief available to you during labour.

Natural Pain Relief

Emotional support

Emotional support during labour is important and can minimise the need for pain relief drugs during delivery. Mothers who have a birthing partner throughout are less likely to need analgesia, are more likely to have a vaginal delivery without the need for ventouse or forceps and are more satisfied with their labour [722]. Being in a calm and joyous state can reduce pain levels [723]. The birthing partner can be anyone who you are comfortable with, for example your partner, mother, sister, doula, midwife, etc.

Massage

Having a massage is well known to induce feelings of relaxation. Research has shown that having repeated pregnancy massages before going into labour can help reduce stress and pain levels, allowing for a better labour experience [724] [725]. I would recommend only having a pregnancy massage from a qualified and accredited massage therapist.

Music

Music can be an important tool during labour as it helps to induce feelings of calm and relaxation, which in turn helps to maintain a steady flow of the labour hormone oxytocin to the uterus. Soft, gentle music is often preferred. Find some music that works for you and have it downloaded on to your device, just in case you lose your Internet connection.

Staying active

Staying active and being able to walk around and find a comfortable position is important in managing pain. Pain is often made worse when lying flat on your back unable to move. Positions such as squatting, being on all fours, or sitting on a birthing ball or chair can reduce pain levels and the need for pain relief medication. Birthing balls are often available in hospitals, which means that you may not have to bring your own unless you want to.

Most women in the UK and US give birth lying on their backs with their hips flexed in what is known as the lithotomy position or a semi-sitting position. These positions are weight bearing through the sacrum and coccyx (tailbone) and can restrict movement of joints during labour [726]. Additionally, they do not allow for gravity to assist in the descent of your baby through the birth canal.

Birthing pools (warm baths)

The use of birthing pools or warm baths has been shown to reduce pain, shorten labour and the need for regional analgesics such as epidurals [727]. However, they should not be used within two hours of taking opioid analgesics as they can cause drowsiness.

A warm pool or bath can help muscles and ligaments to relax and aid in feelings of relaxation, which help the labour hormone oxytocin to flow. The temperature of the bath water should be set at an ideal temperature for the baby, which is 36.5–37.5°C (97.7–99.5°F) [728]. If it is hotter than this (38.5°C/101.3°F), it can increase the baby's heart rate and cause them distress.

Most maternity wards in the UK will have several birthing pools that mothers can use, while in other countries such as the USA most hospitals do not. Within hospitals, the birthing pools are usually on a first come, first served basis and cannot be reserved as no one can predict when labour will actually start. You can also use a birthing pool at home. Most water births in the USA occur at home. New guidelines issued by the American College of Obstetricians and Gynaecologists recommend using birthing pools during the first stage of labour but not in the second stage due to increased risk of infection from poorly cleaned pools [727]. They also state the lack of evidence from having a water birth in stage two of labour, so if you have decided that this is what you want and you live in the US, you may be met with opposition. However, if you feel your labour would be easier and more comfortable, then you should go with it. New research now advices the use of home water births. If you have been diagnosed with COVID-19, you cannot give birth in a birthing pool as there is a risk that you may transmit the virus to the baby [729].

Acupressure

Acupressure can help with labour pain. Certain acupuncture points can be stimulated by a birthing partner to help give pain relief, such as Hegu (LI 4) – see page 205. Acupressure is useful when you are in a relaxed state and are going with the pace of delivery. In other instances, when the pain is greater and the mother is in distress, acupressure may not be strong enough to provide adequate pain relief. It is then necessary to use pharmacological drugs instead.

TENS machines

TENS stands for transcutaneous electrical nerve stimulation. It involves placing electro pads on to the painful area, which are connected by wires to a small battery-powered stimulator. You give yourself small amounts of an electric current through the electrodes to the pads. The pads will contract and stimulate nerves to produce endorphins and stimulate the acupuncture points they sit on. The amount of stimulation is controlled by you. You can still move around while using a TENS machine.

Some hospitals supply TENS machines in their delivery wards. If your hospital does not stock any TENS machines, you can buy your own or rent one. TENS is more effective during the early stages of labour, when many women experience lower back pain. It can also be used on the acupuncture point Sanyinjiao (SP 6) to help dilate the cervix (see page 205).

TENS may be useful if this is your second child and you plan to give birth at home. If you are interested in TENS, learn how to use it in the later months of your pregnancy during your acupuncture pre-birth treatments. Ask your acupuncturist to show you how the TENS machine works as most acupuncturists use it in their practice. You should not use a TENS machine if:

- you experience an allergic skin reaction to the electro pads
- you have a pacemaker or another type of implanted electrical device fitted
- you have broken skin, varicose veins or recent scarring in the area where you want to place the electrodes
- you have epilepsy or a heart rhythm disorder (check with your

obstetrician first)

- you plan to use a birthing pool or warm bath

Breathing

Breathing is one of the most important pain relief methods used during labour. Because your mind has to focus on something and because you need to breathe, you can put the two together to relax your mind and aid contractions. By focusing on your breath you can relax your mind and perform controlled pushes. A simple breathing exercise I advise a lot of my patients to do is to take a breath in through the nose and say 'I', and then breathe out through the mouth and say 'surrender'. This allows you to let go of any tension and be present in the now, helping you to relax, which reduces pain levels. Alternatively, if you already know of a breathing meditation, you can use this instead. Remember that the mind creates stress, while the body gives birth. Breathing out your stress gets your mind out of the way of your body!

Herbal supplements

There are several natural herbs and oils that you can take to help encourage labour, which in turn should reduce the duration of delivery and pain levels (see Chapter Fifteen). Generally, a stalled labour causes more pain and discomfort. A stalled labour is termed stasis (stagnation) in Chinese medicine and stasis causes pain. These herbs can help to kick-start a stalled labour and reduce stasis in the uterus. I would recommend consulting with a qualified and accredited herbalist before taking any herbs during pregnancy.

- bethroot *(trillium erectum)*
- black cohosh *(rhizoma cimicifugae)*
- castor oil *(ricinus communis)*
- clary sage *(salvia sclarea)*
- cottonroot *(gossypium thurberi)*
- motherwort *(leonorus cardiaca)*

- raspberry leaf *(rubus idaeus)*
- shepherd's purse *(capsella bursa-pastoris)*
- valerian *(valeriana officinalis L.)*

Sterile water injections (SWIs)

SWIs or water blocks involves injecting sterile water intradermally into the lower back, usually in four spots (foramens) over the borders of the sacrum (coccyx – tailbone), to relieve pain in early labour [(730)]. These injections are administered by midwives as they do not contain any drugs, just sterile water. There are generally two midwives with four syringes of sterile water.

Unknown to most midwives, these four spots in the tailbone are the acupuncture points Shangliao (UB 31) and Ciliao (UB 31). The injection of water causes the water to apply pressure to these acupuncture points, like acupressure or a massage. However, this procedure is very painful and only works for one to two hours.

I believe this is an out-of-date way of giving pain relief to a mother who is already stressed and in pain. A qualified acupuncturist or midwife who is qualified and accredited in acupuncture can painlessly insert four acupuncture needles into the four acupuncture points located on the tailbone, which will give better pain relief for longer without causing distress to the mother. Alternatively, a TENS machine can be placed on the tailbone instead.

Pharmacological Pain Relief

Pharmacological pain relief comes in several forms from the gas and air to stronger forms of pain control such as epidurals. Let's now look at the different types of pain relief that you may be offered and the pros and cons of each.

Inhaled analgesics (gas and air)

Gas and air are commonly used during labour and is sold under the brand name Entonox. It is a 50 per cent mix of oxygen and nitrous oxide and is considered safe, although it may cause nausea, vomiting, drowsiness and light-headedness in the mother and reduce the baby's breathing [3] [99]. It offers mild pain relief when compared to other anaesthetic gases such as isoflurane, desflurane and sevoflurane, which are less commonly used.

Woman should not be given this gas for long periods as it can cause anaemia (by affecting levels of vitamin B_{12}, which affects iron absorption) and affects white blood cell production thereby weakening the immune system [99]. Vegetarians and vegans are at greater risk of developing anaemia. Most women will notice the bad taste the gas has, which can make them feel nauseous. This is normal. Carrying on will lessen the taste. However, if it makes you want to vomit, stop using it.

Systemic opioid analgesia

Systemic opioid analgesics are morphine-like medicines injected into the bloodstream that affect the whole body. These medications have a limited effect on pain relief and can make you feel slightly disconnected from reality. Known as diamorphine or pethidine, they are derived from the poppy plant but will not make you an addict as they are only used during labour. However, they do pass the placenta and can affect the baby.

These medications can be given as an injection in the thigh (every four hours) or intravenously so you can decide when you need it, which is termed patient-controlled analgesia (PCA). Side effects of diamorphine and pethidine include nausea, vomiting, dry mouth, low heart rate, an irregular heart rate, palpitations, swelling, hypotension, hallucinations, vertigo, unease, mood swings, disturbed sleep, headaches, visual disturbances, sweating, rashes and itching [99]. Antiemetics (drugs to stop nausea and vomiting) are often given together with opioid analgesics, but unfortunately have their own side effects, which include reduced appetite, physical weakness, upset tummy, constipation and headaches [3] [99]. Other side effects to be aware of when given diamorphine or pethidine include:

- Babies whose mothers had pethidine in labour may feed less frequently in the first 48 hours as it can make them drowsy for several days.

- If the medication has not worn off towards the end of labour it can make it difficult to push. You might prefer to ask for half a dose initially to see how it works for you.

- If pethidine or diamorphine are given too close to the time of delivery, they may affect the baby's breathing.

- It can make some women feel woozy, sick and forgetful.

- Pethidine can cross over the placenta to the baby.

- You cannot use a birthing pool or warm bath for around four hours after being given pethidine until the effects have worn off fully [731].

Anaesthesia

There are several types of anaesthesia that can be used during labour. These types of pain relief techniques offer a strong form of pain relief should you need it. The different types are:

1. local block

2. epidural block

3. spinal anaesthesia

4. combined spinal-epidural

5. general anaesthesia

Local block (pudenal analgesia)

A local block is the numbing of the pudendal nerve that serves the external vagina area below to the anus where pain might be felt during delivery. A local anaesthetic such as lidocaine or chloroprocaine is injected at the end of the tailbone to numb the area. It takes about twenty minutes to work after the injection and lasts between two and four hours.

The side effects of these drugs include anxiety, paraesthesia (pins and needles), dizziness, blurred vision, tinnitus, headaches, nausea, vomiting, muscle twitches, tremors, convulsions, depression, drowsiness, respiratory failure, unconsciousness, coma, hypotension, slow heart rate and heart failure [99]. Heart failure can be caused by hypotension (low blood pressure). If you have low blood pressure, take adequate levels of iron during pregnancy (see page 148). Nerve damage occurs in fewer than 3 out of every 100 local nerve blocks [732].

Epidural block and spinal anaesthesia (regional analgesia)

A regional analgesic involves injecting an analgesic drug (bupivacaine hydrochloride, ropivacaine hydrochloride, lignocaine/lidocaine hydrochloride) into either the spinal canal or epidural space. Often opioid medications are combined with the analgesic drug. In general, spinal canal injections are used for caesarean deliveries while epidural injections are used for vaginal deliveries [3]. This form of pain relief has an increased risk of forceps delivery as mothers cannot feel when they are having contractions and when to push.

Side effects from bupivacaine hydrochloride and ropivacaine hydrochloride include arrhythmias (fast heart rate), back pain, chills, dizziness, hypotension, hypertension, nausea, paraesthesia (pins and needles), urinary retention and vomiting [99]. Side effects from lignocaine/lidocaine hydrochloride are more severe and include anxiety, arrhythmias (fast heart rate), heart failure, confusion, dizziness, drowsiness, headaches, loss of consciousness, methemoglobinemia (lack of oxygen to the blood), muscle twitching, nausea, neurological effects, pain, psychosis, respiratory disorders, seizures, altered temperature, tinnitus, tremors, blurred vision and vomiting [99]. Epidurals can also prolong labour. Caesarean deliveries will use this form of pain relief.

A research study found that mothers who had epidurals were less positive about them five years later [202]. Having acupuncture during labour reduces the need for epidurals [204]. Areas that can be numbed by an epidural include:

- abdomen
- chest
- legs
- pelvic area

The procedure involves lying on your side or sitting up in a curled position while an anaesthetist cleans your back with an antiseptic. They will then numb a small area with a local anaesthetic and introduce a needle into your back. A very thin tube will be passed through the needle into your back near the nerves that carry pain impulses from the uterus. The drugs listed above are usually mixed together with opioid medications and are administered through this tube. It takes about 10 minutes to set up the epidural and another 10–15 minutes for it to start working. It does not always work perfectly at first and may need adjusting. For example, you may feel more of a feeling in one leg than another. After it has been set up, the tube is left in your back and you can lie down.

Your midwife can top up the epidural, or you may be able to top it up yourself through a machine, usually every two hours. Your contractions and the baby's heart rate will need to be continuously monitored. This means having a belt around your abdomen and not being able to move. When it is time to deliver the baby, you will be told when you are having contractions by the midwife and when to push as you will no longer feel the contractions yourself.

Epidurals have been routinely used for many years and are widely accepted as an effective method of pain relief during labour. However, as with all medical procedures, there are some associated risks that, although, small, you should be aware of before deciding whether to have one. Possible risks include:

- nerve damage – occurs between 1 in 1,000 (spinal) and 1 in 100,000 (epidural) [732]

- puncture of the dura headache (PDPH) – occurs in 1 in 100 women [733]

Combined spinal-epidural

A combined spinal-epidural involves the combination of the above two techniques: spinal anaesthesia and epidural block [4].

General anaesthesia

General anaesthesia is not commonly used during labour, as it is difficult to manage in pregnant women. It is used during a caesarean delivery in special cases [3] [4].

Caesarean Section

A caesarean section is known as a C-section or caesarean delivery. It involves the use of surgery to deliver the baby. It is the most frequent type of major surgery performed in the US [4]. In the UK, one in four women has a caesarean birth [734]. Caesarean deliveries are only recommended by your obstetrician if there is a medical need for it, for example:

- absolute cephalopelvic disproportion (CPD)
- breech baby
- extreme maternal anxiety
- failure to progress in labour
- infant complications
- older mums
- placenta complications
- previous caesarean delivery
- twins or more
- uterine complications

A caesarean delivery is generally not performed before week 39 unless the baby's lungs are mature or it is an emergency [4]. Most caesareans are carried out using spinal or epidural anaesthetic. During the procedure, you will be awake, but the lower part of your body is numbed and you will not feel anything. The procedure will be carried out behind a screen so you cannot see. A cut about 10–20cm (4–8in) long will be made across your lower abdomen, just below your bikini line, then through eight layers of muscle (your core muscles) and into your womb (uterus), hence why this procedure is classified as major surgery. You may feel some tugging and pulling during the procedure, which is normal. The scar is usually hidden in your pubic hair. After the baby is delivered, it takes around 5 minutes to stitch each layer of muscle, therefore 40 minutes in total.

There are emerging side effects that are being noticed as more women select to have a caesarean birth. They include:

- A reduction in breast milk levels due to irregular hormone levels.

- A uterus with a scar is less able to contract properly, possibly leading to another caesarean section in a future pregnancy.

- Babies born from caesareans are more likely to develop respiratory problems, such as asthma [735] [736]. This is most likely caused by the baby's lungs not being fully mature before the caesarean birth.

- Increased risk of infection or bleeding [4].

- Sluggish bowel movements. New research has shown that acupuncture can speed up bowels movements thereby reducing constipation [737].

- The scar that is left on the uterus wall can cause problems for future pregnancies as the placenta may attach on or close to it, thereby increasing the risk of a miscarriage or a retained placenta, which will require emergency surgery.

Emergency caesareans

Emergency caesareans are needed when complications develop during pregnancy or labour and the baby needs to be delivered quickly. If your midwife or obstetrician is concerned about the safety of you or your baby, they will suggest that you have a caesarean straightaway. For instance, this could be if your cervix does not dilate fully during labour and birth is not progressing properly or if you bleed heavily during labour or the baby is in distress.

Elective caesareans

A caesarean is elective if it is planned in advance. This usually happens when your obstetrician or midwife believes that labour will be dangerous for you or your baby. For example, if your baby is in the breech position or your pelvic canal is not wide enough (CPD – normally measured by your foot size, see page 196), or if the placenta is obstructing the womb exit.

If you ask for a caesarean when there are no medical reasons, your obstetrician or midwife will explain the risks of having a caesarean delivery compared to a vaginal birth. Most hospitals in the UK do not support elective caesareans unless there is a medical reason for it. Being anxious or worried about childbirth or that it is your first birth will often not persuade them to allow you to have an elective caesarean. If they refuse and you still want an elective caesarean then you can either try another hospital or opt to have a caesarean performed privately.

Natural caesareans

A 'natural' caesarean is where obstetricians make an incision through your abdomen and into your uterus around where the baby's head is located. The obstetrician then pulls the baby's head through and leaves the baby, allowing it to wriggle its way out by itself. It is supposed to create a 'calmer and slower' entry into the world, thereby causing less distress to the baby. It also allows the mother and child to bond better as the baby is allowed to lie on the mother's chest as the umbilical cord is cut [738].

Recovering from a caesarean section

In most cases, it takes longer to recover from a caesarean section than from a vaginal delivery. You should be able to get out of bed around

24 hours after having a caesarean and your wound dressing may be removed. Women generally stay in hospital for around three days after having a caesarean section. However, if you and your baby are well and want to go home earlier, you should be able to leave after 24 hours and have your follow-up care at home.

In the first few weeks after giving birth, try to rest as much as possible. Avoid walking up and down stairs too often, as your tummy may be sore. However, you should take gentle daily walks to reduce the risk of blood clots. You will be given pain medication, i.e. paracetamol (acetaminophen, Tylenol), ibuprofen (non-steroidal anti-inflammatory drugs (NSAIDs) such as Brufen, along with Advil, Motrin, and Nurofen) or codeine (co-codamol). Your midwife will advise you on how to look after your wound to prevent infection, such as wearing loose, comfortable clothing and cotton underwear, and gently cleaning and drying the wound daily.

In general, it will take about six weeks for all your tissues to heal completely. Before this time, basic activities, such as caring for your new baby and looking after yourself, should be possible, but may be difficult. For example, lifting up your baby becomes harder without the use of your abdominal (core) muscles, which are still healing.

You may not be able to do some activities straightaway, such as driving a car, exercising, carrying heavy things and having sex. Only start to do these activities when you feel able to do so. Ask your midwife for advice if you are unsure.

If you drive, check your insurance cover for any restrictions about driving after having a caesarean as it is classified as a major operation. Some companies require your obstetrician or doctor to certify that you are fit to drive. Most women do not feel fit to drive for a few weeks after a caesarean and many wait until after their six-week postnatal check.

Future pregnancies

If you had a delivery by caesarean section, it does not necessarily mean that you will need to have another caesarean again in the future. It depends on the next pregnancy, where the placenta attaches to in the uterus, etc. You can discuss future pregnancy options with your midwife, obstetrician or doctor in the hospital, who will take account of:

- the overall risks and benefits of a caesarean section
- the reason for your first caesarean
- the risk of tearing the wall of your womb (uterine rupture) along the scar from your previous caesarean section
- the risk to your own and your baby's health at the time of birth
- your preferences and priorities

If the caesarean was carried out for a health reason that will not change in your next pregnancy, for instance, if you have a very narrow birth canal, it is likely that a caesarean section will be necessary for each subsequent delivery.

Chapter 18

Entering Labour

Starting labour can be a mixture of joyous anticipation of meeting your new baby together with the anxiety of labour. In this chapter, I will discuss ways to make this a more joyous occasion by reducing the duration of labour and pain.

Labour is essentially divided into four stages:

1. Dilation of the cervix.
2. Delivery of your baby.
3. Delivery of the placenta.
4. Recovery.

It is important to remember that every woman is different and therefore every pregnancy is different. How labour starts can vary from woman to woman. For example, some women may experience their 'show', then their waters breaking and then contractions, whereas others may experience their show, contractions and then their waters breaking, while others may experience contractions, their show and then their waters breaking. There is no set rule to labour. For the sake of simplicity, I will describe one path of labour within this book, but try not to get stuck on to this one route, as all routes lead to the birth of your baby.

Pre-Stage One

Going into labour is an active process. As it develops, different positions will be comfortable and birthing plans may change, so be prepared to 'go with the flow' and try not to let yourself feel overwhelmed and stressed when things do not go the way you imagined. The more relaxed you are, the smoother labour will be and the less need you will have for pain relief medication.

As a general rule, before stage one begins, your cervical plug will fall down from the head of the cervix and out through your vagina. The mucus plug forms at the start of pregnancy and acts as a barrier preventing any foreign objects from entering the womb that could cause an infection and harm the baby. It naturally falls away before labour starts and is known as 'the show' or 'the bloody show' as sometimes the thick white discharge is mixed with blood, which is normal. What causes it to fall away is the cervix ripening (dilating). Some women may experience premenstrual symptoms, similar to when their menstrual cycle begins.

Your waters may also break around this time too, but this occurs in only 6–12 per cent of labours [3]. Contractions can then start or intensify and are caused by the hormone oxytocin being released by the pituitary gland. Staying relaxed helps to maintain a steady release of oxytocin. If you become stressed, your adrenals release cortisol, which reduces the release of oxytocin. Having acupuncture from week 35 of pregnancy helps to reduce stress and benefits labour [739]. Acupuncture has also been shown in research to increase levels of prostaglandin E_2, which help to initiate labour and shorten its duration [740].

Some women will vomit or have diarrhoea when their contractions start. This is normal and is the body clearing the way for labour. You have to use the same muscles to push the baby out as you do to push a poo out. It is therefore better for you to empty your bowels now instead of when the baby is being delivered to prevent the two mixing together. It is still important to keep on eating and drinking to ensure you have good energy levels for pushing, therefore do not stop eating for the sake of preventing a bowel movement later. It is also important to try to rest and sleep even when your contractions start and are not frequent, to conserve your energy levels for later.

If you are being induced, you will need to be monitored and may be given an epidural as the contractions will be artificially strong, and are often too painful to bear without any pain relief medication.

Stage One: Established Labour

The first stage of labour starts from the diagnosis of labour, otherwise known as established labour, which can sometimes be difficult to determine [3]. Stage one ends when your cervix is fully dilated at 10cm (4in). Dilation of the cervix is when the head of the cervix (opening to the uterus) starts to open and expands from being closed shut, allowing the baby to pass out of your uterus and through your vagina. Your midwife will check your cervix to see how many centimetres dilated you are. This check via the vagina can be uncomfortable as they insert two fingers up into the vagina to find the head of the cervix. To increase dilatation of your cervix, you can stimulate the acupuncture point Sanyinjiao (SP 6) – see page 205. Sometimes women can spend hours or days waiting, which can make the mother tired, therefore speeding up this process will be better for both the mother and the baby.

When your waters break (the membrane that holds the baby), the liquid can exit your vagina like a gush or a trickle. It may also be green or brown. If it is, then the baby has pooed inside you, as it may have been uncomfortable or stressed. Your midwife will test the water to see if it contains any of the baby's poo. If you are having a home birth and the baby has pooed inside you, you may be admitted to hospital to check for any possible infection. If after 24 hours of your waters breaking you still have not entered the first stage of labour (your cervix is not dilating), your hospital will ask you to come in to be medically induced. This is because once the membrane has been broken, there is a slight increased risk of infection, 1 in 100 – compared to 1 in 200 if the membrane is not broken and is still protecting the baby from bacteria and viruses from the outside world [741]. If your waters break and you do not go into labour, research has shown that acupuncture can help to initiate the start of labour [679].

Contractions will often accompany the dilation of your cervix and can feel like your bump is hardening. When contractions first start, some first-time mothers will think labour is starting, panic a bit and rush to the hospital, only to be turned away as their cervix is not dilated enough. Most hospitals want the cervix to be at least 4cm (1.5in) dilated before admitting the mother to the delivery ward. Contractions will start off coming every 60 minutes, then 50, 40, 30, 20 and 10, then every 3 minutes. When contractions are every 10 minutes it is a good time to go to the hospital, if that is where you have chosen to give birth. Once you are having contractions every three minutes that last for around three minutes, your cervix should be fully dilated and you are ready to enter stage two of labour.

It is quite common for a woman to enter hospital, see the sterile, clinical surroundings, which makes it feel a lot more real and then panic, feel stressed and the contractions stop. This is caused by the release of the stress hormone cortisol, which impacts on the hypothalamus and pituitary system and shuts down the release of the labour hormone oxytocin. In such cases, women are often sent home as they tend to feel more relaxed in their own surroundings, which allows the hormone oxytocin to be released and for contractions to resume. This is why home births are now considered a better place to give birth.

You and your baby's heart will be monitored around every 15 minutes and your cervix every hour depending on how many midwives are on the ward and how busy they are. Two monitors may be attached to you, one for the contractions and the other to monitor the baby's heart rate. Being monitored does not allow you to move around, which can cause pain. If you feel the need to move around, then tell your midwife. However, if you are having an epidural, you will not need to move around to relieve pain, but you might develop bedsores. Your midwife will take measures to try to prevent this from happening. Most hospitals will make you wear long, tight socks, which help to prevent deep vein thrombosis (DVT) from developing (see page 60).

It is normal for some mothers to develop lower back pain during this stage. You can ask your partner to firmly massage your lower back. They should look out for any tender points and massage them, concentrating around the tailbone area (coccyx). Ask them to massage firmly in a clockwise fashion. If this does not help to relieve the pain, try using a TENS machine (see page 213). Moving around, sitting on a birthing ball or using a birthing pool can help reduce the pain. It can also help to prevent blood clots from forming. You can take paracetamol (acetaminophen, Tylenol) or codeine at this point for pain relief as it will not harm the baby. All these options will take the edge off the pain, but may not take it away completely.

Here are some useful positions to be in during labour:

- If possible, stay on your feet. Lean forward and rock your hips from side to side and up and down with each contraction.

- Keep your bottom wiggling during contractions. Lean forward over a beanbag if you find this more comfortable.

- Hang on to something well above waist height and let your body sag, turning your knees outwards.

- Sit your partner on a chair, kneel on the floor with your knees apart and lean on their thighs.

- Get on all fours either on the bed or the floor, whichever you find the most comfortable.

Stage Two: Active Stage

The second stage of labour (active stage) begins when the cervix is 10cm (4in) dilated (open). The opening to your uterus has now reached its maximum, allowing your baby to move from the uterus and into the vaginal canal with the aid of uterine contractions. Entering the second stage of labour will be confirmed by your midwife inserting two fingers up into the vagina and parting their fingers as far as they can at the head of the cervix. Delivery of your baby is now ready!

Once the cervix is fully dilated, the midwife will allow one hour for the baby to descend their head out of the uterus (cervix), which it should do naturally with the aid of uterine contractions. This will be checked by the midwife by inserting two fingers up into the vagina and feeling for the baby's skull. Your midwife will then allow around two hours for the head to come through the pelvis and appear at the entrance of the vagina, known as crowning, as you can see the top of the baby's head through the vaginal opening.

During the second stage of labour, a combination of bones including your sacrum move backwards and in doing so, increases the diameter of your pelvis thereby providing more space for your baby to travel down the birth canal. This is perfectly normal and is known as 'opening the back'. It allows your baby the maximum amount of space for your baby to turn as they navigate their way out of the vaginal canal. In order to facilitate the opening of your back, you should use active birth positions where you are upright and leaning forwards rather than lying down.

This is the time when energy is needed to either push or breathe the baby out. Eating and drinking as well as sleeping beforehand will have prepared you for this. You should only push when you have a contraction and not otherwise. It is all about working with your body's rhythm and not forcing it. The aim of a good delivery is to just breathe the baby out by allowing the contractions to gently push the baby through.

As the contractions push the baby down, the baby will go up slightly when the contractions stop, making it seem like the baby is not coming down. This is normal. This can be made worse from lying down rather than standing or kneeling. Do not panic, the baby is in fact descending out. When the baby's head begins to show through the entrance to the vagina, you might feel some stinging of the vagina. This is normal. Some women will panic at this point and try to finish delivery by forcibly pushing the baby out. Do not do this! Doing this is the main cause of tearing of the vagina. At this point, tiny pushes are needed with each contraction, to gently push the baby's head through, allowing time for the vagina to stretch. Change your breathing to a short breath, as if you were blowing out candles, and make tiny pushes. Your midwife or doula will guide you through this last process and will tell you when you need to change your breathing and make tiny pushes.

The baby's heart rate will be monitored every five minutes to ensure the baby is not distressed. It is also a tiring and a difficult process for the baby and its heart rate may drop. This is normal. If the baby is descending too slowly or is a bit stuck, a suction cup (ventouse) can be placed on their head to help pull them out. If the baby becomes stuck for more than one hour, the midwife may ask if they can cut your vagina to allow for more space (episiotomy). You must agree to this before they do it. If this is needed, then a local anaesthetic will be injected into the labia of the vagina before making the cut and, once the baby is out, the cut will be stitched up. A natural tear heals better than a medically made cut. Forceps can also be used to pull the baby down and out. The use of forceps can take up space within the vaginal canal as extra space is needed either side of the baby's head, whereas a suction cup does not.

It is likely that a greater percentage of first-time mums will tear a little. There are four degrees of tearing:

1. Tearing to the vagina and vulva skin only.

2. Tearing to the perineal muscles but not the anal sphincter (rectum muscle).

3. Tearing to the perineum (the area between the anus and the vulva) and the anal sphincter.

4. Tearing to the perineum, anal sphincter and rectal bowel[3].

If you have teared during labour, your medical team will ensure that it will be stitched up using a local anaesthetic afterwards. Sexual intercourse may be painful for a few months until the tear has properly healed.

Once the head is through, your baby will turn to allow its shoulders and body to pass through. As the head is delivered, a lot of babies will have their umbilical cord wrapped around their neck, one to three times. Some women may panic upon seeing this, but it is normal. It does not mean that the baby is being strangled. Your midwife will simply unwrap it and allow labour to continue. The rest of the baby's body should then just slide out.

Once your baby has been delivered, the fluid covering the baby is dried off as a wet baby loses heat. Your baby will then be wrapped in a blanket and a hat put on their head to keep them warm. Your baby will then be given to you for you to place on to your chest. It is important that your baby's skin touches yours, not only to keep your baby warm, but also to help with bonding and to calm your baby from its ordeal as they can listen to your heartbeat, which relaxes them as they have been listening to it for the last nine months.

The normal blood loss during labour is around 300ml (10oz) compared to a caesarean delivery, which is around 1,000ml (34oz) [3] [8]. The umbilical cord will be pulsating still and, once it stops, if the father is present, they are often asked if they want to cut the cord, otherwise the midwife will do it. At this point, 9 out of 10 babies will start crying. A few will not and that is normal. If they do not start crying, the midwife will check their airways for any mucus that might be blocking it. After that, they usually start crying. When babies are born, they often have a bluish or purple tinge, which is normal. It can take a few minutes for them to gain their natural colour. They may also be covered in vernix, a waxy white substance that covers the skin of newborn babies (see page 178). This is normal.

An Apgar score test is used to assess newborn babies one and five minutes immediately after birth [742]. The Apgar score evaluates your baby on five different criteria: appearance, pulse, grimace, activity and respiration. Each is measured on a scale from zero to two, then summing up the values together. The resulting Apgar score ranges from zero to ten. The one-minute score determines how well the baby tolerated labour. The five-minute score shows how well your baby is doing outside of your womb.

Stage Three: Delivery of the Placenta

Stage three is the delivery of the placenta. Delivery of the placenta is given 30 minutes. Around 90 per cent of placentas are delivered 15 minutes after the baby. In 2–3 per cent of vaginal labours, the placenta is not delivered within 30 minutes [3] [57]. During most vaginal deliveries conducted within hospitals, active management is used during the third stage of labour as it has been shown to reduce internal bleeding [3] [57]. Active management involves an injection of the hormone oxytocin into the mother's leg, which causes a large contraction of the uterus, which releases the placenta from the uterus wall. If the placenta is not delivered within 30 minutes, it is considered to be retained.

Retention of the placenta is a serious condition and can be aggravated by a previous caesarean (the placenta attaches to the scar left from the previous caesarean thereby not allowing it to detach properly). A retained placenta can also happen in older mothers, those who have had previous terminations or a history of endometriosis. It can occur in 2–3 per cent of vaginal deliveries [3]. If this should occur, oxytocin is often administered to the mother and she is encouraged to start breastfeeding, which will naturally increase oxytocin levels in the body. If after one hour the placenta has still not been delivered, surgery is used to extract it [3]. A natural alternative is to take shepherd's purse (*capsella bursa-pastoris*), which has a long history of being used to release a sticky placenta (see page 189).

Delayed cord clamping

Clamping the umbilical cord immediately after birth has been a standard practice for decades. Recently, medical textbooks and research advise obstetricians and midwives to delay clamping by 30–60 seconds as it improves the health of the baby [743] [744] [745]. The theory is that by delaying clamping of the umbilical cord, more blood is passed on to the baby, which increases their levels of blood and iron, thereby reducing the chances of them developing anaemia as they grow [746] [747].

Young children with anaemia is a global problem. Around 43 per cent of children younger than 5 years (approximately 273 million) have anaemia, which is attributed to iron deficiency in 42 per cent [748]. Children with anaemia and iron deficiency have associated impaired neurodevelopment, affecting their cognitive, motor and behavioural abilities [748].

New research has shown that delaying the clamping of the umbilical cord by up to three minutes rather than the textbook advice of one minute, reduces anaemia in children at the age of eight and twelve months [748]. It has also been shown to improve neurodevelopment too [749]. This technique is worth discussing with your midwife and obstetrician before entering labour. In babies born by caesarean delivery, umbilical cord milking can be used to increase blood levels, body temperature and blood pressure [750] [751].

Stage Four: Recovery

Straight after birth you may feel exhausted, happy and bruised in your groin area. This is normal. If you gave birth in a hospital, you can go home after four to six hours once you have passed urine and a bowel movement and your medical team are happy to discharge you. Or you can stay longer if needed, depending on your delivery and the hospital.

Some mothers will feel that shot of love for their baby straightaway, while for others it can take several months. This is normal as everyone is different. Most women may look like they are several months pregnant for weeks after giving birth as it takes time for the uterus to shrink back to its original size, which is normal. Some women may benefit from wearing a band around their lower abdomen to give them support in that area and pull things back into place. I would not recommend starting strenuous postnatal exercises once you have given birth. In China, new mothers are encouraged to stay in bed for a month to help them recover from labour. This is called 'sitting the month' (zuo yuezi). New mothers are encouraged to drink warm fluids and eat no raw vegetables to help them heal faster. This practice dates back 2,000 years.

You may continue to bleed for several weeks afterwards, which is normal if you had a vaginal delivery and is known as lochia. You can use either maternity sanitary towels, which can feel big and bulky or maximum strength night-time sanitary towels. These can also act as a cushion if you had a perineal tear and needed stitches. It is a balance between finding ones that are comfortable and also very absorbent.

It is important to start taking a breastfeeding multivitamin supplement. I would also recommend taking Chinese herbs to help your uterus recover. Chinese herbs are safe to take while breastfeeding. I would also recommend keeping your placenta to consume. The practice of consuming your placenta is widely practised in East Asia and is becoming more popular in the West with many companies now offering to encapsulate the placenta. By consuming your placenta, it helps to nourish your body, which may have become weakened from pregnancy and aids physical recovery. You can either cook and eat your placenta or have is converted into capsules. Most people opt for encapsulation.

You will be visited at home by a healthcare professional to check you and your baby who will offer advice, for example on breastfeeding. You may then see your doctor several weeks after giving birth.

Enjoy this wonderful miracle you have created.

Pregnancy Dictionary

Acupoints: specific points on the body where acupuncture or moxa are applied.

Acupuncture: the insertion of fine pins into acupuncture points along the meridian channels of the body.

Adrenocorticotropic hormone (ACTH): a hormone produced by the pituitary gland that influences the production of hormones by the adrenals.

Androgens: hormones that are made up of testosterone, androstenedione and sex hormone-binding globulin (SHBG).

Blood: the same in both Western and Chinese medicines.

Blood stasis: the impairment of normal blood flow.

BMI (body mass index): a mathematical equation (divide your weight in kilograms by your height in metres squared) that tries to measure a person's body fat.

Chinese herbs: parts of plants mixed together to heal the body.

Chinese medicine: a system of medicine that uses observations in Nature to maintain good health. This system of medicine exists not only in China but surrounding countries such as Japan, Korea, Vietnam, etc.

Chorioamnionitis: an inflammation of the foetal membranes due to a bacterial infection caused by an open uterus, also known as intra-amniotic infection (IAI).

CMV (cytomegalovirus): a herpes virus, which can cause birth defects [752].

Colostrum: first breast milk that is high in fat and has low levels of lactose.

Contraction stress test (CST): a test that temporarily reduces blood flow to the baby. A healthy baby is able to compensate for this.

Corpus luteum: the reformation of the collapsed follicle (egg) sac, which releases progesterone and relaxin.

Corticotrophic-releasing hormone (CRH): affects levels of the stress hormone cortisone and the timing of delivery.

Cretinism: learning difficulties due to hypothyroidism brought about by a lack of iodine in the mother.

Crown–rump length (CRL): the measurement of the length of your baby from the top of the head (crown) to the bottom of the buttocks (rump) during an ultrasound.

Cryptorchidism: a male baby with undescended testes.

Cyst: a sac-like pocket of tissue that contains fluid, air or other substances.

Decidua: the uterus lining (endometrium or endometrial lining).

Dermoid cyst: a small collection of bodily tissues such as hair, teeth, blood, bone, fat, eyes, etc.

Down's syndrome: a trisomy 21 genetic disorder.

Eclampsia: a combination of pre-eclampsia together with convulsions (grand mal seizures).

Ectopic: growth of a fertilised egg outside of the uterus.

ECV (external cephalic version): a medical procedure used to turn a breech baby.

Edwards' syndrome: a trisomy 18 genetic disorder.

Endometrium/endometrial: the lining of the uterus (womb) wall.

Endomyometritis: infection of the uterus.

Extremely low birth weight (ELBW): a birth weight of less than 1,000g (35.27oz).

Fallopian tubes: the tubes that join the ovaries to the uterus.

False labour: when pain is felt in the lower abdomen but does not intensify.

Femur length (FL): measures the length of the baby's femur (leg bone) during pregnancy using an ultrasound. A shorter-than-expected femur can indicate a higher risk of skeletal dysplasia (dwarfism) [753].

Fibroids: non-cancerous tumours, made up of muscle and fibrous tissue that grow in or around the uterus in various sizes.

Foetal echocardiography: similar to an ultrasound. It checks your baby's heart.

Foetal heart tones: foetal heartbeat.

Gestation: the period of pregnancy.

GGD: global growth delay.

Harmony test: a blood test that measures the likelihood of carrying a Down's syndrome, Edwards' syndrome or Patau's syndrome baby.

HCG (human chorionic gonadotropin): used by pregnancy tests to detect pregnancy.

HGH: human growth hormone.

HPT: home pregnancy test.

Hypothalamus: the area in the brain that produces gonadotrophin-releasing hormone (GnRH) and oxytocin.

IUGR (intrauterine growth restriction): where the foetus fails to grow at the rate it is predicted to.

Jing: also known as essence; a more concentrated form of yin that is housed in the kidneys.

Leydig cells: found in male testes and produce testosterone.

Linea nigra: Latin for 'black line'. It is a dark vertical line that appears on the abdomen, between the belly button and the pubic area.

Lipids: organic compounds made up of fats and oils.

Lochia: the post-birth vaginal discharge that contains a mixture of blood, mucus and uterine tissue.

Low birth weight (LBW): a birth weight of less than 2,501g (88.22oz).

Macrosomia: excessive foetal growth and size. Weight varies but generally more than 4,500g (10lb).

Meconium: a newborn's first poo, which is dark green in colour.

MIA (maternal immune activation): an immune response to a virus during pregnancy.

Moxibustion: the use of heat therapy (moxa) on specific acupoints.

ng (nanogram): a unit of substance equal to one billionth of a gram.

Oedema: fluid retention in areas of the body.

Oestradiol: the most abundant and dominant hormone from the group of oestrogens.

Oestrogen: the group of hormones secreted during pregnancy.

Oxytocin: a hormone that induces labour and the release of breast milk.

P4: progesterone.

Patau's syndromes: a trisomy 13 genetic disorder.

Pertussis: whooping cough.

Phytoestrogens: naturally-occurring oestrogens found in plants.

Pituitary gland: the gland that secretes oxytocin.

Placenta: an organ solely for pregnancy that facilities the interaction between mother and baby.

Placental abruption: when the placenta separates from the uterus wall before birth.

Placenta accreta: when the placenta grows too deeply into the uterine wall.

Placenta previa: when the placenta partially or wholly blocks the neck of the uterus, thereby preventing normal delivery of a baby.

pmol (picomole): a unit of substance equal to one trillionth (10-12) of a mole.

Pre-eclampsia (PE): a disorder of pregnancy characterised by high blood pressure and a large amount of protein in the urine.

Primip: an abbreviation for primigravida, which means a woman who is pregnant for the first time.

Progesterone: a steroid hormone secreted by the *corpus luteum* and the placenta.

Progestins: a group of steroid hormones produced by the *corpus luteum* and placenta. The main progestin is progesterone.

Progestogens: a group of steroid hormones produced by the *corpus luteum* and the placenta. The main progestogen is progesterone.

Prolactin: a hormone that stimulates breast development and lactation.

PROM: an abbreviation for pre-labour rupture of membranes.

Proteinuria: too much protein in the urine (>30mg/mmol).

Qi: energy; from food, air and a person's constitution.

Relaxin: a female hormone produced by the *corpus luteum* and placenta that relaxes the uterus during implantation, pregnancy and labour.

TRH: thyrotropin-releasing hormone.

Trimester: a three-month period of pregnancy.

Trophoblasts: the outer cells of an embryo (blastocyst) that form the connection to the uterus and later develop into the placenta.

TSH: thyroid-stimulating hormone.

Very low birth weight (VLBW): a birth weight of less than 1,501g (52.94oz).

Yang: male, the sun, active, midday, hot, summer, etc.

Yin: female, the moon, passive, midnight, cold, winter, etc.

Zika virus: a virus transmitted sexually or via mosquito bites that causes congenital birth defects [754].

References

1. *Viral infection of the pregnant cervix predisposes to ascending bacterial infection.* **Racicot, Karen.** 2, s.l. : J Immunol, 2013, Vol. 191.

2. **Jacobson, John and Zieve, David.** Eating right during pregnancy. *Medline Plus.* [Online] 04 October 2016. [Cited: 02 June 2017.] https://medlineplus.gov/ency/patientinstructions/000584.htm.

3. **Magowan, Brian, Owen, Philip and Thomson, Andrew.** *Clinic Obstretics & Gynaecology.* Edinburgh : Elsevier, 2014.

4. **Beckmann, Charles, et al.** *Obstretics and Gynecology.* Philadelphia : Wolters Kluwer, 2010.

5. *Green tea polyphenols: versatile cosmetic ingredient.* **Sandeep, Kumar.** 4, s.l. : International Journal of Advanced Research in Pharmaceutical & Bio Sciences, 2012, Vol. 1.

6. **Martini, Frederic.** *Fundamentals of Anatomy and Physiology.* Upper Saddle River : Prentice Hall Inc, 1998.

7. **Tortora, Gerard and Derrickson, Bryan.** *Principles of Anatomy & Physiology.* [ed.] 14th Edition. Hoboken : Wiley, 2014.

8. **Norwitz, Errol.** *Obstetrics & Gynecology at a Glance.* Oxford : Blackwell Sciences Ltd, 2001.

9. *Acupuncture Increases Nocturnal Melatonin Secretion and Reduces Insomnia and Anxiety: A Preliminary Report.* **Warren Spence, D.** s.l. : The Journal of Neuropsychiatry and Clinical Neurosciences, 2004, Vol. 16.

10. *Effects of acupuncture therapy on insomnia.* **Sok, S.** 4, s.l. : Journal of Advanced Nursing, 2003, Vol. 44.

11. *Auricular Acupuncture Treatment for Insomnia: A Systematic Review.* **Chen, Hai Yong.** 6, s.l. : The Journal of Alternative and Complementary Medicine, 2007, Vol. 13.

12. *Restless Leg Syndrome: A Neglected Diagnosis.* **Einollahi, Behzad.** 5, s.l. : Nephrourol Mon, 2014, Vol. 6.

13. *Evaluation of Acupuncture in the Treatment of Restless Legs Syndrome: A Randomized Controlled Trial.* **Raiss, Gholam.** 5, s.l. : Journal of Acupuncture and Meridian Studies, 2017, Vol. 10.

14. **JOHN BRAXTON HICKS (1823-1897).** *National Center for Biotechnology Information, U.S. National Library of Medicine.* [Online] J. H. Young. [Cited: 30 July 2020.] https://www.ncbi. nlm.nih.gov/pmc/articles/PMC1034548/pdf/medhist00175-0075.pdf.

15. *Effectiveness and Analysis of Applying the Principle of Myofascial Trigger Points (MTrPs) to Treat Lower Extremity Varicose Veins (LEVVs): A Prospective Clinical Therapeutic Study.* **Wu, Zonghui.** s.l. : SSRN, 2020.

16. *Application of acupuncture in the treatment of venous insufficiency and varicose veins.* **Alp, Hayriye.** 2, s.l. : Cardiovasc Surg Int, 2019, Vol. 7.

17. *Case report: successful treatment of varicose veins with acupuncture.* **Bodenheim, R.** s.l. : merican Journal of Acupuncture, 1999, Vol. 27.

18. *Treatment of vulvar and perineal varicose veins.* **Van Cleef, Jean-François.** 1, s.l.: Phlebolymphology, 2011, Vol. 18.

19. *Not-patient and not-visitor: A metasynthesis fathers' encounters with pregnancy, birth and maternity care.* **Steen, Mary.** s.l. : Midwifery, 2012, Vol. 28.

20. *Fathers' involvement during pregnancy and childbirth: An integrative literature review.* **Xue, Weilin.** s.l. : Midwifery, 2018, Vol. 62.

21. *The Three Phases of Fatherhood in Pregnancy.* **May, K.** 6, s.l. : Nursing Research, 1982, Vol. 31.

22. *The Missing Link in MCH: Paternal Involvement in Pregnancy Outcomes.* **Bond, M.** 4, s.l. : American Journal of Men's Health, 2010, Vol. 4.

23. *Resident Fathers' Pregnancy Intentions, Prenatal Behaviors, and Links to Involvement With Infants.* **Bronte-Tinkew, Jacinta.** s.l. : Journal of Marriage and Family, 2007, Vol. 69.

24. *Positive Health Outcomes of Fathers' Involvment in Pregnancy and Childbirth Paternal Support: A Scope Study Literature Review.* **Plantin, L.** 1, s.l. : Fathering, 2011, Vol. 9.

25. *Fathers' engagement in pregnancy and childbirth: evidence from a national survey.* **Redshaw, Maggie.** 70, s.l. : BMC Pregnancy and Childbirth, 2013, Vol. 13.

26. *The Effects of Father Involvement during Pregnancy on Receipt of Prenatal Care and Maternal Smoking.* **Martin, Laurie.** s.l. : Matern Child Health J, 2007, Vol. 11.

27. **National Health Service.** *NHS Maternity Services Quantitative Research (October), Prepared by TNS System Three for Kate Hawkins.* London : Department of Health, 2005.

28. *Higher Maternal Levels of Free Estradiol in First Compared to Second Pregnancy: Early Gestational Differences.* **Bernstein, Leslie.** 6, s.l. : JNCI, 1986, Vol. 76.

29. *T-cell subsets (Th1 versus Th2).* **Romagnani, Sergio.** 1, s.l. : Ann Allergy Asthma Immunol, 2000, Vol. 85.

30. *The immune response during the luteal phase of the ovarian cycle: a Th2-type response?* **Faas, Marijke**, et al. 5, s.l. : Fertility and Sterility, 2000, Vol. 74.

31. *Second trimester corticotropin-releasing hormone levels in relation to preterm delivery and ethnicity.* **Holzman, Claudia.** 5, s.l. : Obstetrics & Gynecology, 2001, Vol. 97.

32. *Maternal Prenatal Anxiety and Corticotropin-Releasing Hormone Associated With Timing of Delivery.* **Mancuso, Roberta.** 5, s.l. : Psychosomatic Medicine, 2004, Vol. 66.

33. *Maternal Corticotropin-Releasing Hormone Is Increased with Impending Preterm Birth.* **Korebrits, C.** 5, s.l. : Journal of Clinical Endocrinology and Metabolism, 1998, Vol. 83.

34. *Maternal plasma corticotropin-releasing hormone associated with stress at 20 weeks' gestation in pregnancies ending in preterm delivery.* **Hobel, Calvin.** 1, s.l.: American Journal of Obstetrics and Gynecology, 1999, Vol. 180.

35. *Effects of electro-acupuncture on corticotropin-releasing factor in rats with experimentally-induced polycystic ovaries.* **Stener-Victorin**, E. 5-6, s.l. : Neuropeptides, 2001, Vol. 35.

36. *Effect of acupuncture on anxiety-like behavior during nicotine withdrawal and relevant mechanisms.* **Chae, Younbyoung.** 2, s.l. : Neuroscience Letters, 2008, Vol. 430.

37. *Effect of Acupuncture on Hypothalamic–Pituitary–Adrenal System in Maternal Separation Rats.* **Park, Hae.** s.l. : Cell Mol Neurobiol, 2011, Vol. 31.

38. *The effects of acupuncture stimulation at PC6 (Neiguan) on chronic mild stress-induced biochemical and behavioral responses.* **Kim, Hyunyoung.** s.l. : Neuroscience Letters, 2009, Vol. 460.

39. *Effects from acupuncture in treating anxiety: integrative review.* **Goyatá, Sueli.** 3, s.l. : Rev Bras Enferm, 2016, Vol. 69.

40. *Effects of an integrative treatment, therapeutic acupuncture and conventional treatment in alleviating psychological distress in primary care patients - a pragmatic randomized controlled trial.* **Arvidsdotter, Tina.** s.l. : BMC Complementary and Alternative Medicine, 2013, Vol. 13.

41. *Acupuncture and electroacupuncture for anxiety disorders: A systematic review of the clinical research.* **Amorim, Diogo.** s.l. : Complementary Therapies in Clinical Practice, 2018, Vol. 31.

42. *Effects of Acupuncture on Anxiety Levels and Prefrontal Cortex Activity Measured by Near-Infrared Spectroscopy: A Pilot Study.* **Sakatani, K.** s.l. : Oxygen Transport to Tissue XXXVII, 2016.

43. *Current evidence regarding the management of mood and anxiety disorders using complementary and alternative medicine.* **Bazzan, Anthony.** 4, s.l. : Expert Rev. Neurother, 2014, Vol. 14.

44. *Effect of Acupressure, Acupuncture and Moxibustion in Women With Pregnancy-Related Anxiety and Previous Depression: A Preliminary Study.* **Suzuki, Shunji and Tobe, Chiharu.** 6, s.l. : J Clin Med Res, 2017, Vol. 9.

45. **Brownstein, David.** *Iodine: Why You Need It, Why You Can't Live Without It.* West Bloomfield : Medical Alternative Press, 2014.

46. *Increased risk of iodine deficiency with vegetarian nutrition.* **Remer, Thomas.** 1, s.l. : British Journal of Nutrition, 1999, Vol. 81.

47. *Inadequate Iodine Intake in Population Groups Defined by Age, Life Stage and Vegetarian Dietary Practice in a Norwegian Convenience Sample.* **Brantsæter, Anne Lise.** 230, s.l. : Nutrients, 2018, Vol. 10.

48. *Are vegetarians an 'at risk group' for iodine deficiency?* **Davidsson, Lena.** 3-4, s.l.: British Journal of Nutrition, 1999, Vol. 81.

49. **Fields, Cheryl.** *Comprehensive Handbook of Iodine.* s.l. : Elsevier , 2009.

50. *Thyroid-Stimulating Hormone Values in Pregnancy: Cutoff Controversy Continues?* **Khadilkar, Suvarna.** s.l. : The Journal of Obstetrics and Gynecology of India, 2019, Vol. 69.

51. *Endocrine Disorders in Pregnancy Guideline.* Greater Manchester and Eastern Cheshire SCN. [Online] NHS, 2018. [Cited: 1 July 2021.] https://www.england.nhs.uk/north-west/wp-content/uploads/sites/48/2019/03/GMEC-SCN-Endocrine-Disorders-Pregnancy-Guideline-v1.pdf.

52. *The antinociceptive effect of non-noxious sensory stimulation is mediated partly through oxytocinergic mechanisms.* **Uvnäs-Moberg, K,** et al. 2, s.l. : Acta Physiol Scand, 1993, Vol. 149.

53. *Brain Oxytocin: A Key Regulator of Emotional and Social Behaviours in Both Females and Males.* **Neumann, D.** s.l. : Journal of Neuroendocrinology, 2008, Vol. 20.

54. *Microbial Reconstitution Reverses Maternal Diet-Induced Social and Synaptic Deficits in Offspring.* **Buffington, S A,** et al. 7, s.l. : Cell, 2016, Vol. 165.

55. *The Fat-Induced Satiety Factor Oleoylethanolamide Suppresses Feeding through Central Release of Oxytocin.* **Gaetani, Silvana,** et al. 24, s.l. : The Journal of Neuroscience, 2010, Vol. 30.

56. *Peripheral oxytocin treatment ameliorates obesity by reducing food intake and visceral fat mass.* **Maejima, Yuko and Iwasaki, Yusaku.** 12, s.l. : Aging, 2011, Vol. 3.

57. **Impey, L and Child, T.** *Obstetrics & Gynaecology.* Chichester : John Wiley & Sons, 2012.

58. *Control of GnRH neuronal activity by metabolic factors: the role of leptin and insulin.* **Gamba, Marcella and Pralong, Francois.** s.l. : Molecular and Cellular Endocrinology, 2006.

59. *Artificial Sweetener Use and One-Year Weight Change among Women.* **Stellman, Steven and Lawrence, Garfinkel.** s.l. : Preventive Medicine, 1986, Vol. 15.

60. *Low-Frequency Electro-Acupuncture and Physical Exercise Improve Metabolic Disturbances and Modulate Gene Expression in Adipose Tissue in Rats with Dihydrotestosterone-Induced Polycystic Ovary Syndrome.* **Manneräs, Louise** , et al. 7, s.l. : Endocrinology, 2008, Vol. 149.

61. **Johnson, Wendy.** *Developing Difference.* s.l. : Macmillan International Higher Education, 2013.

62. *Severity of ASD Symptoms and Their Correlation with the Presence of Copy Number Variations and Exposure to First Trimester Ultrasound.* **Webb, Sara.** 3, s.l. : Autism Research, 2017, Vol. 10.

63. *Is ultrasound unsound? A review of epidemiological studies of human exposure to ultrasound.* **Salvesen , K.** 4, s.l. : Ultrasound Obstet Gynecol, 1995, Vol. 6.

64. *Prenatal diagnosis and pregnancy outcome analysis of thickened nuchal fold in the second trimester.* **Li, Lushan.** s.l. : Medicine, 2018, Vol. 46.

65. *Thromboprophylaxis improves the live birth rate in women with consecutive recurrent miscarriages and hereditary thrombophilia.* **Carp, H, Dolitzky, M and Inbal, A.** s.l. : Journal of Thrombosis and Haemostasis, 2003, Vol. 1.

66. *Effect of electro-acupuncture stimulation of different frequencies and intensities on ovarian blood flow in anaesthetized rats with steroid-induced polycystic ovaries.* **Stener-Victorin, Elisabet** , et al. 16, s.l. : Reproductive Biology and Endocrinology, 2004, Vol. 2.

67. *Data and Statistics on Down Syndrome. Centers for Disease Control and Prevention.* [Online] **U.S. Department of Health & Human Services,** 23 October 2020. [Cited: 24 July 2021.] https://www.cdc.gov/ncbddd/birthdefects/downsyndrome/data.html.

68. *Survival of trisomy 18 (Edwards syndrome) and trisomy 13 (Patau Syndrome) in England and Wales: 2004-2011.* **Wu, Jianhua.** s.l. : Am J Med Genet A, 2013.

69. *Antenatal Screening. Queen Mary University of London.* [Online] December 2016. [Cited: 08 October 2020.] https://www.qmul.ac.uk/wolfson/media/wolfson/1in300.pdf.

70. *Non-Invasive Prenatal Testing (NIPT) – The SAFE Test.* St George's University Hospitals. [Online] NHS. [Cited: 7 July 2021.] https://www.stgeorges.nhs.uk/service/maternity-services/your-pregnancy/fetal-medicine-unit/the-safe-test/.

71. *For a range of conditions. Harmony Test.* [Online] [Cited: 7 July 2021.] https://www.harmonytest.com/global/en/nipt-test-for-expecting-parents-cell-free-dna/nipt/what-does-nipt-test-for-with-cell-free-dna-cfdna.html.

72. *Prevention of Maternal–Fetal Transmission of Cytomegalovirus.* **Adler, Stuart.** s.l. : EBioMedicine, 2015, Vol. 2.

73. *Prevention of Primary Cytomegalovirus Infection in Pregnancy.* **Revello, Maria.** s.l. : EBioMedicine, 2015, Vol. 2.

74. *Routine CMV screening during pregnancy.* **Collinet, P.** s.l. : European Journal of Obstetrics & Gynecology and Reproductive Biology, 2004, Vol. 114.

75. *A study on the traditional chinese medicine jinyebaidu for prevention and treatment of intrauterine infection with guinea pigs cytomegalovirus.* **Chen, Suhu.** s.l. : Journal of Huazhong University of Science and Technology, 2005, Vol. 25.

76. *Effects of Jinye Baidu Granule on Fetal Growth and Development With Maternal Active Human Cytomegalovirus Infection.* **Jiang, Hong.** 4, s.l. : Chin J Integr Med, 2006, Vol. 12.

77. *Group B strep.* **NHS.** [Online] 1 February 2018. [Cited: 30 December 2020.] https://www.nhs.uk/conditions/group-b-strep/.

78. *What are the risks of scarlet fever during pregnancy?* **NHS.** [Online] 28 November 2019. [Cited: 30 December 2020.] https://www.nhs.uk/common-health-questions/pregnancy/what-are-the-risks-of-scarlet-fever-during-pregnancy/.

79. *Traditional Chinese medicine.* **Nestler, Gary.** 1, s.l. : Medical Clinics of North America, 2002, Vol. 86.

80. *What are the risks of chickenpox during pregnancy?* **NHS.** [Online] 27 May 2020. [Cited: 30 December 2020.] https://www.nhs.uk/common-health-questions/pregnancy/what-are-the-risks-of-chickenpox-during-pregnancy/.

81. *How is chickenpox treated during pregnancy?* **NHS.** [Online] 17 October 2018. [Cited: 30 December 2020.] https://www.nhs.uk/common-health-questions/pregnancy/how-is-chickenpox-treated-during-pregnancy.

82. *Review of Clinical Studies of Oral Herbal Medicine Treatment for Pediatric Chickenpox using CNKI Database - Focused on Chinese Randomized Controlled Trials after 2000s.* **Choi, Jung.** 3, s.l. : The Journal of Pediatrics of Korean Medicine, 2020, Vol. 34.

83. *What are the risks of shingles during pregnancy?* **NHS.** [Online] 8 October 2018. [Cited: 30 December 2020.] https://www.nhs.uk/common-health-questions/pregnancy/what-are-the-risks-of-shingles-during-pregnancy/.

84. *Oral Chinese herbal medicine for post-herpetic neuralgia: A systematic review and meta-analysis of randomized controlled trials.* **Liang, Haiying.** s.l. : European Journal of Integrative Medicine, 2017, Vol. 10.

85. *Placental Pathology in COVID-19.* **Shanes, Elisheva.** s.l. : Am J Clin Pathol, 2020.

86. *Placenta lacks major molecules used by SARS-CoV-2 virus to cause infection.* **National Institutes of Health.** [Online] 14 July 2020. [Cited: 04 September 2020.] https://www.nih.gov/news-events/news-releases/placenta-lacks-major-molecules-used-sars-cov-2-virus-cause-infection.

87. *Clinical manifestations, risk factors, and maternal and perinatal outcomes of coronavirus disease 2019 in pregnancy: living systematic review and meta-analysis.* **Allotey, John.** s.l. : BMJ, 2020.

88. *Maternal transmission of SARS-COV-2 to the neonate, and possible routes for such transmission: A systematic review and critical analysis.* **Walker , Kate.** s.l. : BJOG, 2020.

89. *Rates of Maternal and Perinatal Mortality and Vertical Transmission in Pregnancies Complicated by Severe Acute Respiratory Syndrome Coronavirus 2 (SARS-Co-V-2) Infection.* **Huntley, Benjamin.** s.l. : Obstetrics & Gynecology, 2020.

90. *AMSTERDAM HOSPITAL STUDYING WHETHER BREAST MILK CAN PROTECT AGAINST CORONAVIRUS.* **NL Times.** [Online] 24 April 2020. [Cited: 04 September 2020.] https://nltimes.nl/2020/04/24/amsterdam-hospital-studying-whether-breast-milk-can-protect-coronavirus?fbclid=IwAR0417s3cwBRsxUCtXP7mI6P15KhuDSQgF2EiGH2L6FcyO_lFFdPrOKLAfk.

91. *Transmitting biological effects of stress in utero: Implications for mother and offspring.* **Reynolds, Rebecca,** et al. 2013, Psychoneuroendocrinology, Vol. 38, pp. 1843-49.

92. *Effect of Lavender Cream with or without Foot-bath on Anxiety, Stress and Depression in Pregnancy: a Randomized Placebo-Controlled Trial.* **Effati-Daryani, Fatemeh.** 1, s.l. : J Caring Sci., 2015, Vol. 4.

93. *Women with nausea and vomiting in pregnancy demonstrate worse health and are adversely affected by odours.* **Swallow, B.** s.l. : Journal of Obstetrics and Gynaecology , 2005, Vol. 25.

94. *Auriculotherapy as a means of managing nausea and vomiting in pregnancy: A double-blind randomized controlled clinical trial.* **Negarandeh , Reza.** s.l.: Complement Ther Clin Pract, 2020.

95. *Morning sickness control in early pregnancy by Neiguan point acupressure.* de **Aloysio, D.** 5, s.l. : Obstetrics and Gynecology, 1992, Vol. 80.

96. *P6 Acupressure Reduces Morning Sickness.* **Dundee, J.** 8, s.l. : Journal of the Royal Society of Medicine, 1988, Vol. 81.

97. *Increase in the Vagal Modulation by Acupuncture at Neiguan Point in the Healthy Subjects.* **Huang, Sheng-Teng.** 1, s.l. : The American Journal of Chinese Medicine, 2005, Vol. 33.

98. *Effect of Nei–Guan point (P6) acupressure on ketonuria levels, nausea and vomiting in women with hyperemesis gravidarum.* **Shin, Hye Sook.** 5, s.l. : JAN, 2007, Vol. 59.

99. Royal Pharmaceutical Society. British National Formulary - 76. London : BNF, 2018.

100. *Gastroesophageal reflux disease in pregnancy.* **Raja Ali, R.** 5, s.l. : Best Practice & Research Clinical Gastroenterology, 2007, Vol. 21.

101. **Acid-suppressive medications during pregnancy and risk of asthma and allergy in children: A systematic review and meta-analysis. Devine, Rebecca.** s.l. : J Allergy Clin Immunol, 2016.

102. *Clinical trial: acupuncture vs. doubling the proton pump inhibitor dose in refractory heartburn.* **Dickman, R.** s.l. : Alimentary Pharmacology & Therapeutics, 2007, Vol. 26.

103. *Acupuncture for Dyspepsia in Pregnancy: A Prospective, Randomised, Controlled Study.* **Guerreiro da Silva, Joao.** s.l. : Acupunct Med, 2009, Vol. 27.

104. *Gastrointestinal motility disorders and acupuncture.* **Yin, Jieyun.** s.l. : Autonomic Neuroscience: Basic and Clinical, 2010, Vol. 157.

105. *Acupuncture to treat hypertension: a recent systematic review and implications for subsequent research.* **Leem, Jungtae.** s.l. : Integrative Medicine Research, 2016.

106. *The Effect of Acupuncture on Essential Hypertension.* **Kwong-Chuen, T.** 4, s.l. : The American Journal of Chinese Medicine, 1975, Vol. 3.

107. *Acupuncture, a promising adjunctive therapy for essential hypertension: a double-blind, randomized, controlled trial.* **Yin, C.** s.l. : Neurological Research, 2007, Vol. 29.

108. *Acupuncture for essential hypertension.* **Wang, J.** 5, s.l. : International Journal of Cardiology, 2013, Vol. 169.

109. *Effects of Acupuncture on Preeclampsia in Chinese Women: A Pilot Prospective Cohort Study.* **Zeng, Y.** s.l. : Acupuncture in Medicine, 2015, Vol. 33.

110. *Anaemia, prenatal iron use, and risk of adverse pregnancy outcomes: systematic review and meta-analysis.* **Haider, B.** s.l. : BMJ, 2013, Vol. 346.

111. *Maternal Use of Acetaminophen, Ibuprofen, and Acetylsalicylic Acid During Pregnancy and Risk of Cryptorchidism.* **Jensen, Morten.** 6, s.l. : Epidemiology, 2010, Vol. 21.

112. *Intrauterine exposure to mild analgesics during pregnancy and the occurrence of cryptorchidism and hypospadia in the offspring: the Generation R Study.* **Snijder, Claudia.** 4, s.l. : Human Reproduction, 2012, Vol. 27.

113. *Intrauterine exposure to mild analgesics is a risk factor for development of male reproductive disorders in human and rat.* **Kristensen, David.** 1, s.l. : Human Reproduction, 2011, Vol. 26.

114. *Aspirin use during pregnancy and the risk of bleeding complications: A Swedish population-based cohort study.* **Hastie, Roxanne.** s.l. : American Journal of Obstetrics and Gynecology, 2020.

115. *Role of calcium during pregnancy: Maternal and fetal needs.* **Hacker, Andrea.** 7, s.l. : Nutrition Reviews, 2012, Vol. 70.

116. *A randomised controlled trial of intravenous magnesium sulphate versus placebo in the management of women with severe pre-eclampsia.* **Coetzee, E.** s.l. : British Journal of Obstetrics and Gynaecology, 1998, Vol. 105.

117. *Nicotinamide benefits both mothers and pups in two contrasting mouse models of preeclampsia.* **Li, Feng.** 47, s.l. : Proceedings of the National Academy of Sciences, 2016, Vol. 113.

118. *Effects of Acupuncture on Preeclampsia in Chinese Women: A Pilot Prospective Cohort Study.* **Zeng, Yingchun.** 2, s.l. : Acupuncture in Medicine, 2016, Vol. 34.

119. *Integrating Acupuncture for Preeclampsia with Severe Features and HELLP Syndrome in a High-Risk Antepartum Care Setting.* **Kocher, Zena.** 6, s.l. : Medical Acupuncture, 2019, Vol. 31.

120. https://www.nhs.uk/conditions/urinary-tract-infections-utis/. **NHS.** [Online] 17 December 2017. [Cited: 28 November 2020.] https://www.nhs.uk/conditions/urinary-tract-infections-utis/.

121. *Haemorrhoids during pregnancy.* **Avsar, A.** 3, s.l. : Journal of Obstetrics and Gynaecology, 2010, Vol. 30.

122. *Efficacy and safety of acupuncture for functional constipation: a randomised, sham-controlled pilot trial.* **Lee, Hye-Yoon.** 186, s.l. : BMC Complementary and Alternative Medicine, 2018, Vol. 18.

123. *Gastrointestinal motility disorders and acupuncture.* **Yin, Jieyun.** s.l. : Autonomic Neuroscience: Basic and Clinical, 2010, Vol. 157.

124. *Interventions for treating constipation in pregnancy (Review).* **Jewell, D.** 2, s.l. : Cochrane Database of Systematic Reviews, 2001.

125. *Treating constipation during pregnancy.* **Trottier, Magan.** s.l. : Canadian Family Physician, 2012, Vol. 58.

126. *Pregnancy-related constipation.* **Prather, C.** s.l. : Curr Gastroenterol Rep, 2004, Vol. 6.

127. *Constipation and pregnancy.* **Cullen, Garret.** 5, s.l. : Best Practice & Research Clinical Gastroenterology, 2007, Vol. 21.

128. *Psyllium is superior to ducusate sodium for treatment of chronic constipation.* **McRorie, J.** s.l. : Aliment Pharmacol Ther, 1998, Vol. 12.

129. *Haemorrhoids and anal fissures during pregnancy and after childbirth: a prospective cohort study.* **Poskus, T.** 13, s.l. : BJOG, 2014, Vol. 121.

130. *Conservative management of symptomatic and/or complicated haemorrhoids in pregnancy and the puerperium.* **Quijano, C.** 3, s.l. : Cochrane Database of Systematic Reviews, 2005.

131. *Hemorrhoids during pregnancy: Sitz bath vs. ano-rectal cream: A comparative prospective study of two conservative treatment protocols.* **Shirah, Bader.** 4, s.l. : Women and Birth, 2018, Vol. 31.

132. *A meta-analysis of the clinical efficacy of the combination of acupuncture and Chinese medicine in the treatment of haemorrhoids.* **Zeng, Mengjie.** 2, s.l. : Acupuncture & Electro-Therapeutics Research, 2019, Vol. 44.

133. *Acupuncture for tension-type headache in pregnancy: A prospective, randomized, controlled study.* **Guerreiro da Silva, J.** s.l. : European Journal of Integrative Medicine, 2012.

134. *Non-pharmacological management of migraine during pregnancy.* **Airola, Gisella.** s.l. : Neurol Sci, 2010, Vol. 31.

135. *Acupuncture for tension-type headache in pregnancy: A prospective, randomized, controlled study.* **Guerreiro da Silva, J.** 4, s.l. : European Journal of Integrative Medicine, 2012, Vol. 4.

136. *Acupuncture for Chronic Headaches—An Epidemiological Study.* **Melchart, Dieter.** 4, s.l. : Headache, 2006, Vol. 46.

137. *Acupuncture relieves pelvic and low-back pain in late pregnancy.* **Kvorning, Nina.** s.l. : Acta Obstet Gynecol Scand, 2004, Vol. 83.

138. *A prospective randomized study comparing acupuncture with physiotherapy for low-back and pelvic pain in pregnancy.* **Wedenberg, Kaj.** s.l. : Acta Obstet Gynecol Scand, 2000, Vol. 79.

139. *Acupuncture for Low Back Pain in Pregnancy – a Prospective, Quasi- Randomised, Controlled Study.* **Guerreiro da Silva, João.** 2, s.l. : Acupuncture in Medicine, 2004, Vol. 22.

140. *Auricular acupuncture as a treatment for pregnant women who have low back and posterior pelvic pain: a pilot study.* **Wang, Shu-Ming.** 3, s.l. : American Journal of Obstetrics and Gynecology, 2009, Vol. 201.

141. *Acupuncture for Lower Back and Pelvic Pain in Late Pregnancy: A Retrospective Report on 167 Consecutive Cases.* **Kvorning Ternov, Nina.** 3, s.l. : Pain Medicine, 2001, Vol. 2.

142. *Meta-Analysis: Acupuncture for Low Back Pain.* **Manheimer, Eric.** s.l. : Ann Intern Med, 2005, Vol. 142.

143. *Low Back Pain in Pregnancy.* **Forrester, Max.** s.l. : Acupuncture in Medicine, 2003, Vol. 21.

144. *Acupuncture in treatment of carpal tunnel syndrome: A randomized controlled trial study.* **Khosrawi, Saeid.** 1, s.l. : J Res Med Sci., 2012, Vol. 17.

145. *Acupuncture for Carpal Tunnel Syndrome: A Systematic Review of Randomized Controlled Trials.* **Sim, Hoseob.** 3, s.l. : The Journal of Pain, 2011, Vol. 12.

146. *Treatment of Carpal Tunnel Syndrome With Medical Acupuncture.* **Schulman, Robert.** 3, s.l. : Medical Acupuncture, 2008, Vol. 20.

147. *Efficacy of Acupuncture versus Night Splinting for Carpal Tunnel Syndrome: A Randomized Clinical Trial.* **Kumnerddee , Wipoo.** 12, s.l. : J Med Assoc Thai, 2010, Vol. 93.

148. *Healthcare utilisation of pregnant women who experience sciatica, leg cramps and/or varicose veins: A cross-sectional survey of 1835 pregnant women.* **Hall, Helen.** 1, s.l. : Women and Birth, 2016, Vol. 29.

149. *Does Acupuncture Have a Place as an Adjunct Treatment During Pregnancy? A Review of Randomized Controlled Trials and Systematic Reviews.* **Smith, C.** 3, s.l. : Birth, 2009, Vol. 36.

150. *Clinical study on effect of Chinese herbal medicine for supplementing kidney and qi and activating blood circulation in treating intrauterine growth retardation of fetus.* **Huang , G.** 8, s.l. : Chinese Journal of Integrated Traditional and Western Medicine, 1999, Vol. 19.

151. *Clinical study on effect of Chinese herbal medicine for supplementing kidney and Qi and activating blood circulation in treating intrauterine growth retardation of fetus.* **Huang, G.** s.l. : CJIM, 2000, Vol. 6.

152. *Effects of the Prescription of Reinforcing Kidney, Replenishing Qi and Promoting Blood Circulation on the Umbilical Serum Level of Nitric Oxide and Lipid Peroxidation in Intrauterine Growth Retardation.* **Shu , Yimin.** s.l. : Chinese Journal of Microcirculation, 1999.

153. *The utero-placental circulation, eugenics and the prevention and treatment of high risk pregnancies.* **Xi-rui, W.** s.l. : Journal of Tongji Medical University, 1994, Vol. 14.

154. *Gestational diabetes.* **NHS.** [Online] 6 August 2019. [Cited: 26 June 2020.] https://www.nhs.uk/conditions/gestational-diabetes/.

155. *Myo-inositol may prevent gestational diabetes onset in overweight women: a randomized, controlled trial.* **Santamaria, Angelo.** 19, s.l. : The Journal of Maternal-Fetal & Neonatal Medicine, 2016, Vol. 29.

156. *Myo-Inositol Supplementation and Onset of Gestational Diabetes Mellitus in Pregnant Women With a Family History of Type 2 Diabetes.* **D'Anna, Rosario.** 4, s.l. : Diabetes Care, 2013, Vol. 36.

157. *Myoinositol in the Prevention of Gestational Diabetes Mellitus: Is It Sensible?* **Sobota-Grzeszyk, Angelika.** s.l. : Journal of Diabetes Research, 2019.

158. *Myo-Inositol Supplementation to Prevent Gestational Diabetes Mellitus.* **Celentano, C.** 30, s.l. : Curr Diab Rep, 2016, Vol. 16.

159. *Acupuncture: is it effective for treatment of insulin resistance?* **Liang, F.** 7, s.l. : Diabetes, Obesity and Metabolism, 2010, Vol. 12.

160. *Acupuncture for type 2 diabetes mellitus: A systematic review and meta-analysis of randomized controlled trials.* **Chen, Chao.** s.l. : Complementary Therapies in Clinical Practice, 2019, Vol. 36.

161. *Therapeutic effects of acupuncture on blood glucose level among patients with type-2 diabetes mellitus: A randomized clinical trial.* **Kazemi, Amir.** 1, s.l. : Journal of Traditional Chinese Medical Sciences, 2019, Vol. 6.

162. *Effect of bilateral needling at an acupuncture point, ST-36 (Zusanli) on blood glucose levels in type 2 diabetes mellitus patients: A pilot randomized placebo controlled trial.* **Mooventhan, A.** s.l. : Journal of Complementary & Integrative Medicine, 2020.

163. *Influence of Acupuncture on HPA Axis in a Rat Model of Chronic Stress-induced Depression.* **Sun, Dong-wei, Wang, Long and Sun, Zhong-ren.** 4, s.l. : Journal of Acupuncture and Tuina Science, 2007, Vol. 5.

164. *Acupuncture: a promising treatment for depression during pregnancy.* **Manber, Rachel.** 1, s.l. : Journal of Affective Disorders, 2004, Vol. 83.

165. *Acupuncture for Depression during Pregnancy: a Randomized Controlled Trial.* **Manber, R.** s.l. : Dtsch Z Akupunkt, 2010, Vol. 53.

166. *Acupuncture for Mild to Moderate Emotional Complaints in Pregnancy – a Prospective, Quasi-Randomised, Controlled Study.* **Guerreiro da Silva, J.** 3, s.l.: Acupuncture in Medicine, 2007, Vol. 25.

167. *Women's experiences of having depression during pregnancy and receiving acupuncture treatment—A qualitative study.* **Ormsby, Simone.** 6, s.l. : Women and Birth, 2017, Vol. 31.

168. *Maternal age over 40 years and pregnancy outcome: a hospital-based survey.* **Marozioa, Luca.** s.l. : The Journal of Maternal-Fetal & Neonatal Medicine, 2017.

169. *Placental abruption: epidemiology, risk factors and consequences.* **Tikkanen, Minna.** 2, s.l. : Acta Obstetricia et Gynecologica Scandinavica, 2011, Vol. 90.

170. *Placental abruption and perinatal death.* **Kyrklund-Blomberga, Nina.** s.l. : Paediatric and Perinatal Epidemiology, 2001, Vol. 15.

171. *Placental Abruption Associated with Cocaine Abuse.* **Townsend, Ronald.** s.l. : AJR, 1988, Vol. 150.

172. *Pregnancy-related complications and perinatal outcomes resulting from transfer of cryopreserved versus fresh embryos in vitro fertilization: a meta-analysis.* **Sha, Tingting.** 2, s.l. : Fertility and Sterility, 2018, Vol. 109.

173. *Are intracytoplasmic sperm injection and high serum estradiol compounding risk factors for adverse obstetric outcomes in assisted reproductive technology?* **Royster, Greene.** 2, s.l. : Fertility and Sterility, 2016, Vol. 106.

174. *Assisted reproductive technology and the risk of pregnancy-related complications and adverse pregnancy outcomes in singleton cohort studies.* **Qin, Jiabi.** 1, s.l. : Fertility and Sterility, 2016, Vol. 105.

175. *Pregnancy Outcome at Maternal Age 40 and Older.* **Jahromi, Bahia.** 3, s.l. : Taiwanese Journal of Obstetrics and Gynecology, 2008, Vol. 47.

176. *MR Imaging in the Evaluation of Placental Abruption: Correlation with Sonographic Findings.* **Masselli, Gabriele.** 1, s.l. : Radiology, 2011, Vol. 259.

177. *Treating oligohydramnios with extract of Salvia miltiorrhiza: A randomized control trial.* **Chu, Hong-nü.** 1, s.l. : Ther Clin Risk Manag, 2008, Vol. 4.

178. *The Effect of Ear Acupuncture on BPS of Oligohydramnios.* **Han , Yuhuan.** s.l. : Tianjing Medical Journal, 1994, Vol. 10.

179. *Chinese Herbal Medicine in Treatment of Polyhydramnios: a Meta-analysis and Systematic Review.* **Zhou, Fen.** 2, s.l. : Chinese Medical Sciences Journal, 2013, Vol. 28.

180. *Betts, Debra. The Essential Guide to Acupuncture in Pregnancy & Childbirth.* Hove : The Journal of Chinese Medicine, 2006.

181. **Rochat De La Vallee, Elisabeth.** *A Study of Qi.* London : Monkey Press, 2013.

182. **Zhen, Li Shi.** *Pulse Diagnosis.* Brookline : Paradigm Pblications, 1985.

183. **Wiseman, Nigel.** *A Practical Dictionary of Chinese Medicine.* Brookline : Paradigm Publications, 1998.

184. *Complete mapping of the tattoos of the 5300-year-old Tyrolean Iceman.* **Samadelli, Marco** , et al. 5, s.l. : Journal of Cultural Heritage, 2015, Vol. 16.

185. **Cheng, Xinnong.** *Chinese Acupuncture and Moxibustion.* Beijing : Foreign Languages Press, 1999.

186. *The safety of acupuncture during pregnancy: a systematic review.* **Park, Jimin.** s.l. : Acupunct Med, 2014, Vol. 32.

187. *Safety of Acupuncture: Results of a Prospective Observational Study with 229,230 Patients and Introduction of a Medical Information and Consent Form.* **Witt, Claudia,** et al. s.l. : Forsch Komplementmed, 2009, Vol. 16.

188. *The Primo Vascular System as a New Anatomical System.* **Stefanov, Miroslav** , et al. 6, s.l. : Journal of Acupuncture and Meridian Studies, 2013, Vol. 6.

189. *Bonghan Circulatory System as an Extension of Acupuncture Meridians.* **Soh, Kwang-Sup.** 2, s.l. : J Acupunct Meridian Stud, 2009, Vol. 2.

190. *Structure and Distribution of an Unrecognized Interstitium in Human Tissues.* **Benias, Petros,** et al. s.l. : Nature, 2018.

191. *Tratamiento con acupuntura: evaluación multidimensional del dolor lumbar en gestantes.* **Eveliny, Martins.** s.l. : Rev. esc. enferm. USP, 2018, Vol. 52.

192. *The use of acupuncture in maternity care: a pilot study evaluating the acupuncture service in an Australian hospital antenatal clinic.* **Hope-Allan, N.** 4, s.l. : Midwifery, 2004, Vol. 10.

193. *Changes in Levels of Serum Insulin, C-Peptide and Glucose after Electroacupuncture and Diet Therapy in Obese Women.* **Cabıoglu , Mehmet and Ergene, Neyhan.** 3, s.l. : The American Journal of Chinese Medicine, 2006, Vol. 34.

194. *Electroacupuncture reduces uterine artery blood flow impedance in infertile women.* **Ming, Ho,** et al. 2, s.l. : Taiwan J Obstet Gynecol, 2009, Vol. 48.

195. *Ovarian blood flow responses to electroacupuncture stimulation depend on estrous cycle and on site and frequency of stimulation in anesthetized rats.* **Stener-Victorin, Elisabet , Fujisawa, Shigeko and Kurosawa, Mieko.** s.l. : J Appl Physiol, 2006, Vol. 101.

196. *Role of acupuncture in the treatment of female infertility.* **Chang, Raymond, Chung, Pak and Rosenwaks, Zev.** 6, s.l. : Fertility and Sterility, 2002, Vol. 78.

197. *Effects of acupuncture and stabilising exercises as adjunct to standard treatment in pregnant women with pelvic girdle pain: randomised single blind controlled trial.* **Elden, Helen.** s.l. : BMJ, 2005.

198. *Acupuncture for Dyspepsia in Pregnancy: A Prospective, Randomised, Controlled Study.* **da Silva, J.** 2, s.l. : Acupuncture in Medicine, 2009, Vol. 27.

199. *Effect of acupuncture on nausea of pregnancy: a randomized, controlled trial.* **Knight, Beatrice.** 2, s.l. : Obstetrics & Gynecology, 2001, Vol. 97.

200. *Effects of Acupuncture on Anxiety Levels and Prefrontal Cortex Activity Measured by Near-Infrared Spectroscopy: A Pilot Study.* **Sakatani, K,** et al. s.l. : Adv Exp Med Biol, 2016.

201. *The relationship between perceived stress, acupuncture, and pregnancy rates among IVF patients: a pilot study.* **Balk, J,** et al. s.l. : Complementary Therapies in Clinical Practice, 2010.

202. *Acupuncture or acupressure for pain management during labour.* **Smith, C.** 2, s.l. : Cochrane Database of Systematic Reviews, 2020.

203. *The effects of acupuncture during labour on nulliparous women: A randomised controlled trial.* **Hantoushzadeh, Sedigheh.** s.l. : Australian and New Zealand Journal of Obstetrics and Gynaecology, 2007, Vol. 47.

204. *Acupuncture treatment during labour—a randomised controlled trial.* **Ramnero, Agneta.** s.l. : BJOG, 2002, Vol. 109.

205. *The effect of acupuncture on uterine contraction induced by oxytocin.* **Pak, S,** et al. 1, s.l. : Am J Chin Med, 2000, Vol. 28.

206. *Effect of acupuncture treatment on uterine motility and cyclooxygenase-2 expression in pregnant rats.* **Kim, J, Shin, K and Na, C.** 4, s.l. : Gynecol Obstet Invest, 2000, Vol. 50.

207. *Changes in Serum Leptin and Beta Endorphin Levels with Weight Loss by Electroacupuncture and Diet Restriction in Obesity Treatment.* **Cabıoğlu, Mehmet Tuğrul and Ergene , Neyhan.** 1, s.l. : The American Journal of Chinese Medicine, 2006, Vol. 34.

208. *Acupuncture on the Endometrial Morphology, the Serum Estradiol and Progesterone Levels, and the Expression of Endometrial Leukaemia-inhibitor Factor and Osteopontin in Rats.* **Fu, Houju,** et al. s.l. : Evidence-Based Complementary and Alternative Medicine, 2011.

209. *Compounds of Natural Origin and Acupuncture for the Treatment of Diseases Caused by Estrogen Deficiency.* **Thakur, A, Mandal, S and Banerjee, S.** 3, s.l. : Journal of Acupuncture and Meridian Studies, 2016, Vol. 9.

210. *Changes in serum cortisol and prolactin associated with acupuncture during controlled ovarian hyperstimulation in women undergoing in vitro fertilization-embryo transfer treatment.* **Magarelli, P, Cridennda, D and Cohen, M.** 6, s.l.: Fertility and Sterility, 2009, Vol. 92.

211. *Postdates pregnancy and complementary therapies.* **Evans, Maggie.** s.l. : Complementary Therapies in Clinical Practice, 2009, Vol. 15.

212. *Methods of Cervical Ripening and Labor Induction.* **Summers, Lisa.** 2, s.l. : Journal of Nurse-Midwifery, 1997, Vol. 42.

213. *One hundred years of aspirin.* **Jack, David.** s.l. : The Lancet, 1997, Vol. 350.

214. **Wilson, Edward.** *The Diversity Of Life.* s.l. : The Belknap Press Of Harvard University Press, 1993.

215. **Singleton , Mary Lou.** *Saving Our Endangered Midwifery Aiiies.* Midwifery Todoy. 2004.

216. *Efficacy of the Kampo Medicine Xiong-Gui-Jiao-Ai-Tang, a Traditional Herbal Medicine, in the Treatment of Threatened Abortion in Early Pregnancy.* **Ushiroyama, Takahisa.** 5, s.l. : The American Journal of Chinese Medicine, 2006, Vol. 34.

217. *Evidence-based interventions of threatened miscarriage.* **Li, Juan.** 1, s.l. : World J Tradit Chin Med, 2017, Vol. 3.

218. *Herbs and natural therapies for pregnancy, birth and breastfeeding.* **Walls, D.** 2, s.l. : International Journal of Childbirth Education, 2009, Vol. 24.

219. *Clinical evidence of Chinese medicine therapies for depression in women during perimenopause and menopause.* **Di, Yuan Ming.** s.l. : Complementary Therapies in Medicine, 2019, Vol. 47.

220. *The Relationship between Traditional Chinese Medicine and Modern Medicine.* **Dong, Jingcheng.** s.l. : Evidence-Based Complementary and Alternative Medicine, 2013.

221. *Prevalance And Economic Burden Of Medication Errors In The NHS In England.* **Elliot, Rachel,** et al. s.l. : Policy Research Unit in Economic Evaluation of Health & Care Interventions (EEPRU), 2018.

222. **Williams, Steven.** *Health and social care directorate.* s.l. : National Institute of Health and Care Excellence, 2015.

223. *Medical error—the third leading cause of death in the US.* **Makary, Martin and Daniel, Michael.** s.l. : BMJ, 2016.

224. *Paracetamol-induced endocrine disruption in human fetal testes.* **Jégou, Bernard.** s.l. : Nature Reviews Endocrinology, 2015, Vol. 11.

225. *Prenatal paracetamol exposure is associated with shorter anogenital distance in male infants.* **Fisher, B.** 11, s.l. : Human Reproduction, 2016, Vol. 31.

226. *Paracetamol, Aspirin, and Indomethacin Induce Endocrine Disturbances in the Human Fetal Testis Capable of Interfering With Testicular Descent.* **Mazaud-Guittot, Séverine.** s.l. : J Clin Endocrinol Metab, 2013, Vol. 98.

227. *Prolonged exposure to acetaminophen reduces testosterone production by the human fetal testis in a xenograft model.* **van den Driesche, Sander.** 288, s.l. : Science Translational Medicine, 2015, Vol. 7.

228. *Intrauterine Exposure to Paracetamol and Aniline Impairs Female Reproductive Development by Reducing Follicle Reserves and Fertility.* **Holm, Jacob,** et al. 1, s.l. : TOXICOLOGICAL SCIENCES, 2016, Vol. 150.

229. *Use of prescription paracetamol during pregnancy and risk of asthma in children: a population-based Danish cohort study.* **Andersen, Ane.** s.l. : Clinical Epidemiology, 2012, Vol. 4.

230. *Acetaminophen use in pregnancy and neurodevelopment: attention function and autism spectrum symptoms.* **Avella-Garcia, Claudia.** 9, s.l. : International Journal of Epidemiology, 2016, Vol. 1.

231. *Acetaminophen Use During Pregnancy, Behavioral Problems, and Hyperkinetic Disorders.* **Liew, Zeyan.** 4, s.l. : JAMA Pediat, 2014, Vol. 168.

232. *Prenatal paracetamol exposure and child neurodevelopment: a sibling-controlled cohort study.* **Brandlistuen, Ragnhild.** s.l. : International Journal of Epidemiology, 2013, Vol. 42.

233. *Paracetamol, Aspirin, and Indomethacin Induce Endocrine Disturbances in the Human Fetal Testis Capable of Interfering With Testicular Descent.* **Mazaud-Guittot, Séverine.** s.l. : J Clin Endocrinol Metab, 2013, Vol. 98.

234. *Acupuncture in pregnancy.* **da Silva, João.** s.l. : Acupunct Med, 2015, Vol. 33.

235. *Nausea, vomiting, and heartburn in pregnancy: a prospective look at risk, treatment, and outcome.* **Naumann, Christopher.** 8, s.l. : The Journal of Maternal-Fetal & Neonatal Medicine, 2012, Vol. 25.

236. *Antibiotics in Pregnancy: Are They Safe?* **Norwitz, Errol.** 3, s.l. : Rev Obstet Gynecol, 2009, Vol. 2.

237. **Balen, Adam.** *Infertility in Practice.* Fourth Edition. Boca Raton : CRC Press, 2014.

238. *Use of antibiotics during pregnancy and risk of spontaneous abortion.* **Muanda, Flory, Sheehy, Odile and Bérard, Anick.** 17, 2017, CMAJ, Vol. 189, pp. E625-33.

239. *Over-the-Counter Medications in Pregnancy.* **Black, R.** 12, s.l. : Am Fam Physician, 2003, Vol. 67.

240. *Topical Antiviral and Antifungal Medications in Pregnancy: A Review of Safety Profiles.* **Patel, V.** s.l. : J Eur Acad Dermatol Venereol, 2017, Vol. 31.

241. *Antifungal Therapy During Pregnancy.* **King, Coleman.** s.l. : Clinical Infectious Diseases, 1998, Vol. 27.

242. *A Review of Antiviral and Antifungal Use and Safety during Pregnancy.* **Cottreau, Jessica.** 6, s.l. : Pharmacotherapy, 2016, Vol. 36.

243. *Antifungal drugs in pregnancy: a review.* **Varsha, V.** 5, s.l. : Expert Opinion on Drug Safety, 2003, Vol. 2.

244. *A review of antihistamines used during pregnancy.* **Kar, Sumit.** 2, s.l. : J Pharmacol Pharmacother, 2012, Vol. 3.

245. *Safety of antihistamines during pregnancy and lactation.* **So, Miranda.** s.l. : Canadian Family Physician, 2010, Vol. 56.

246. *The Risk of Adverse Pregnancy Outcome After First Trimester Exposure to H1 Antihistamines: A Systematic Review and Meta-Analysis.* **Etwel, Fatma.** s.l. : Drug Safety, 2017, Vol. 40.

247. **Duncan , Pamela.** *Four million people in England are long-term users of antidepressants.* s.l. : The Guardian, 2018.

248. **Wehrwein, Peter.** *Astounding increase in antidepressant use by Americans.* s.l. : Harvard Health, 2020.

249. *Increasing use of antidepressants in pregnancy.* **Cooper, William.** 6, s.l. : American Journal of Obstetrics and Gynecology, 2007, Vol. 196.

250. *Use of antidepressant medications during pregnancy: a multisite study.* **Andrade, Susan.** 2, s.l. : American Journal of Obstetrics & Gynecology, 2008, Vol. 198.

251. *Pregnancy Outcomes Following Use of Escitalopram: A Prospective Comparative Cohort Study.* **Klieger-Grossmann, Chagit.** s.l. : Journal of Clinical Pharmacology, 2012, Vol. 52.

252. *The safety profile of escitalopram in pregnancy and breastfeeding.* **C, Bellantuono.** 6, s.l. : Rivista di Psichiatria, 2013, Vol. 48.

253. *The safety of escitalopram during pregnancy and breastfeeding: a comprehensive review.* **Bellantuono, Cesario.** 6, s.l. : Huamn Psychopharmacology, 2012, Vol. 27.

254. *Antidepressant Use During Pregnancy and the Risk of Autism Spectrum Disorder in Children.* **Boukhris, Takoua.** s.l. : JAMA Pediatr, 2015.

255. *Antidepressant use during pregnancy and the risk of major congenital malformations in a cohort of depressed pregnant women: an updated analysis of the Quebec Pregnancy Cohort.* **Bérard, Anick.** s.l. : BMJ Open, 2017, Vol. 7.

256. *Are Selective Serotonin Reuptake Inhibitors Cardiac Teratogens? Echocardiographic Screening of Newborns with Persistent Heart Murmur.* **Merlob, Paul.** s.l. : Birth Defects Research, 2009, Vol. 85.

257. *Association of Selective Serotonin Reuptake Inhibitor Exposure During Pregnancy With Speech, Scholastic, and Motor Disorders in Offspring.* **Brown, Alan.** s.l. : JAMA Psychiatry, 2016.

258. *Birth Outcomes in Pregnant Women Taking Fluoxetine.* **Chambers, Christina.** s.l. : The New England Journal of Medicine, 1996, Vol. 335.

259. *First Trimester Exposure to Paroxetine and Risk of Cardiac Malformations in Infants: The Importance of Dosage.* **Bérard, Anick.** s.l. : Birth Defects Research, 2007, Vol. 80.

260. *Fluoxetine and infantile hypertrophic pylorus stenosis: a signal from a birth defects—drug exposure surveillance study.* **Bakker, Marian.** 8, s.l. : Pharmaoepidemiology & Drug Safety, 2010, Vol. 19.

261. *Major Congenital Malformations Following Prenatal Exposure to Serotonin Reuptake Inhibitors and Benzodiazepines Using Population-Based Health Data.* **Oberlander, Tim.** s.l. : Birth Defects Research, 2008, Vol. 83.

262. *Maternal Use of Selective Serotonin Reuptake Inhibitors and Risk of Congenital Malformations.* **Wogelius, Pia.** 6, s.l. : Epidemiology, 2006, Vol. 17.

263. *Paroxetine and Congenital Malformations: Meta-Analysis and Consideration of Potential Confounding Factors.* **Bar-Oz, Benjamin.** 5, s.l.: Clinical Therapeutics, 2007, Vol. 29.

264. *Paroxetine and fluoxetine in pregnancy: a prospective, multicentre, controlled, observational study.* **Diav-Citrin, Orna.** 5, s.l. : British Journal of Clinical Pharmacology, 2008, Vol. 66.

265. *Paroxetine in the first trimester and the prevalence of congenital malformations.* **Alexander Cole, J.** s.l. : Pharmacoepidemiology and Drug Safety, 2007, Vol. 16.

266. *Selective Serotonin Reuptake Inhibitor (SSRI) Antidepressants in Pregnancy and Congenital Anomalies: Analysis of Linked Databases in Wales, Norway and Funen, Denmark.* **Jordan, Sue.** s.l. : PLOS ONE, 2016.

267. *Selective serotonin reuptake inhibitors and adverse pregnancy outcomes.* **Wen, Shi Wu.** s.l. : American Journal of Obstetrics and Gynecology, 2006, Vol. 194.

268. *The Use of Antidepressant Medications During Pregnancy and the Risk of Neonatal Seizures.* **Faruk, Uguz.** 5, s.l. : ournal of Clinical Psychopharmacology, 2019, Vol. 39.

269. *The Safety of Newer Antidepressants in Pregnancy and Breastfeeding.* **Gentile, Salvatore.** 2, s.l. : Drug Safety, 2005, Vol. 28.

270. *Use of antidepressants and anxiolytics in early pregnancy and the risk of preeclampsia and gestational hypertension: a prospective study.* **Bernard, Nathalie.** 146, s.l. : BMC Pregnancy and Childbirth volume, 2019, Vol. 19.

271. *Selective serotonin reuptake inhibitors in pregnancy and congenital malformations: population based cohort study.* **Pedersen, Lar.** s.l. : BMJ, 2009, Vol. 339.

272. *First-Trimester Use of Paroxetine and Congenital Heart Defects: A Population-Based Case-Control Study.* **Bakker, Marian.** s.l. : Birth Defects Research, 2010, Vol. 88.

273. *Selective serotonin reuptake inhibitors in pregnant women and neonatal withdrawal syndrome: a database analysis.* **Sanz, E.** 9458, s.l. : The Lancet, 2005, Vol. 365.

274. *Antidepressant use during pregnancy and the risk of gestational diabetes mellitus: a nested case–control study.* **Dandjinou, M.** s.l. : BMJ Open, 2019, Vol. 9.

275. *Tricyclic antidepressants in pregnancy and puerperium.* **Gentile, Salvatore.** 2, s.l. : Expert Opinion on Drug Safety, 2014, Vol. 13.

276. *Pharmacological treatment of unipolar depression during pregnancy and breast-feeding—A clinical overview.* **Nielsen, René.** 3, s.l. : Nordic Journal of Psychiatry , 2012, Vol. 66.

277. *Use of Prescribed Psychotropics during Pregnancy: A Systematic Review of Pregnancy, Neonatal, and Childhood Outcomes.* **Creeley , Catherine.** 9, s.l. : Brain Sci., 2019, Vol. 9.

278. *Toxic Neonatal Effects Following Maternal Clomipramine Therapy.* **Schimmell, Michael.** 4, s.l. : Journal of Toxicology: Clinical Toxicology, 1991, Vol. 29.

279. *Clomipramine concentration and withdrawal symptoms in 10 neonates.* **ter Horst, Peter.** 2, s.l. : British Journal of Clinical Pharmacology, 2011, Vol. 73.

280. *New changes in pregnancy and lactation labelling: Review of dermatologic drugs.* **Koh, Yun.** s.l. : International Journal of Women's Dermatology, 2019, Vol. 5.

281. *The safety of antidepressant use in pregnancy.* **Kalraa, Sanjog.** 2, s.l. : Expert Opinion on Drug Safety, 2005, Vol. 4.

282. *Psychotropic medication during pregnancy and lactation.* **Menon, Sharmila.** s.l.: Arch Gynecol Obstet, 2008, Vol. 277.

283. *Use of psychotropic drugs during pregnancy and breast-feeding.* **Damkier, Larsen.** s.l. : Acta Psychiatr Scand, 2015, Vol. 132.

284. *Pharmacotherapy of Depression in Pregnancy.* **Patkar, Ashwin.** 2, s.l. : Annals of Clinical Psychiatry, 2004, Vol. 16.

285. *A Benefit-Risk Assessment of Agomelatine in the Treatment of Major Depression.* **Howland, R.** s.l. : Drug-Safety, 2011, Vol. 34.

286. *Evaluating the safety of St. John's Wort in human pregnancy.* **Moretti, Myla.** s.l. : Reproductive Toxicology, 2009, Vol. 28.

287. *St John's wort for depression—an overview and meta-analysis of randomised clinical trials.* **Linde, Klaus.** s.l. : BMJ, 1996, Vol. 313.

288. *St John's wort for major depression.* **Linde , K.** 4, s.l. : Cochrane Database of Systematic Reviews, 2008.

289. *St John's Wort During Pregnancy.* **Grush, Lynn.** 18, s.l. : JAMA, 1998, Vol. 280.

290. *The benefit from whole body acupuncture in major depression.* **Röschke, J.** 1-3, s.l. : Journal of Affective Disorders, 2000, Vol. 57.

291. *The Neuroscience of Nonpharmacological Traditional Chinese Therapy (NTCT) for Major Depressive Disorder: A Systematic Review and Meta-Analysis.* **Ye, Jiajia.** s.l. : Evidence-Based Complementary and Alternative Medicine, 2019.

292. *Acupuncture for depression during pregnancy: a randomized controlled trial.* **Manber, Rachel.** 3, s.l. : Obstet Gynecol, 2010, Vol. 115.

293. *Second-generation antiepileptic drugs and pregnancy: a guide for clinicians.* **Reimers, Arne.** s.l. : Expert Review of Neurotherapeutics , 2012, Vol. 12.

294. *Lamotrigine and the risk of malformations in pregnancy.* **Cunnington, Marianne.** 6, s.l. : Neurology, 2005, Vol. 64.

295. *Lamotrigine clearance during pregnancy.* **Tran, T.** 2, s.l. : Neurology, 2002, Vol. 59.

296. *Preliminary Results on Pregnancy Outcomes in Women Using Lamotrigine.* **Tennis, Patricia.** 10, s.l. : Epilepsia, 2002, Vol. 43.

297. *Lamotrigine in Pregnancy: Pharmacokinetics During Delivery, in the Neonate, and During Lactation.* **Ohman, Inger.** 6, s.l. : Epilqisin, 2000, Vol. 41.

298. *Oxcarbazepine in pregnancy: clinical experience in Argentina.* **Meischenguiser, Ricardo.** s.l. : Epilepsy & Behavior , 2004, Vol. 5.

299. *Safety profile of oxcarbazepine: Results from a prescription-event monitoring study.* **Buggy, Yvonne.** 5, s.l. : Epilepsia, 2010, Vol. 51.

300. *Safety of the newer antiepileptic drug oxcarbazepine during pregnancy.* **Montouris, Georgia.** 5, s.l. : Current Medical Research and Opinion, 2005, Vol. 21.

301. *The fetal safety of Levetiracetam: A systematic review.* **Chaudhry, Shahnaz.** s.l.: Reproductive Toxicology, 2014, Vol. 46.

302. *Levetiracetam in pregnancy: Results from the UK and Ireland epilepsy and pregnancy registers.* **Mawhinney, Ellen.** 4, s.l. : Neurology, 2013, Vol. 80.

303. *Levetiracetam: More Evidence of Safety in Pregnancy: Levetiracetam in Pregnancy.* **Koubeissi, Mohamad.** s.l. : Epilepsy Currents, 2013.

304. *Outcome of children born to epileptic mothers treated with carbamazepine during pregnancy.* **Ornoy, A.** s.l. : Archives of Disease in Childhood, 1996, Vol. 75.

305. *Pattern of Malformations in the Children of Women Treated with Carbamazepine during Pregnancy.* **Lyons Jones, Kenneth.** s.l. : N Engl J Med, 1989, Vol. 320.

306. *The teratogenic effect of carbamazepine: a meta-analysis of 1255 exposures.* **Matalon, S.** 1, s.l. : Reproductive Toxicology, 2002, Vol. 16.

307. *Transient Hepatic Dysfunction in an Infant of an Epileptic Mother Treated with Carbamazepine during Pregnancy and Breastfeeding.* **Reed, M.** 12, s.l.: Annals of Pharmacotherapy, 1992, Vol. 26.

308. *The Effects of Lithium, Valproic Acid, and Carbamazepine During Pregnancy and Lactation.* **Iqbal, Mohammad.** 4, s.l. : Clinical Toxicology, 2001, Vol. 39.

309. *Spina Bifida in Infants of Women Treated with Carbamazepine during Pregnancy.* **Rosa, Franz.** s.l. : N Engl J Med, 1991, Vol. 324.

310. *Lamotrigine and the risk of malformations in pregnancy.* **Cunnington, Marianne.** 6, s.l. : Neurology, 2005, Vol. 64.

311. *Levetiracetam in pregnancy: Preliminary experience from the UK Epilepsy and Pregnancy Register.* **Hunt, J.** 10, s.l. : Neurology, 2006, Vol. 67.

312. *Comparative safety of antiepileptic drugs during pregnancy.* **Hernandez-Díaz, S.** s.l. : Neurology, 2012, Vol. 78.

313. *Pregnancy outcome following maternal exposure to pregabalin may call for concern.* **Winterfeld, Ursula.** s.l. : American Academy of Neurology, 2016.

314. *Adverse pregnancy outcomes in women exposed to gabapentin and pregabalin: data from a population-based study.* **Mostacci, Barbara.** s.l. : J Neurol Neurosurg Psychiatry Month, 2017.

315. *Exposition in utero à l'acide valproïque et aux autres traitements de l'épilepsie et des troubles bipolaires et risque de malformations congénitales majeures (MCM) en France.* **Raguideau, F,** et al. 2017, Synthèse.

316. *A brief history of vaccines & vaccination in India.* **Lahariya, Chandrakant.** 4, s.l. : Indian J Med Res., 2014, Vol. 139.

317. *Pandemic 2009 Influenza A(H1N1) Virus Illness Among Pregnant Women in the United States.* **Siston, Alicia.** 15, s.l. : JAMA, 2018, Vol. 303.

318. *British Broadcasting Corporation. Pregnant women should be offered Covid vaccine.* **BBC.** [Online] 16 April 2021. [Cited: 18 July 2021.] https://www.bbc.co.uk/news/health-56778146.

319. *Covid unlocking risk for pregnant women, say doctors.* **BBC.** [Online] 15 July 2021. [Cited: 18 July 2021.] https://www.bbc.co.uk/news/health-57840159.

320. *Whooping cough.* **NHS.** [Online] 13 November 2019. [Cited: 16 November 2020.] https://www.nhs.uk/conditions/whooping-cough/.

321. *Safety of pertussis vaccination in pregnant women in UK: observational study.* **Donegan, Katherine.** s.l. : BMJ, 2014, Vol. 349.

322. *Pertussis (Whooping Cough).* **Centers for Disease Control and Prevention.** [Online] U.S. Department of Health & Human Services, 7 August 2017. [Cited: 16 November 2020.] https://www.cdc.gov/pertussis/about/signs-symptoms.html.

323. *A comparison of temporal trends in United States autism prevalence to trends in suspected environmental factors.* **Nevison, Cynthia.** 73, s.l. : Nevison Environmental Health, 2014, Vol. 13.

324. *Prevalence and Characteristics of Autism Spectrum Disorder Among Children Aged 8 Years — Autism and Developmental Disabilities Monitoring Network, 11 Sites, United States, 2012.* **Centers for Disease Control and Prevention.** 3, s.l. : U.S. Department of Health and Human Services, 2016, Vol. 65.

325. *Genetic Syndromes, Maternal Diseases and Antenatal Factors Associated with Autism Spectrum Disorders (ASD).* **Ornoy, Asher.** s.l. : Front. Neurosci, 2016.

326. *Sex differences in autism spectrum disorders.* **Werling, Donna.** 2, s.l. : Curr Opin Neurol. , 2013, Vol. 26.

327. *Perinatal risk factors and infantile autism.* **Maimburg, R.** s.l. : Acta Psychiatr Scand, 2006, Vol. 114.

328. *Ruling on doctor in MMR scare.* **NHS.** [Online] 29 January 2010. [Cited: 30 December 2020.] https://www.nhs.uk/news/medical-practice/ruling-on-doctor-in-mmr-scare.

329. *The role of mercury in the pathogenesis of autism.* **Bernard, S.** s.l. : Molecular Psychiatry, 2002, Vol. 7.

330. *Thiomersal in vaccines.* **Clements, C.** s.l. : The Lancet, 2000, Vol. 355.

331. *An Assessment of Thimerosal Use in Childhood Vaccines.* **Ball, Leslie.** 5, s.l. : PEDIATRICS, 2001, Vol. 107.

332. *Mercury in Vaccines from the Australian Childhood Immunization Program Schedule.* **Austin, David.** s.l. : Journal of Toxicology and Environmental Health, Part A, 2010, Vol. 73.

333. *Aluminum salts in vaccines—US perspective.* **Baylor, Norman.** s.l. : Vaccine, 2002, Vol. 20.

334. *Elimination of aluminum adjuvants.* **Hem, Stanley.** s.l. : Vaccine, 2002, Vol. 20.

335. *Aluminum compounds as vaccine adjuvants.* **Gupta, Rajesh.** 3, s.l. : Advanced Drug Delivery Reviews, 1998, Vol. 32.

336. *Aluminium compounds for use in vaccines.* **Lindblad, Erik.** 5, s.l. : Immunology & Cell Biology, 2004, Vol. 82.

337. *Vaccine Ingredients - Aluminum. The Children's Hospital of Philadelphia.* [Online] 22 March 2018. [Cited: 06 June 2020.] https://www.chop.edu/centers-programs/vaccine-education-center/vaccine-ingredients/aluminum#:~:text=Aluminum%20adjuvants%20are%20used%20in,%2C%20rubella%2C%20varicella%20and%20rotavirus..

338. *Aluminum.* **PubChem.** [Online] [Cited: 08 June 2020.] https://pubchem.ncbi.nlm.nih.gov/element/Aluminum#:~:text=Although%20aluminum%20is%20the%20most,(Al2O3)..

339. *Aluminium in brain tissue in autism.* **Mold, M.** s.l. : Journal of Trace Elements in Medicine and Biology, 2018, Vol. 46.

340. *The Health Effects of Aluminum Exposure.* **Klotz, Katrin.** 39, s.l. : Dtsch Arztebl Int., 2017, Vol. 114.

341. *Aluminium salts.* **Unilever.** [Online] 2020. [Cited: 06 June 2020.] https://www.unilever.com/brands/Our-products-and-ingredients/Your-ingredient-questions-answered/Aluminium-salts.html.

342. *Association Between Maternal Use of Folic Acid Supplements and Risk of Autism Spectrum Disorders in Children.* **Suren, Pal.** 6, s.l. : JAMA, 2013, Vol. 309.

343. *Maternal periconceptional folic acid intake and risk of autism spectrum disorders and developmental delay in the CHARGE (CHildhood Autism Risks from Genetics and Environment) case-control study.* **Schmid, Rebecca.** s.l. : Am J Clin Nutr, 2012, Vol. 96.

344. *New Perspective on Impact of Folic Acid Supplementation during Pregnancy on Neurodevelopment/Autism in the Offspring Children – A Systematic Review.* **Gao, Yunfei.** 11, s.l. : PLoS One, 2016, Vol. 11.

345. *Association of Maternal Use of Folic Acid and Multivitamin Supplements in the Periods Before and During Pregnancy With the Risk of Autism Spectrum Disorder in Offspring.* **Levine, Stephen.** 2, s.l. : JAMA Psychiatry, 2018, Vol. 75.

346. *The association between maternal use of folic acid supplements during pregnancy and risk of autism spectrum disorders in children: a meta-analysis.* **Wang, Meiyun.** 51, s.l. : Molecular Autism, 2017, Vol. 8.

347. *Chemicals, Nutrition, and Autism Spectrum Disorder: A Mini-Review.* **Fujiwara, Takeo.** s.l. : Front. Neurosci, 2016, Vol. 10.

348. *Environmental contributions to autism: Explaining the rise in incidence of autistic spectrum disorders.* **Scott, James.** 2, s.l. : Journal of Environmental Immunology and Toxicology, 2014, Vol. 1.

349. *Maternal Dietary Fat Intake in Association With Autism Spectrum Disorders.* **Lyall, Kristen.** 2, s.l. : American Journal of Epidemiology, 2013, Vol. 178.

350. *How nutritional status, diet and dietary supplements can affect autism. A review.* **Kawicka, Anna.** 1, s.l. : Rocz Panstw Zakl Hig, 2013, Vol. 64.

351. *Maternal high-fat diet programming of the neuroendocrine system.* **Sullivan, Elinor.** s.l. : Hormones and Behavior, 2015.

352. *The Gut Microbiota and Autism Spectrum Disorders.* **Li, Qinrui.** s.l. : Front. Cell. Neurosci, 2017, Vol. 11.

353. *Mothers of Autistic Children: Lower Plasma Levels of Oxytocin and Arg-Vasopressin and a Higher Level of Testosterone.* **Xiu, Xin-Jie.** 9, s.l. : PLoS One, 2013, Vol. 8.

354. *Oxytocin-Mediated GABA Inhibition During Delivery Attenuates Autism Pathogenesis in Rodent Offspring.* **Tyzio, Roman.** 6171, s.l. : Science, 2014, Vol. 343.

355. *Vitamin D treatment during pregnancy prevents autism-related phenotypes in a mouse model of maternal immune activation.* **Vuillermot, Stephanie.** 9, s.l. : Vuillermot et al. Molecular Autism, 2017, Vol. 8.

356. *Autism and vitamin D.* **Cannell, John.** s.l. : Medical Hypotheses, 2008, Vol. 70.

357. *Autism: Will vitamin D supplementation during pregnancy and early childhood reduce the recurrence rate of autism in newborn siblings?* **Stubbs, G.** s.l. : Medical Hypotheses, 2016, Vol. 88.

358. *Autism spectrum disorder and low vitamin D at birth: a sibling control study.* **Fernell, E.** 3, s.l. : Molecular Autism, 2015, Vol. 6.

359. *Vitamin D and autism: Clinical review.* **Kocovska, Eva.** s.l. : Research in Developmental Disabilities, 2012, Vol. 33.

360. *Vitamin D hormone regulates serotonin synthesis. Part 1: relevance for autism.* **Patrick, Rhonda.** 6, s.l. : The FASEB Journal, 2014, Vol. 28.

361. *Vitamin D and autism, what's new?* **Cannell, J.** s.l. : Rev Endocr Metab Disord, 2017, Vol. 18.

362. *Maternal vitamin D deficiency and the risk of autism spectrum disorders: population-based study.* **Magnusson, Cecilia.** s.l. : BJPsych Open, 2016, Vol. 2.

363. *Shank and zinc mediate an AMPA receptor subunit switch in developing neurons.* **Ha, Huong.** 405, s.l. : Front. Mol. Neurosci, 2018, Vol. 11.

364. *Prenatal zinc prevents communication impairments and BDNF disturbance in a rat model of autism induced by prenatal lipopolysaccharide exposure.* **Kirsten, Thiago.** s.l. : Life Sciences, 2015, Vol. 130.

365. *Infantile zinc deficiency: Association with autism spectrum disorders.* **Yasuda, Hiroshi.** s.l. : Sci Rep, 2011, Vol. 1.

366. *Gender Dependent Evaluation of Autism like Behavior in Mice Exposed to Prenatal Zinc Deficiency.* **Grabrucker, Stefanie.** s.l. : Behav. Neurosci, 2016.

367. *Lipopolysaccharide Exposure Induces Maternal Hypozincemia, and Prenatal Zinc Treatment Prevents Autistic-Like Behaviors and Disturbances in the Striatal Dopaminergic and mTOR Systems of Offspring.* **Kirsten, Thiago.** 7, s.l. : PLoS One, 2015, Vol. 10.

368. *Zinc in Gut-Brain Interaction in Autism and Neurological Disorders.* **Vela, Guillermo.** s.l. : Neural Plasticity, 2015.

369. *Mercury, Lead, and Zinc in Baby Teeth of Children with Autism Versus Controls.* **Adams, James.** 12, s.l. : Journal of Toxicology and Environmental Health, Part A, 2007, Vol. 70.

370. *The role of zinc and copper in autism spectrum disorders.* **Bjørklund, Geir.** s.l. : Acta Neurobiol Exp, 2013, Vol. 73.

371. *Zinc status in autistic children.* **Yorbik, Ozgur.** s.l. : The Journal of Trace Elements in Experimental Medicine, 2004, Vol. 17.

372. *Maternal immune activation yields offspring displaying mouse versions of the three core symptoms of autism.* **Malkova, Natalia.** s.l. : Brain, Behavior, and Immunity, 2012, Vol. 26.

373. *Maternal infection and immune involvement in autism.* **Patterson, Paul.** 7, s.l.: Trends in Molecular Medicine, 2011, Vol. 17.

374. *Maternal Immune Activation and Autism Spectrum Disorder: Interleukin-6 Signaling as a Key Mechanistic Pathway.* **Parker-Athill, E.** s.l.: Neurosignals, 2010, Vol. 18.

375. *Maternal immune activation and abnormal brain development across CNS disorders.* **Knuesel, Irene.** s.l. : Nature Reviews Neurology, 2014, Vol. 10.

376. *Autism Spectrum Disorder and Particulate Matter Air Pollution before, during, and after Pregnancy: A Nested Case–Control Analysis within the Nurses' Health Study II Cohort.* **Raz, Raanan.** 3, s.l. : Environmental Health Perspectives, 2015, Vol. 123.

377. *In Utero Exposure to Toxic Air Pollutants and Risk of Childhood Autism.* **von Ehrenstein, Ondine.** s.l. : Epidemiology, 2014, Vol. 25.

378. *Traffic-Related Air Pollution, Particulate Matter, and Autism.* **Volk, Heather.** 1, s.l. : JAMA Psychiatry, 2013, Vol. 70.

379. *Ambient Air Pollution and Autism in Los Angeles County, California.* **Becerra, Tracy.** 3, s.l. : Environmental Health Perspectives, 2013, Vol. 121.

380. *Childhood autism spectrum disorders and exposure to nitrogen dioxide, and particulate matter air pollution: A review and meta-analysis.* **Flores-Pajo, Marie-Claire.** s.l. : Environmental Research, 2016, Vol. 151.

381. *Air Pollution and Autism Spectrum Disorders: Causal or Confounded.* **Weisskopf, Marc.** s.l. : Curr Envir Health Rpt, 2015, Vol. 2.

382. *Autism spectrum disorder: interaction of air pollution with the MET receptor tyrosine kinase gene.* **Volk, Heather.** 1, s.l. : Epidemiology , 2014, Vol. 25.

383. *Fine particulate matter and the risk of autism spectrum disorder.* **Talbott, Evelyn.** s.l. : Environmental Research, 2015, Vol. 140.

384. *Residential Proximity to Freeways and Autism in the CHARGE Study.* **Volk, Heather.** 6, s.l. : Environmental Health Perspectives, 2011, Vol. 119.

385. *Environmental Chemical Exposures and Autism Spectrum Disorders: A Review of the Epidemiological Evidence.* **Kalkbrenner, Amy.** s.l. : Curr Probl Pediatr Adolesc Health Care, 2014.

386. *Prenatal Valproate Exposure and Risk of Autism Spectrum Disorders and Childhood Autism.* **Christensen, Jakob** , et al. 16, s.l. : JAMA, 2013, Vol. 309.

387. *Autism Spectrum Disorders Following in Utero Exposure to Antiepileptic Drugs.* **Bromley, R.** 23, s.l. : Neurology, 2008, Vol. 71.

388. *Prospective assessment of autism traits in children exposed to antiepileptic drugs during pregnancy.* **Wood, A.** 7, s.l. : Epilepsia, 2015, Vol. 56.

389. *In utero exposure to valproic acid and autism — A current review of clinical and animal studies.* **Roullet, F.** s.l. : Neurotoxicol Teratol, 2013, Vol. 36.

390. *Characteristics of fetal anticonvulsant syndrome associated autistic disorder.* **Rasalam, A.** s.l. : Developmental Medicine & Child Neurology, 2005, Vol. 47.

391. *The prevalence of neurodevelopmental disorders in children prenatally exposed to antiepileptic drugs.* **Bromley, R.** s.l. : J Neurol Neurosurg Psychiatr, 2013, Vol. 84.

392. *Autism genes are selectively targeted by environmental pollutants including pesticides, heavy metals, bisphenol A, phthalates and many others in food, cosmetics or household products.* **Carter, C.** s.l. : Neurochemistry International, 2016, Vol. 101.

393. *The association of environmental toxicants and autism spectrum disorders in children.* **Ye, B.** s.l. : Environmental Pollution, 2017, Vol. 227.

394. *Plasma phthalate and bisphenol a levels and oxidant-antioxidant status in autistic children.* **Kondolot, Meda.** s.l. : Environmental Toxicology and Pharmacology, 2016, Vol. 43.

395. *Questions about Prenatal Ultrasound and the Alarming Increase in Autism.* **Rodgers, Caroline.** 80, s.l. : Midwifery Today, 2006.

396. *Juvenile manifestation of ultrasound communication deficits in the neuroligin-4 null mutant mouse model of autism.* **Ju, Anes.** s.l. : Behavioural Brain Research, 2014, Vol. 270.

397. *Is there a link between autism and glyphosate-formulated herbicides?* **Beecham, James.** 1, s.l. : Journal of Autism, 2016, Vol. 3.

398. *Autism: Transient in utero hypothyroxinemia related to maternal flavonoid ingestion during pregnancy and to other environmental antithyroid agents.* **Román, Gustavo.** 1-2, s.l. : Journal of the Neurological Sciences, 2007, Vol. 262.

399. *Allergies, asthma, ADHD: Is it the food we eat?* **Peper, Erik.** s.l. : Western Edition, 2015, Vol. 10.

400. *Environmental factors in the development of autism spectrum disorders.* **Sealey, L.** s.l. : Environment International, 2016, Vol. 88.

401. *Prenatal and infant exposure to ambient pesticides and autism spectrum disorder in children: population based case-control study.* **von Ehrenstein, Ondine.** 1962, s.l. : BMJ, 2019, Vol. 364.

402. *Maternal glyphosate exposure causes autism-like behaviors in offspring through increased expression of soluble epoxide hydrolase.* **Pu, Yaoyu.** 21, s.l.: PNAS , 2020, Vol. 117.

403. *Evidence the U.S. autism epidemic initiated by acetaminophen (Tylenol) is aggravated by oral antibiotic amoxicillin/clavulanate (Augmentin) and now exponentially by herbicide glyphosate (Roundup).* **Good, Peter.** s.l. : Clinical Nutrition ESPEN, 2017.

404. *Low dose mercury toxicity and human health.* **Zahir, Farhana,** et al. 2, s.l. : Environmental Toxicology and Pharmacology, 2005, Vol. 20.

405. *Mercury and autism: Accelerating Evidence?* **Mutter, Joachim.** 5, s.l. : Neuroendocrinology Letters, 2005, Vol. 26.

406. *A prospective study of prenatal mercury exposure from maternal dental amalgams and autism severity.* **Geier, David.** s.l. : Acta Neurobiol Exp, 2009, Vol. 69.

407. *A comprehensive review of mercury provoked autism.* **Geier, D.** s.l. : Indian J Med Res, 2008, Vol. 128.

408. *The relationship between mercury and autism: A comprehensive review and discussion.* **Kern, Janet.** s.l. : Journal of Trace Elements in Medicine and Biology, 2016, Vol. 37.

409. *Mercury as a possible link between maternal obesity and autism spectrum disorder.* **Skalny, Anatoly.** s.l. : Medical Hypotheses, 2016, Vol. 91.

410. *Combined prenatal and postnatal butyl paraben exposure produces autism-like symptoms in offspring: Comparison with valproic acid autistic model.* **Ali, Elham.** s.l. : Pharmacology, Biochemistry and Behavior, 2013, Vol. 111.

411. *Interplay between pro-inflammatory cytokines and brain oxidative stress biomarkers: Evidence of parallels between butyl paraben intoxication and the valproic acid brain physiopathology in autism rat model.* **Hegazy, Hoda.** s.l. : Cytokine, 2015, Vol. 71.

412. *Prenatal phenol and paraben exposures in relation to child neurodevelopment including autism spectrum disorders in the MARBLES study.* **Barkoski, Jacqueline.** s.l. : Environmental Research, 2019, Vol. 179.

413. *Bayesian modeling of time-dependent vulnerability to environmental hazards: an example using autism and pesticide data.* **Roberts, Eric.** s.l. : Statist. Med, 2012.

414. *Increased Serum Phthalates (MEHP, DEHP) and Bisphenol A Concentrations in Children With Autism Spectrum Disorder: The Role of Endocrine Disruptors in Autism Etiopathogenesis.* **Kardas, Fatih.** s.l. : Journal of Child Neurology, 2015.

415. *Endocrine disruptors and childhood social impairment.* **Miodovnik, Amir.** s.l. : NeuroToxicology, 2011, Vol. 32.

416. *The role of phthalate esters in autism development: A systematic review.* **Jeddi, Maryam.** s.l. : Environmental Research, 2016, Vol. 151.

417. *The plausibility of maternal toxicant exposure and nutritional status as contributing factors to the risk of autism spectrum disorders.* **Nuttall, Johnathan.** 4, s.l. : Nutritional Neuroscience, 2017, Vol. 20.

418. *Prenatal and perinatal analgesic exposure and autism: an ecological link.* **Bauer, A.** 41, s.l. : Environ Health, 2013, Vol. 12.

419. *Maternal use of acetaminophen during pregnancy and risk of autism spectrum disorders in childhood: A Danish national birth cohort study.* **Liew, Zeyan.** s.l. : Autism Research, 2015, Vol. 9.

420. *Evidence that Increased Acetaminophen use in Genetically Vulnerable Children Appears to be a Major Cause of the Epidemics of Autism, Attention Deficit with Hyperactivity, and Asthma.* **Shaw, William.** s.l. : Journal of Restorative Medicine , 2013, Vol. 2.

421. *Prenatal Exposure to Acetaminophen and Risk for Attention Deficit Hyperactivity Disorder and Autistic Spectrum Disorder: A Systematic Review, Meta-Analysis, and Meta-Regression Analysis of Cohort Studies.* **Masarwa, Reem.** 8, s.l. : American Journal of Epidemiology, 2018, Vol. 187.

422. *Is acetaminophen safe in pregnancy?* **Toda, Katsuhiro.** 1, s.l. : Scandinavian Journal of Pain, 2017, Vol. 17.

423. *Maternal cannabis use in pregnancy and child neurodevelopmental outcomes.* **Corsi, D.** s.l. : Nat Med, 2020.

424. *Antidepressant Use During Pregnancy and Childhood Autism Spectrum Disorders.* **Croen, Lisa.** 11, s.l. : Arch Gen Psychiatry, 2011, Vol. 68.

425. *Parental depression, maternal antidepressant use during pregnancy, and risk of autism spectrum disorders: population based case-control study.* **Rai, Dheeraj.** s.l.: BMJ, 2013, Vol. 346.

426. *Antidepressant Use During Pregnancy and the Risk of Autism Spectrum Disorder in Children.* **Boukhris, Takoua.** 2, s.l. : JAMA Pediatr, 2016, Vol. 170.

427. *Acupuncture and good prognosis IVF patients: Synergy.* **Magarelli, P.** s.l. : Fertility & Sterility, 2004, Vol. 82.

428. *Does acupuncture have a role in the treatment of threatened miscarriage? Findings from a feasibility randomised trial and semi-structured participant interviews.* **Betts, D.** s.l. : BMC Pregnancy and Childbirth, 2016, Vol. 16.

429. *Acupuncture as a therapeutic treatment option for threatened miscarriage.* **Betts, D.** 20, s.l. : BMC Complement Altern Med, 2012, Vol. 12.

430. *Warm tub bath and sauna in early pregnancy: risk of malformation uncertain.* **Waldenström, Ulla.** 6, s.l. : Acta Obstetricia et Gynecologica Scandinavica, 1994, Vol. 73.

431. *Exercise during pregnancy mitigates negative effects of parental obesity on metabolic function in adult mouse offspring.* **Laker, Rhianna.** 3, s.l. : Journal of Applied Physiology, 2021, Vol. 130.

432. *Can I give blood?* [Online] **NHS Blood and Transplant.** [Cited: 09 June 2020.] https://www.blood.co.uk/who-can-give-blood/can-i-give-blood/.

433. *Socioeconomic Status and Adverse Birth Outcomes: A Population-Based Canadian Sample.* **Campbell, Emily,** et al. s.l. : Cambridge University Press, 2017, J. Biosoc. Sci., pp. 1-12.

434. *Environmental pollution and the fetus.* **Yurdakök, Kadriye.** 1, s.l. : Journal of Pediatric and Neonatal Individualized Medicine, 2012, Vol. 1.

435. *Environmental estrogen-like endocrine disrupting chemicals and breast cancer.* **Morgan, Marisa** , et al. s.l. : Molecular and Cellular Endocrinology, 2017, Vol. 457.

436. *Fetuses suffer from extra oestrogen exposure.* **Khamsi , Roxanne.** s.l. : Nature, 2005.

437. *The effects of environmental hormones on reproduction.* **Danzo, B.** s.l. : CMLS, Cell. Mol. Life Sci, 1998, Vol. 54.

438. *Hormones in international meat production: biological,sociological and consumer.* **Galbraith, H.** s.l. : Nutrition Research Reviews, 2002, Vol. 15.

439. *Human infertility: are endocrine disruptors to blame?* **Marques-Pinto, A and Carvalho, D.** 3, s.l. : Endocr Connect, 2013, Vol. 2.

440. *What is glyphosate? Soil Association.* [Online] [Cited: 08 June 2020.] https://www.soilassociation.org/our-campaigns/not-in-our-bread/what-is-glyphosate/.

441. *Association of gestational maternal hypothyroxinemia and increased autism risk.* **Román, Gustavo.** 5, s.l. : Annals of Neurology, 2013, Vol. 74.

442. *A comparison of temporal trends in United States autism prevalence to trends in suspected environmental factors.* **Nevison, Cynthia.** 73, s.l. : Nevison Environmental Health, 2014, Vol. 13.

443. *Glyphosate Use Predicts Healthcare Utilization for ADHD in the Healthcare Cost and Utilization Project net (HCUPnet): A Two-Way Fixed-Effects Analysis.* **Fluegge, Keith and Fluegge, Kyle.** 4, s.l. : Pol. J. Environ. Stud, 2016, Vol. 25.

444. *Aluminum and Glyphosate Can Synergistically Induce Pineal Gland Pathology: Connection to Gut Dysbiosis and Neurological Disease.* **Seneff, S.** s.l. : Agricultural Sciences, 2015, Vol. 6.

445. *Agency for Toxic Substances and Disease Registry (ATSDR).* Toxicological Profile for DDT, DDE, DDD. Atlanta : U.S. Department of Health and Human Services, Public Health Service, 2002.

446. *Science linking environmental contaminant exposures with fertility and reproductive health impacts in the adult female.* **Mendola, Pauline , Messer, Lynne and Rappazzo, Kristen.** 2, s.l. : Fertility and Sterility, 2008, Vol. 89.

447. *Thyroid Hormones in Pregnancy in Relation to Environmental Exposure to Organochlorine Compounds and Mercury.* **Takser, Larissa.** 8, s.l. : Environmental Health Perspectives, 2005, Vol. 113.

448. *Occurrence of pharmaceuticals and hormones in drinking water treated from surface waters.* **Vulliet, Emmanuelle , Cren-Olivé, Cécile and Grenier-Loustalot, Marie-Florence.** 1, s.l. : Environ Chem Lett, 2011, Vol. 9.

449. *Miscarriages associated with drinking water disinfection byproducts, study says.* **Betts, Kellyn.** s.l. : Environmental Science & Technology, 1998.

450. *Drinking water contaminants and adverse pregnancy outcomes: a review.* **Bove, Frank.** 1, s.l. : Environmental Health Perspectives, 2002, Vol. 110.

451. *A Prospective Study of Spontaneous Abortion: Relation to Amount and Source of Drinking Water Consumed in Early Pregnancy.* **Shanna , H.** 2, s.l.: Epidemiology, 1998, Vol. 9.

452. *Adverse Pregnancy Outcomes in Relation to Water Consumption: A Re-Analysis of Data from the Original Santa Clara County Study, California, 1980-1981.* **Deane, Margaret.** 2, s.l. : Epidemiology, 1992, Vol. 3.

453. *Contamination, bioaccumulation and toxic effects of perfluorinated chemicals (PFCs) in the water environment: a review paper.* **Suja, Fatihah.** 6, s.l. : Water Sci Technol, 2009, Vol. 60.

454. *The use of household cleaning products during pregnancy and lower respiratory tract infections and wheezing during early life.* **Casas, Lidia.** s.l. : Int J Public Health, 2013, Vol. 58.

455. *Frequent use of chemical household products is associated with persistent wheezing in pre-school age children.* **Sherriff, A.** s.l. : Thorax, 2005, Vol. 60.

456. *Early infancy microbial and metabolic alterations affect risk of childhood asthma.* **Arrieta, Marie-Claire.** 307, s.l. : Science Translational Medicine, 2015, Vol. 7.

457. *Exposure During Pregnancy to Glycol Ethers and Chlorinated Solvents and the Risk of Congenital Malformations.* **Cordier, Sylvaine.** 6, s.l. : Epidemiology, 2012, Vol. 23.

458. *Polybrominated Diphenyl Ether (PBDE) Flame Retardants and Thyroid Hormone during Pregnancy.* **Chevrier, Jonathan.** 10, s.l. : Environmental Health Perspectives, 2010, Vol. 118.

459. *Maternal body burdens of PCDD/Fs and PBDEs are associated with maternal serum levels of thyroid hormones in early pregnancy: a cross-sectional study.* **Lignell, Sanna.** s.l. : Environmental Health, 2016, Vol. 15.

460. *Associations between Polybrominated Diphenyl Ether (PBDE) Flame Retardants, Phenolic Metabolites, and Thyroid Hormones during Pregnancy.* **Stapleton, Heather.** 10, s.l. : Environmental Health Perspectives, 2011, Vol. 119.

461. *Concentrations of polybrominated diphenyl ethers (PBDEs) and 2,4,6-tribromophenol in human placental tissues.* **Leonetti, Christopher.** s.l.: Environment International, 2016, Vol. 88.

462. *Polybrominated Diphenyl Ethers (PBDEs) in Aborted Human Fetuses and Placental Transfer during the First Trimester of Pregnancy.* **Zhao, Yaxian.** 11, s.l. : Environ. Sci. Technol., 2013, Vol. 47.

463. *Prenatal exposure to polychlorinated biphenyls (PCBs) and polybrominated diphenyl ethers (PBDEs) may influence birth weight among infants in a Swedish cohort with background exposure: a cross-sectional study.* **Lignell, Sanna.** s.l. : Environmental Health, 2013, Vol. 12.

464. *Prenatal Exposure to PBDEs and Neurodevelopment.* **Herbstman, Julie.** 5, s.l.: Environmental Health Perspectives, 2010, Vol. 118.

465. *House Dust Concentrations of Organophosphate Flame Retardants in Relation to Hormone Levels and Semen Quality Parameters.* **Meeker, John and Stapleton, Heather.** 3, s.l. : Environmental Health Perspectives, 2010, Vol. 118.

466. *Organophosphate exposures during pregnancy and child neurodevelopment: Recommendations for essential policy reforms.* **Hertz-Picciotto, Irva.** s.l. : PLoS Med, 2018, Vol. 10.

467. *Residential proximity to organophosphate and carbamate pesticide use during pregnancy, poverty during childhood, and cognitive functioning in 10-year-old children.* **Rowe, Christopher.** s.l. : Environmental Research, 2016, Vol. 150.

468. *Prenatal exposure to organophosphate esters and behavioral development in young children in the Pregnancy, Infection, and Nutrition Study.* **Brett T and Doherty, Brett.** s.l. : Environmental Research, 2019, Vol. 169.

469. *Nonylphenol in pregnant women and their matching fetuses: Placental transfer and potential risks of infants.* **Huang, Yu-Fang.** s.l. : Environmental Research, 2014, Vol. 134.

470. *Induction of Calbindin-D9k Messenger RNA and Protein by Maternal Exposure to Alkylphenols During Late Pregnancy in Maternal and Neonatal Uteri of Rats.* **Hong, Eui-Ju.** 2, s.l. : Biology of Reproduction, 2004, Vol. 71.

471. *In utero reproductive study in rats exposed to nonylphenol.* **Hossaini, Alireza** , et al. s.l. : Reproductive Toxicology, 2001, Vol. 15.

472. *Cumulative Chemical Exposures During Pregnancy and Early Development.* **Mitro, Susanna.** 4, s.l. : Curr Environ Health Rep, 2016, Vol. 2.

473. *Exposure to food contaminants during pregnancy.* **Chan-Hon-Tong, Anne.** s.l.: Science of the Total Environment, 2013, Vols. 458-460.

474. *The influence of maternal dietary exposure to dioxins and PCBs during pregnancy on ADHD symptoms and cognitive functions in Norwegian preschool children.* **Caspersen, Ida.** s.l. : Environment International, 2016.

475. *Detrimental effects of flame retardant, PBB153, exposure on sperm and future generations.* **Greeson, K.** 8567, s.l. : Sci Rep, 2020, Vol. 10.

476. *Emerging endocrine disrupters: perfluoroalkylated substances.* **Jensen, Allan and Leffers, Henrik.** s.l. : International Journal of Andrology, 2008, Vol. 31.

477. *Exposure sources and thyroid effects of perfluorinated compounds (PFCs) during pregnancy.* **Webster, Glenys.** Vancover : The University of British Columbia, 2011.

478. *Serum levels of perfluoroalkyl compounds in human maternal and umbilical.* **Monroy, Rocio.** s.l. : Environmental Research, 2008, Vol. 108.

479. *Maternal Concentrations of Polyfluoroalkyl Compounds during Pregnancy and Fetal and Postnatal Growth in British Girls.* **Maisonet, Mildred.** 10, s.l.: Environmental Health Perspectives, 2012, Vol. 120.

480. *The Association of Prenatal Exposure to Perfluorinated Chemicals with Maternal Essential and Long-Chain Polyunsaturated Fatty Acids during Pregnancy and the Birth Weight of Their Offspring: The Hokkaido Study.* **Kishi, Reiko.** 10, s.l. : Environmental Health Perspectives, 2015, Vol. 123.

481. *Indoor Sources of Poly- and Perfluorinated Compounds (PFCS) in Vancouver, Canada: Implications for Human Exposure.* **Shoeib, Mahiba.** 19, s.l. : Environ. Sci. Technol., 2011, Vol. 45.

482. *Mapping a Course for PFCs: Transfer Between Mothers' Milk and Serum.* **Fields, Scott.** 2, s.l. : Environmental Health Perspectives, 2007, Vol. 115.

483. *Exposure to Polyfluoroalkyl Chemicals and Attention Deficit/Hyperactivity Disorder in U.S. Children 12–15 Years of Age.* **Hoffman, Kate.** 12, s.l. : Environmental Health Perspectives, 2010, Vol. 118.

484. *National Collaborating Centre for Environmental Health. Potential human health effects of perfluorinated chemicals (PFCs).* British Columbia : British Columbia Centre for Disease Control, 2010.

485. *Environmental oestrogens, cosmetics and breast cancer.* **Darbre, P D.** 1, s.l. : Best Practice & Research Clinical Endocrinology & Metabolism, 2006, Vol. 20.

486. *Triclosan and triclocarban exposure and thyroid function during pregnancy—A randomized intervention.* **Ley, Catherine.** s.l. : Reproductive Toxicology, 2017, Vol. 74.

487. *Associations of maternal exposure to triclosan, parabens, and other phenols with prenatal maternal and neonatal thyroid hormone levels.* **Berger, Kimberly.** s.l. : Environmental Research, 2018, Vol. 165.

488. *Maternal Exposure to Triclosan Impairs Thyroid Homeostasis and Female Pubertal Development in Wistar Rat Offspring.* **Rodríguez, Pablo.** s.l. : Journal of Toxicology and Environmental Health, Part, 2010, Vol. 73.

489. *Urinary triclosan concentrations during pregnancy and birth outcomes.* **Etzel, Taylor.** s.l. : Environmental Research, 2017, Vol. 156.

490. *Urinary and air phthalate concentrations and self-reported use of personal care products among minority pregnant women in New York city.* **Just, A,** et al. s.l. : Journal of Exposure Science and Environmental Epidemiology, 2010, Vol. 20.

491. *Phthalate exposure among pregnant women in Jerusalem, Israel: results of a pilot study.* **Berman, T,** et al. s.l. : Environment International, 2009, Vol. 35.

492. *Maternal phthalate exposure promotes allergic airway inflammation over two generations via epigenetic modifications.* **Jahreis, Susanne,** et al. 2017, Journal of Allergy and Clinical Immunology.

493. *Ambient black carbon particles reach the fetal side of human placenta.* **Bové, H.** s.l. : Nature Communications, 2019, Vol. 10.

494. *Airborne pollution and pregnancy.* **Jauniaux, E.** 3, s.l. : BJOG, 2020, Vol. 127.

495. *Air pollution combustion emissions: characterization of causative agents and mechanisms associated with cancer, reproductive, and cardiovascular effects.* **Lewtas, J.** s.l. : Mutat Res, 2007, Vol. 636.

496. *Cadmium: Toxic effects on the reproductive system and the embryo.* **Thompson, Jennifer and Bannigan, John.** 2008, Reproductive Toxicology, pp. 304-315.

497. *Cadmium Determination in Mexican-Produced Tobacco.* **Saldivar De R, Liliana,** et al. 1991, Environmental Research, Vol. 55, pp. 91-96.

498. *Impact of heavy metals on the female reproductive system.* **Rzymski, Piotr** , et al. 2, s.l. : Annals of Agricultural and Environmental Medicine, 2015, Vol. 22.

499. *Carbon monoxide poisoning — a public health perspective.* **Raub, James.** s.l.: Toxicology, 2000, Vol. 145.

500. *Exposure to mobile phone (900–1800 MHz) during pregnancy: tissue oxidative stress after childbirth.* **Toossi, Mohammad.** 10, s.l. : The Journal of MaternalFetal & Neonatal Medicine, 2018, Vol. 31.

501. *Ultra high frequency-electromagnetic field irradiation during pregnancy leads to an increase in erythrocytes micronuclei incidence in rat offspring.* **Ferreira, Amâncio.** s.l. : Life Sciences, 2006, Vol. 80.

502. *Wi-Fi (2.45 GHz)- and Mobile Phone (900 and 1800 MHz)-Induced Risks on Oxidative Stress and Elements in Kidney and Testis of Rats During Pregnancy and the Development of Offspring.* **Özorak, A.** s.l. : Biol Trace Elem Res, 2013, Vol. 156.

503. *The influence of microwave radiation from cellular phone on fetal rat brain.* **Ji ,Jing.** 1, s.l. : Electromagnetic Biology and Medicine, 2012, Vol. 31.

504. *Maternal cell phone use during pregnancy and child behavioral problems in five birth cohorts.* **Birks, Laura.** s.l. : Environment International, 2017, Vol. 104.

505. *Associations of Maternal Cell-Phone Use During Pregnancy With Pregnancy Duration and Fetal Growth in 4 Birth Cohorts.* **Tsarna, Ermioni.** 7, s.l. : American Journal of Epidemiology, 2019, Vol. 188.

506. *Study on Microwave Absorbing of Tourmaline and Dravite/ZnO Complex Powders.* **Zhang, Xiaohui and Ma, Hongwen.** s.l. : Advanced Materials Research Vols, 2014.

507. *Actual Wearing State of Aged Pregnant Women for the Development of Electromagnetic Waves Shielding Maternity Wear.* **Kim, Young-im.** 5, s.l. : Fashion & Textile Research Journal, 2019, Vol. 21.

508. *Determination of bisphenol A concentrations in human biological fluids reveals significant early prenatal exposure.* **Ikezuki, Yumiko** , et al. 11, s.l. : Human Reproduction, 2002, Vol. 17.

509. *Late pregnancy is vulnerable period for exposure to BPA.* **Ohtani, Naoko.** 3, s.l.: J Vet Med Sci, 2018, Vol. 80.

510. *Prenatal exposure to bisphenol A and phthalates and childhood respiratory tract infections and allergy.* **Gascon, Mireia.** 2, s.l. : Journal of Allergy and Clinical Immunology, 2015, Vol. 135.

511. *Risk Assessment of Using Aluminum Foil in Food Preparation.* **Bassioni, Ghada.** s.l. : Int. J. Electrochem. Sci, 2012.

512. *Neurobiology of gender identity and sexual orientation.* **Roselli, C.** 7, s.l. : Journal of Neuroendocrinology, 2017, Vol. 30.

513. *Sexual differentiation of the human brain in relation to gender identity and sexual orientation.* **Savic, Ivanka.** s.l. : Progress in Brain Research, 2010, Vol. 186.

514. *Sexual Hormones and the Brain: An Essential Alliance for Sexual Identity and Sexual Orientation.* **Garcia-Falgueras, A.** s.l. : Pediatric Neuroendocrinology, 2010, Vol. 17.

515. *Prenatal testosterone and gender-related behaviour.* **Hines, Melissa.** s.l. : European Journal of Endocrinology, 2006, Vol. 155.

516. **Pitchford, Paul.** *Healing with Whole Foods.* Third. Berkeley : North Atlantic Books, 2002.

517. *Dehydration-induced oligohydramnios.* **Ross, Michael.** s.l. : Am J Obstet Gynecol, 1990.

518. *Iron-Deficiency Anemia.* **Camaschella, Clara.** s.l. : The New England Journal of Medicine, 2015, Vol. 372.

519. *Raw eggs 'safe for pregnant women'.* **BBC.** [Online] 25 July 2016. [Cited: 30 December 2020.] https://www.bbc.co.uk/news/health-36888285.

520. *How to eat less saturated fat.* **NHS.** [Online] 26 March 2020. [Cited: 04 October 2020.] https://www.nhs.uk/live-well/eat-well/eat-less-saturated-fat/.

521. *Offspring of Normal and Diabetic Rats Fed Saturated Fat in Pregnancy Demonstrate Vascular Dysfunction.* **Koukkou, E.** 25, s.l. : Circulation, 1998, Vol. 98.

522. *Opiate-like effects of sugar on gene expression in reward areas of the rat brain.* **Spangler, Rudolph**, et al. 2, s.l. : Molecular Brain Research, 2004, Vol. 124.

523. *Intake of artificially sweetened soft drinks and risk of preterm delivery: a prospective cohort study in 59,334 Danish pregnant women.* **Halldorsson, Thorhallur.** 3, s.l. : The American Journal of Clinical Nutrition, 2010, Vol. 92.

524. *Association Between Artificially Sweetened Beverage Consumption During Pregnancy and Infant Body Mass Index.* **Azad, Meghan.** s.l. : JAMA Pediatr, 2016.

525. *Consumption of artificial sweeteners in pregnancy increased overweight risk in infants.* **Ali, F.** s.l. : Arch Dis Child Educ Pract Ed, 2017.

526. *Consumption of Artificially-Sweetened Soft Drinks in Pregnancy and Risk of Child Asthma and Allergic Rhinitis.* **Maslova, Ekaterina.** 2, s.l. : PLoS One, 2013, Vol. 8.

527. *Omega-3 Fatty Acid Supplementation During Pregnancy.* **Greenberg, James.** 4, s.l. : Rev Obstet Gynecol, 2008, Vol. 1.

528. *FDA and EPA Issue Fish Consumption Advice.* **U.S. Food and Drug Administration.** [Online] 18 January 2017. [Cited: 10 June 2020.] https://www.fda.gov/food/cfsan-constituent-updates/fda-and-epa-issue-fish-consumption-advice.

529. *Omega-3 Fatty Acids and Pregnancy.* **Coletta, Jaclyn.** 4, s.l. : Rev Obstet Gynecol., 2010, Vol. 3.

530. *Average purchase per person per week of fish in the United Kingdom (UK) from 2006 to 2017/2018.* **Statista.** [Online] [Cited: 31 December 2020.] https://www.statista.com/statistics/284380/weekly-household-consumption-of-fish-in-the-united-kingdom-uk/.

531. *Have a healthy diet in pregnancy.* **NHS.** [Online] 14 February 2020. [Cited: 16 November 2020.] https://www.nhs.uk/conditions/pregnancy-and-baby/healthy-pregnancy-diet/.

532. *Maternal polyunsaturated fatty acids and risk for autism spectrum disorder in the MARBLES high-risk study.* **Huang, Yunru.** 5, s.l. : Autism, 2020, Vol. 24.

533. *Maternal Fatty Acid Status During Pregnancy and Child Autistic Traits. The Generation R Study.* **Steenweg-de Graaff, Jolien.** 9, s.l. : American Journal of Epidemiology, 2016, Vol. 183.

534. *The role of marine omega-3 in human neurodevelopment, including Autism Spectrum Disorders and Attention-Deficit/Hyperactivity Disorder – a review.* **Martins, Bárbara.** 9, s.l. : Critical Reviews in Food Science and Nutrition, 2020, Vol. 60.

535. **Brewer, Sarah.** *The Essential Guide to Vitamins, Minerals and Herbal Supplements.* London : Right Way, 2010.

536. *Effects of omega-3 fatty acids in prevention of early preterm delivery: a systematic review and meta-analysis of randomized studies.* **Kar, Sumit.** s.l.: European Journal of Obstetrics & Gynecology and Reproductive Biology, 2016, Vol. 198.

537. *Fish Consumption, Erythrocyte Fatty Acids, and Preterm Birth.* **Klebanoff, Mark.** 5, s.l. : Obstet Gynecol., 2011, Vol. 117.

538. *Dietary variables and glucose tolerance in pregnancy.* **Wang, Y.** 4, s.l. : Diabetes Care, 2000, Vol. 23.

539. *Prospective Study of Peripregnancy Consumption of Peanuts or Tree Nuts by Mothers and the Risk of Peanut or Tree Nut Allergy in Their Offspring.* **Lindsay Frazier, A.** 2, s.l. : JAMA Pediatr, 2014, Vol. 168.

540. *Selenium status in pregnancy influences children's cognitive function at 1.5 years of age.* **Skroder, Helena.** 5, s.l. : Clinical Nutrition, 2015, Vol. 34.

541. *Meat intake and reproductive parameters among young men.* **Afeiche, Myriam.** 3, s.l. : Epidemiology, 2014, Vol. 25.

542. *Risk Assessment of Growth Hormones and Antimicrobial Residues in Meat.* **Jeong, Sang-Hee.** 4, s.l. : Toxicol Res., 2010, Vol. 26.

543. *Development Initiatives, 2017. Global Nutrition Report 2017.* Bristol : Global Nutrition Report, 2017.

544. *Is caffeine addictive? The most widely used psychoactive substance in the world affects same parts of the brain as cocaine.* **Daly, J.** 95, s.l. : Lakartidningen, 1998, Vol. 16.

545. *Effect of reducing caffeine intake on birth weight and length of gestation: randomised controlled trial.* **Bech, Bodil.** 7590, s.l. : BMJ, 2007, Vol. 334.

546. **Schilter, B.** *Coffee: Recent Developments.* Oxford : Blackwell Science, 2001.

547. *Maternal caffeine consumption has irreversible effects on reproductive parameters and fertility in male offspring rats.* **Dorostghoal, Mehran.** 4, s.l. : Clin Exp Reprod Med, 2012, Vol. 39.

548. *Maternal coffee drinking in pregnancy and risk of small for gestational age birth.* **Parazzini1, F.** s.l. : European Journal of Clinical Nutrition, 2005, Vol. 59.

549. *Coffee and pregnancy.* **Hey, Edmund.** 7590, s.l. : BMJ, 2007, Vol. 334.

550. *Should I limit caffeine during pregnancy?* **NHS.** [Online] 02 May 2018. [Cited: 11 June 2020.] https://www.nhs.uk/common-health-questions/pregnancy/should-i-limit-caffeine-during-pregnancy/.

551. *Caffeine During Pregnancy: Grounds for Concern?* **Eskenazi, Brenda.** 24, s.l. : JAMA, 1993, Vol. 270.

552. *Caffeine Clinical Bottom Line.* **Ulbricht, Catherine.** 6, s.l. : Alternative and Complementary Therapies, 2012, Vol. 18.

553. *The effects of moderate alcohol consumption during pregnancy on fetal growth and morphogenesis.* **Hanson, James.** 3, s.l. : The Journal of Pediatrics, 1978, Vol. 92.

554. *Adverse Effects on Offspring of Maternal Alcohol Abuse during Pregnancy.* **Ouellette, Eileen.** s.l. : N Engl J Med, 1977, Vol. 297.

555. *Effects on the Child of Alcohol Abuse During Pregnancy.* **Olegard, R.** s.l. : Acta Pædiatrica, 1979, Vol. 68.

556. *Consumption of Alcohol During Pregnancy: A Review of Effects on Growth and Development of Offspring.* **Abel, Ernest.** 3, s.l. : Human Biology, 1982, Vol. 54.

557. *Are probiotics safe for use during pregnancy and lactation?* **Elias, Jackie.** 3, s.l. : Canadian Family Physician, 2011, Vol. 57.

558. *Probiotic Safety in Pregnancy: A Systematic Review and Meta-analysis of Randomized Controlled Trials of Lactobacillus, Bifidobacterium, and Saccharomyces spp.* **Dugoua, Jean-Jacques.** 6, s.l. : Journal of Obstetrics and Gynaecology Canada, 2009, Vol. 31.

559. *Ly6Chi Monocytes Provide a Link between Antibiotic-Induced Changes in Gut Microbiota and Adult Hippocampal Neurogenesis.* **Möhle, Luisa**, et al. 9, s.l. : Cell Reports, 2016, Vol. 15.

560. *Microbial lysate upregulates host oxytocin.* **Varian, Bernard.** s.l. : Brain, Behavior, and Immunity, 2017, Vol. 61.

561. *Supplementation with Lactobacillus rhamnosus or Bifidobacterium lactis probiotics in pregnancy increases cord blood interferon-γ and breast milk transforming growth factor-β and immunoglobin A detection.* **Prescott, S.** s.l. : Clinical and Experimental Allergy, 2008, Vol. 38.

562. *Low breast milk TGF-β2 is induced by Lactobacillus reuteri supplementation and associates with reduced risk of sensitization during infancy.* **Böttcher , Malin.** 6, s.l. : Pediatric Allergy & Immunology, 2008, Vol. 19.

563. *Regular consumption of Lactobacillus reuteri-containing lozenges reduces pregnancy gingivitis: an RCT.* **Schlagenhauf, Ulrich.** 11, s.l. : Clinic Periodonotology, 2016, Vol. 43.

564. *Oral Lactobacillus rhamnosus GR-1 and Lactobacillus reuteri RC-14 to reduce Group B Streptococcus colonization in pregnant women: A randomized controlled trial.* **Ho, Ming.** s.l. : Taiwanese Journal of Obstetrics & Gynecology, 2016, Vol. 55.

565. *Maternal probiotic supplementation during pregnancy and breast-feeding reduces the risk of eczema in the infant.* **Rautava, Samuli.** 6, s.l. : Journal of Allergy and Clinical Immunology, 2012, Vol. 130.

566. *Probiotics during pregnancy and breast-feeding might confer immunomodulatory protection against atopic disease in the infant.* **Rautava, Samuli.** 1, s.l. : Journal of Allergy and Clinical Immunology, 2002, Vol. 109.

567. *Effect of polyphenols on production of steroid hormones from human adrenocortical NCI-H295R cells.* **Hasegawa, E,** et al. 2, s.l. : Biol Pharm Bull, 2013, Vol. 36.

568. *The Flavonoid Apigenin Is a Progesterone Receptor Modulator with In Vivo Activity in the Uterus.* **Dean, Matthew,** et al. s.l. : Hormones and Cancer, 2018.

569. *Apigenin: A Promising Molecule for Cancer Prevention.* **Shukla, Sanjeev** and Gupta, Sanjay. 6, s.l. : Pharm Res, 2010, Vol. 27.

570. *Maternal Obesity in Pregnancy, Gestational Weight Gain, and Risk of Childhood Asthma.* **Forno, Erick.** 2, s.l. : Pediatrics, 2014, Vol. 134.

571. *Maternal obesity, gestational weight gain, and risk of asthma and atopic disease in offspring: A study within the Danish National Birth Cohort.* **Harpsøe, Maria.** 4, s.l. : Journal of Allergy and Clinical Immunology, 2013, Vol. 131.

572. *Copper regulates cyclic-AMP-dependent lipolysis.* **Krishnamoorthy, Lakshmi ,** et al. s.l. : Nature Chemical Biology, 2016, Vol. 12.

573. *Behavior of Some Solid Food Simulants in Contact with Several Plastics Used in Microwave Ovens.* **Nerín, Cristina and Acosta, Domingo.** 25, s.l. : J. Agric. Food Chem, 2002, Vol. 50.

574. *Microwave Heating Causes Rapid Degradation of Antioxidants in Polypropylene Packaging, Leading to Greatly Increased Specific Migration to Food Simulants As Shown by ESI-MS and GC-MS.* **Alin, Jonas and Hakkarainen, Minna.** 10, s.l. : J. Agric. Food Chem, 2011, Vol. 59.

575. *Hazards of microwave cooking: direct thermal damage to the pharynx and larynx.* **Ford, G and Horrocks, C.** s.l. : The Journal of Laryngology & Otology, 1994, Vol. 108.

576. *Thermal injury to the upper aerodigestive tract after microwave heating of food.* **Offer, G, Nanan, D and Marshall, J.** s.l. : Journal of Accident and Emergency Medicine, 1995, Vol. 12.

577. *Detection of phytoestrogens in samples of second trimester human amniotic fluid.* **Foster, Warren.** 3, s.l. : Toxicology Letters, 2002, Vol. 129.

578. *Soy but not bisphenol A (BPA) or the phytoestrogen genistin alters developmental weight gain and food intake in pregnant rats and their offspring.* **Cao, Jinyan.** s.l. : Reproductive Toxicology, 2015, Vol. 58.

579. *Phytoestrogens in Human Pregnancy.* **Jarrell, John.** s.l. : Obstetrics and Gynecology International, 2012.

580. **Mindell, Earl and Mundis, Hester.** *Earl Mindell's New Vitamin Bible.* New York : Hachette Book Group, 2011.

581. *The pros and cons of phytoestrogens.* **Patisaul, Heather and Jefferson, Wendy.** 4, s.l. : Frontiers in Neuroendocrinology, 2010, Vol. 31.

582. *Estimated Asian adult soy protein and isoflavone intakes.* **Messina, M, Nagata, C and Wu, A.** 1, s.l. : Nutrition and Cancer, 2006, Vol. 55.

583. *Isoflavone Intake in Early Pregnancy and Hypospadias in the Japan Environment and Children's Study.* **Michikawa, Takehiro.** s.l. : Urology, 2019, Vol. 124.

584. *Maternal Vitamin A Supplementation in Relation to Selected Birth Defects.* **Werler, Martha.** s.l. : Teratology, 1990, Vol. 42.

585. *Safety of vitamin A: recent results.* **Bendich, A.** 2, s.l. : The American Journal of Clinical Nutrition, 1989, Vol. 49.

586. *Vitamin A in pregnancy: requirements and safety limits.* **Azaïs-Braesco, Véronique.** s.l. : Am J Clin Nutr, 2000, Vol. 71.

587. *Beta-carotene, vitamin A and carrier proteins in thyroid diseases.* **Aktuna, D**, et al. s.l. : Acta Medica Austriaca, 1993, Vol. 20.

588. *Marginal biotin deficiency during normal pregnancy.* **Mock, Donald.** 2, s.l. : The American Journal of Clinical Nutrition, 2002, Vol. 75.

589. *Marginal Biotin Deficiency is Common in Normal Human Pregnancy and Is Highly Teratogenic in Mice.* **Mock, Donald.** 1, s.l. : The Journal of Nutrition, 2009, Vol. 139.

590. *Biotin.* **National Institutes of Health.** [Online] U.S. Department of Health & Human Services, 03 June 2020. [Cited: 17 June 2020.] https://ods.od.nih.gov/factsheets/ Biotin-HealthProfessional/.

591. *Calcium.* **National Institutes of Health.** [Online] U.S. Department of Health & Human Services, 26 March 2020. [Cited: 17 June 2020.] https://ods.od.nih.gov/factsheets/ Calcium-HealthProfessional/.

592. *Baby boys and girls receive different nutrients in breast milk.* **The Guardian.** [Online] 14 February 2014. [Cited: 04 September 2020.] https://www.theguardian.com/science/2014/feb/14/ baby-boys-girls-sex-formula-milk.

593. *D'Alberto, Attilio. My Fertility Guide: How To Get Pregnant Naturally.* London : Attilio D'Alberto, 2019.

594. *Choline.* **National Institutes of Health.** [Online] U.S. Department of Health & Human Services, 03 June 2020. [Cited: 17 June 2020.] https://ods.od.nih.gov/factsheets/ Choline-HealthProfessional/.

595. *Altered metabolism of maternal micronutrients and omega 3 fatty acids epigenetically regulate matrix metalloproteinases in preterm pregnancy: A novel hypothesis.* **Sundrani, Deepali.** 5, s.l. : Medical Hypotheses, 2011, Vol. 77.

596. *Copper.* **National Institutes of Health.** [Online] U.S. Department of Health & Human Services, 03 June 2020. [Cited: 17 June 2020.] https://ods.od.nih.gov/factsheets/ Copper-HealthProfessional/.

597. *Polyunsaturated Fatty Acids in Male and Female Reproduction.* **Wathes, Claire, Abayasekara, Robert and Aitken, John.** s.l. : Bioology of Reproduction, 2007, Vol. 77.

598. *Long-chain n-3 PUFA: plant v. marine sources.* **Williams, Christine and Burdge, Graham.** s.l. : Proceedings of the Nutrition Society, 2006, Vol. 65.

599. *Deficient or Excess Folic Acid Supply During Pregnancy Alter Cortical Neurodevelopment in Mouse Offspring.* **Harlan De Crescenzo, Angelo.** bhaa248, s.l. : Cerebral Cortex, 2020.

600. *Use of folic acid for prevention of spina bifida and other neural tube defects--1983-1991.* **Centers for Disease Control (CDC).** 30, s.l. : MMWR Morb Mortal Wkly Rep, 1991, Vol. 40.

601. *Prevalence of spina bifida and anencephaly during the transition to mandatory folic acid fortification in the United States.* **Williams, Laura.** 1, s.l. : Teratology, 2002, Vol. 66.

602. *Folic Acid Supplements in Pregnancy and Severe Language Delay in Children.* **Roth, Christine** , et al. 14, s.l. : JAMA, 2011, Vol. 306.

603. *Recommendations: Women & Folic Acid.* **Centres for Disease Control and Prevention.** [Online] 13 August 2019. [Cited: 16 June 2020.] https://www.cdc.gov/ncbddd/folicacid/recommendations.html#:~:text=The%20Institute%20of%20Medicine's%20Food,with%20a%20neural%20tube%20defect.

604. *Folate.* **National Institutes of Health.** [Online] U.S. Department of Health & Human Services, 03 June 2020. [Cited: 16 June 2020.] https://ods.od.nih.gov/factsheets/Folate-HealthProfessional/.

605. *Iodine.* **National Institutes of Health.** [Online] U.S. Department of Health & Human Services, 01 May 2020. [Cited: 16 June 2020.] https://ods.od.nih.gov/factsheets/Iodine-Consumer/.

606. *The impact of maternal iron deficiency and iron deficiency anemia on child's health.* **Abu-Ouf, Noran.** 2, s.l. : Saudi Med J., 2015, Vol. 36.

607. *Dietary iron intake during early pregnancy and birth outcomes in a cohort of British women.* **Alwan, Nisreen.** 4, s.l. : Hum Reprod., 2011, Vol. 26.

608. *Iron.* **National Institutes of Health.** [Online] U.S. Department of Health & Human Services, 28 February 2020. [Cited: 16 June 2020.] https://ods.od.nih.gov/factsheets/Iron-HealthProfessional/.

609. *Dietary pyrroloquinoline quinone (PQQ) alters indicators of inflammation and mitochondrial-related metabolism in human subjects.* **Harris, Calliandra,** et al. 12, s.l. : The Journal of Nutritional Biochemistry, 2013, Vol. 24.

610. *Pyrroloquinoline Quinone Improves Growth and Reproductive Performance in Mice Fed Chemically Defined Diets.* **Steinberg, Francene.** 2, s.l. : Experimental Biology and Medicine, 2003, Vol. 228.

611. *Potential health benefits of spirulina microalgae.* **Capelli, Bob and Cysewski, Gerald.** 2, s.l. : Nutra Foods, 2010, Vol. 9.

612. *Vitamin A and Pregnancy: A Narrative Review.* **Bastos Maia, S.** s.l. : Nutrients , 2019, Vol. 11.

613. *Vitamin D.* **National Institutes of Health.** [Online] U.S. Department of Health & Human Services, 24 March 2020. [Cited: 16 June 2020.] https://ods.od.nih.gov/factsheets/VitaminD-HealthProfessional/.

614. *Vitamin D in cutaneous carcinogenesis: Part I.* **Tang, Jean,** et al. 5, s.l. : J Am Acad Dermatol, 2012, Vol. 67.

615. *Vitamin D deficiency in pregnant New Zealand women.* **Eagleton, Carl.** 1241, s.l. : The New Zealand Medical Journal, 2006, Vol. 119.

616. *Vitamin D deficiency rickets in breast-fed infants presenting with hypocalcaemic seizures.* **Ahmed, I.** 8, s.l. : Acta Paediatrica, 1995, Vol. 84.

617. *Vitamin K.* **National Institutes of Health.** [Online] U.S. Department of Health & Human Services, 03 June 2020. [Cited: 17 June 2020.] https://ods.od.nih.gov/factsheets/vitaminK-HealthProfessional/.

618. *The Effect of Zinc Supplementation on Pregnancy Outcome.* **Goldenberg, Robert.** 6, s.l. : JAMA, 1995, Vol. 274.

619. *The zinc spark is an inorganic signature of human egg activation.* **Duncan, Francesca,** et al. s.l. : Nature, 2016.

620. *Dietary Supplement Labeling Guide: Appendix C. Daily Values for Infants, Children Less Than 4 Years of Age, and Pregnant and Lactating Women.* **U.S. Food & Food Administration.** [Online] April 2005. [Cited: 18 June 2020.] https://www.fda.gov/food/dietary-supplements-guidance-documents-regulatory-information/dietary-supplement-labeling-guide-appendix-c-daily-values-infants-children-less-4-years-age-and.

621. *Safety of Oral Alpha-Lipoic Acid Treatment in Pregnant Women: A Retrospective Observational Study.* **Parente, E.** s.l. : Eur Rev Med Pharmacol Sci, 2017, Vol. 18.

622. *The Impact of Pollen on the Health Status.* **Michalczyk, Maria.** 1, s.l. : Polis Journal of Natural Sciences, 2019, Vol. 34.

623. *Pollen exposure in pregnancy and infancy and risk of asthma hospitalisation - a register based cohort study.* **Lowe, Adrian.** 17, s.l. : Allergy, Asthma & Clinical Immunology, 2012, Vol. 8.

624. *Chromium.* **National Institutes of Health.** [Online] U.S. Department of Health & Human Services, 27 February 2020. [Cited: 18 June 2020.] https://ods.od.nih.gov/factsheets/Chromium-HealthProfessional/.

625. *An l-arginine-nitric oxide-cyclic guanosine monophosphate system exists in the uterus and inhibits contractility during pregnancy.* **Yallampalli, Chandrasekhar.** 1, s.l. : American Journal of Obstetrics and Gynecology, 1994, Vol. 170.

626. *Gestational changes in l-arginine-induced relaxation of pregnant rat and human myometrial smooth muscle.* **Izumi, Hidetaka.** 5, s.l. : American Journal of Obstetrics and Gynecology, 1993, Vol. 169.

627. *Nω-Nitro-L-arginine, an inhibitor of nitric oxide synthesis, increases blood pressure in rats and reverses the pregnancy-induced refractoriness to vasopressor agents.* **Molnár, Miklós.** 5, s.l. : American Journal of Obstetrics and Gynecology, 1992, Vol. 166.

628. *l-arginine reverses the adverse pregnancy changes induced by nitric oxide synthase inhibition in the rat.* **Helmbrecht, Gary.** 4, s.l. : American Journal of Obstetrics and Gynecology, 1996, Vol. 175.

629. *The Functions of Corticosteroid-Binding Globulin and Sex Hormone-Binding Globulin: Recent Advances.* **Rosner, W.** 1, s.l. : Endocrine Reviews, 1990, Vol. 11.

630. *Hair manganese concentrations in newborns and their mothers.* **Saner, G.** 5, s.l.: The American Journal of Clinical Nutrition, 1985, Vol. 41.

631. *Magnesium.* **National Institutes of Health.** [Online] U.S. Department of Health & Human Services, 24 March 2020. [Cited: 18 June 2020.] https://ods.od.nih.gov/factsheets/Magnesium-HealthProfessional/.

632. *Manganese.* **National Institutes of Health.** [Online] U.S. Department of Health & Human Services, 03 June 2020. [Cited: 18 June 2020.] https://ods.od.nih.gov/factsheets/Manganese-HealthProfessional/.

633. *Herbal Medicine in Pregnancy and Childbirth.* **Westfall, Rachel.** 1, s.l. : Advances In Natural Therapy, 2001, Vol. 18.

634. *Thiamin.* **National Institutes of Health.** [Online] U.S. Department of Health & Human Services, 03 June 2020. [Cited: 18 June 2020.] https://ods.od.nih.gov/factsheets/ Thiamin-HealthProfessional/.

635. *Vitamin B12.* **National Institutes of Health.** [Online] U.S. Department of Health & Human Services, 30 March 2020. [Cited: 18 June 2020.] https://ods.od.nih.gov/factsheets/ VitaminB12-HealthProfessional/.

636. *Riboflavin.* **National Institutes of Health.** [Online] U.S. Department of Health & Human Services, 03 June 2020. [Cited: 18 June 2020.] https://ods.od.nih.gov/factsheets/ Riboflavin-HealthProfessional/.

637. *Niacin.* **National Institutes of Health.** [Online] U.S. Department of Health & Human Services, 03 June 2020. [Cited: 18 June 2020.] https://ods.od.nih.gov/factsheets/ Niacin-HealthProfessional/.

638. *Pantothenic Acid.* **National Institutes of Health.** [Online] U.S. Department of Health & Human Services, 03 June 2020. [Cited: 18 June 2020.] https://ods.od.nih.gov/factsheets/ PantothenicAcid-HealthProfessional/.

639. *Vitamin B6.* **National Institutes of Health.** [Online] U.S. Department of Health & Human Services, 24 February 2020. [Cited: 18 June 2020.] https://ods.od.nih.gov/factsheets/ VitaminB6-HealthProfessional/.

640. *Vitamin C.* **National Institutes of Health.** [Online] U.S. Department of Health & Human Services, 27 Fbruary 2020. [Cited: 18 June 2020.] https://ods.od.nih.gov/factsheets/ VitaminC-HealthProfessional/.

641. *Vitamin E.* **National Institutes of Health.** [Online] U.S. Department of Health & Human Services, 28 February 2020. [Cited: 18 June 2020.] https://ods.od.nih.gov/factsheets/ VitaminE-HealthProfessional/.

642. **Romm, Aviva.** *Botanical Medicine for Women's Health.* s.l. : Churchill Livingstone, 2010.

643. *Coenzyme Q10 in Pregnancy.* **Noia, G.** 4, s.l. : Fetal Diagnosis and Therapy, 1996, Vol. 11.

644. *Coenzyme Q10 supplementation during pregnancy reduces the risk of pre-eclampsia.* **Teran, Enrique.** s.l. : International Journal of Gynecology and Obstetrics, 2009, Vol. 105.

645. *Coenzyme Q10 is increased in placenta and cord blood during preeclampsia.* **Teran, Enrique.** s.l. : BioFactors, 2005, Vol. 25.

646. *Selenium.* **National Institutes of Health.** [Online] U.S. Department of Health & Human Services, 11 March 2020. [Cited: 18 June 2020.] https://ods.od.nih.gov/factsheets/ Selenium-HealthProfessional/.

647. *Detecting Potential Teratogenic Alkaloids from Blue Cohosh Rhizomes Using an in Vitro Rat Embryo Culture.* **Kennelly, Edward.** 10, s.l. : J. Nat. Prod, 1992, Vol. 62.

648. *Herbal therapies in pregnancy: what works?* **Dante, Giulia.** 2, s.l. : Current Opinion in Obstetrics and Gynecology, 2014, Vol. 26.

649. *EBCOG Position Statement about the use of Herbal medication during.* **Savona-Ventura, Charles.** s.l. : European Journal of Obstetrics & Gynecology and Reproductive, 2019.

650. *Safety and Efficacy of Blue Cohosh (Caulophyllum Thalictroides) During Pregnancy and Lactation.* **Dugoua, Jean-Jacques.** 1, s.l. : Can J Clin Pharmacol, 2008, Vol. 15.

651. *Folk beliefs of food avoidance and prescription among menstruating and pregnant Karbi women of Kamrup district, Assam.* **Goswami, Ritu.** 19, s.l. : Journal of Ethnic Foods, 2019, Vol. 6.

652. *Prostaglandin E2 involvement in mammalian female fertility: ovulation, fertilization, embryo development and early implantation.* **Niringiyumukiza, Jean, Cai, Hongcai and Xiang, Wenpei.** 43, s.l. : Reproductive Biology and Endocrinology, 2018, Vol. 16.

653. *Activation of the epithelial Na+ channel triggers prostaglandin E2 release and production required for embryo implantation.* **Ruan, Y.** s.l. : Nature Medicine, 2012, Vol. 18.

654. *Maternal vitamin A supplementation in relation to selected birth defects.* **Werler, Martha,** et al. s.l. : Teratology, 1990, Vol. 42.

655. *Maternal consumption of polyphenol-rich foods in late pregnancy and fetal ductus arteriosus flow dynamics.* **Zielinsky, P.** s.l. : Journal of Perinatology, 2010, Vol. 30.

656. *Association between the serum folate levels and tea consumption during pregnancy.* **Shiraishi, Mie.** 5, s.l. : BioScience Trends, 2010, Vol. 4.

657. *Fetal and Neonatal Outcomes in Women Reporting Ingestion of Licorice (Glycyrrhiza uralensis) during Pregnancy.* **Choi, June-Seek.** 2, s.l. : Planta Med, 2013, Vol. 79.

658. *Birth Outcome in Relation to Licorice Consumption during Pregnancy.* **Strandberg, Timo.** 11, s.l. : American Journal of Epidemiology, 2001, Vol. 153.

659. *Birth preparation acupuncture for normalising birth: An analysis of NHS service routine data and proof of concept.* **Lokugamage, A.** s.l. : Journal of Obstetrics and Gynaecology, 2020.

660. *Complications of Term Pregnancies Beyond 37 Weeks of Gestation.* **Caughey, Aaron.** 1, s.l. : Obstetrics & Gynecology, 2004, Vol. 103.

661. *Maternal complications of pregnancy increase beyond 40 weeks of gestation in low-risk women.* **Caughey, Aaron.** s.l. : Journal of Perinatology, 2006, Vol. 26.

662. *Prolonged pregnancy: evaluating gestation-specific risks of fetal and infant mortality.* **Hilder, Lisa.** s.l. : British Journal of Obstetrics and Gynaecology, 1998, Vol. 105.

663. *Neonatal and Maternal Morbidity Among Low-Risk Nulliparous Women at 39–41 Weeks of Gestation.* **Chen, Han-Yang.** 4, s.l. : Obstetrics Gynecology, 2019, Vol. 133.

664. *Perinatal mortality associated with induction of labour versus expectant management in nulliparous women aged 35 years or over: An English national cohort study.* **Knight, Hannah.** s.l. : PLOS Medicine, 2017.

665. *Forty weeks and beyond: pregnancy outcomes by week of gestation.* **Alexander, James.** 2, s.l. : Obstetrics & Gynecology, 2000, Vol. 96.

666. *Late-Preterm Birth: Does the Changing Obstetric Paradigm Alter the Epidemiology of Respiratory Complications?* **Yoder, Bradley.** 4, s.l. : Obstetrics & Gynecology, 2008, Vol. 111.

667. *Risks of stillbirth and neonatal death with advancing gestation at term: A systematic review and meta-analysis of cohort studies of 15 million pregnancies.* **Muglu, Javaid.** 7, s.l. : PLoS Medicine, 2019, Vol. 16.

668. *The benefits and risks of inducing labour in patients with prior caesarean delivery: a systematic review.* **McDonagh, Marian.** 8, s.l. : BJOG, 2005, Vol. 112.

669. *Safety and Efficacy of Black Cohosh (Cimicifuga Racemosa) During Pregnancy and Latation.* **Dugoua, Jean-Jacques.** 3, s.l. : Can J Clin Pharmacol, 2006, Vol. 13.

670. *Herbal Medicines and Pregnancy.* **Dugoua, Jean-Jacques.** 3, s.l. : J Popul Ther Clin Pharmacol, 2010, Vol. 17.

671. **Romm, Aviva.** *Blue Cohosh: History, Science, Safety, and Midwife Prescribing of a Potentially Fetotoxic Herb.* s.l. : Yale Medicine Thesis Digital Library, 2009.

672. *Complementary and alternative medicine for induction of labour.* **Hall, Helen.** 3, s.l. : Women and Birth, 2012, Vol. 25.

673. *A national survey of herbal preparation use by nurse-midwives for labor stimulation: Review of the literature and recommendations for practice.* **McFarlin, Barbara.** 3, s.l. : Journal of Nurse-Midwifery, 1999, Vol. 44.

674. *A Study on the Safety and Efficacy of Castor Oil for Cervical Ripening and Labour Induction.* **Iravani, M.** 1, s.l. : Jundishapur Scientific Medical Journal, 2006, Vol. 5.

675. *Changes in salivary oxytocin after inhalation of clary sage essential oil scent in term-pregnant women: a feasibility pilot study.* **Tadokoro, Y.** s.l. : BMC Res Notes, 2017, Vol. 10.

676. *Effects of Valerian Consumption During Pregnancy on Cortical Volume and the Levels of Zinc and Copper in the Brain Tissue of Mouse Fetus.* **Mahmoudian, Alireza.** 4, s.l. : Zhong Xi Yi Jie He Xue Bao, 2012, Vol. 10.

677. *Effect of Acupressure on Cervical Ripening.* **Torkzahrani, Shahnaz.** s.l. : Iranian Red Crescent Medical Journal, 2015.

678. *Effect of Acupuncture on Induction of Labor.* **Lim, Chi Eung.** 11, s.l. : The Journal of Alternative and Complementary Medicine, 2009, Vol. 15.

679. *Acupuncture administered after spontaneous rupture of membranes at term significantly reduces the length of birth and use of oxytocin. A randomized controlled trial.* **Gaudernack, Lise.** s.l. : Acta Obstetricia et Gynecologica, 2006, Vol. 85.

680. *The effects of acupuncture during labour on nulliparous women: A randomised controlled trial.* **Hantoushzadeh, S.** 1, s.l. : Australian and New Zealand Journal of Obstetrics and Gynaecology, 2007, Vol. 47.

681. *A gentle start to life. Epi.No Birth Preparation.* [Online] [Cited: 30 July 2020.] https://www.epino.de/en/epi-no.html.

682. *The EpiNo® Device: Efficacy, Tolerability, and Impact on Pelvic Floor—Implications for Future Research.* **Kavvadias, Tilemachos.** s.l. : Obstet Gynecol Int., 2016.

683. *Experience Natural Birth Without Tearing, Interventions & Fear.* **Aniball.** [Online] [Cited: 16 October 2020.] https://aniball.uk.

684. *Steroid receptor coactivators 1 and 2 mediate fetal-to-maternal signaling that initiates parturition.* **Gao, Lu.** 7, s.l. : Journal of Clinical Investigation, 2015, Vol. 125.

685. *Timing of singleton births by onset of labour and mode of birth in NHS maternity units in England, 2005–2014: A study of linked birth registration, birth notification, and hospital episode data.* **Martin, Peter.** s.l. : PLUS ONE, 2018.

686. *Amniocentesis for Fetal Lung Maturity: Will It Become Obsolete?* **Varner, Stephen.** 3-4, s.l. : Rev Obstet Gynecol, 2013, Vol. 6.

687. **Ogbejesi, Chioma.** *Lecithin Sphingomyelin Ratio.* Treasure Island : StatPearls Publishing LLC, 2020.

688. **Caron, J.** *Breech Presentation.* s.l. : StatPearls Publishing LLC, 2020.

689. *Cost-effectiveness of breech version by acupuncture-type interventions on BL 67, including moxibustion, for women with a breech foetus at 33 weeks gestation: a modelling approach.* **van den Berg, Ineke.** 2, s.l. : Complementary Therapies in Medicine, 2010, Vol. 18.

690. *Moxibustion and other acupuncture point stimulation methods to treat breech presentation: a systematic review of clinical trials.* **Li, X.** 4, s.l. : Chin Med, 2009, Vol. 4.

691. *Effectiveness of acupuncture-type interventions versus expectant management to correct breech presentation: A systematic review.* **van den Berg, Ineke.** 2, s.l. : Complementary Therapies in Medicine, 2008, Vol. 16.

692. *Turning Foetal Breech Presentation at 32-35 Weeks of Gestational Age by Acupuncture and Moxibustion.* **Brici, Paolo.** s.l. : Evidence-Based Complementary and Alternative Medicine, 2019.

693. *Effect of stimulating the BL67 point on fetal correction from breech to cephalic presentation and natural delivery after the 36 weeks of pregnancy: A randomized clinical trial.* **Sourani, Khatereh.** 2, s.l. : Reproductive and Developmental Medicine, 2020, Vol. 4.

694. *Correction of nonvertex presentation with moxibustion: a systematic review and metaanalysis.* **Vas, Jorge.** 3, s.l. : American Journal of Obstetrics and Gynecology, 2009, Vol. 201.

695. *'It definitely made a difference': A grounded theory study of yoga for pregnancy and women's self-efficacy for labour.* **Campbell, Virginia.** s.l. : Midwifery, 2019, Vol. 68.

696. *Birthing outcomes from an Australian HypnoBirthing programme.* **Phillips-Moore, Julie.** 8, s.l. : British Journal of Midwifery, 2012, Vol. 20.

697. *Hypnobirthing Increases Pain Tolerane and Reduces Anxiety in Active Phase Labor.* **Nursalam.** 1, s.l. : Jurnal Ners, 2008, Vol. 3.

698. *Unexpected consequences: women's experiences of a self-hypnosis intervention to help with pain relief during labour.* **Finlayson, Kenneth.** s.l. : BNC Pregnancy and Childbirth, 2015, Vol. 15.

699. *Born Too Soon: The global epidemiology of 15 million preterm births.* **Blencowe, Hannah.** s.l. : Reprod Health, 2013, Vol. 10.

700. *Preterm birth associated with maternal fine particulate matter exposure: A global, regional and national assessment.* **Malley, Christopher.** s.l. : Environment International, 2017.

701. *Employment, working conditions, and preterm birth: results from the Europop case-control survey.* **Saurel-Cubizolles, M.** s.l. : Journal of Epidemiology & Community Health, 2004, Vol. 58.

702. *Women's experiences of traditional Chinese acupuncture treatment for threatened preterm labour.* **Robinson, Anneke.** s.l. : Auckland University of Technology, 2005.

703. *Chinese herbal medicines for threatened miscarriage.* **Li, L.** 5, s.l. : Cochrane Database of Systematic Reviews, 2012.

704. *Vaginal progesterone decreases preterm birth and neonatal morbidity and mortality in women with a twin gestation and a short cervix: an updated meta-analysis of individual patient data.* **Romero, Roberto.** 3, s.l. : Ultrasound Obstet Gynecol, 2017, Vol. 49.

705. *Effect of Acupressure on Cervical Ripening.* **Torkzahrani, Shahnaz.** 8, s.l. : Iran Red Crescent Med J, 2015, Vol. 17.

706. *Effects of SP6 Acupressure on Labor Pain and Length of Delivery Time in Women During Labor.* **Lee, Mi Kyeong.** 6, s.l. : The Journal of Alternative and Complementary Medicine, 2004, Vol. 10.

707. *Effects of acupressure at the Sanyinjiao point (SP6) on the process of active phase of labor in nulliparas women.* **Kashanian, Maryam.** 7, s.l. : The Journal of Maternal-Fetal & Neonatal Medicine, 2010, Vol. 23.

708. *Effects of SP6 Acupuncture Point Stimulation on Labor Pain and Duration of Labor.* **Yesilcicek Calik, Kiymet.** 10, s.l. : Iran Red Crescent Med J, 2014, Vol. 16.

709. *Comparison of the effect of Hoku Point (LI4) acupressure with that of San-Yin-Jiao (SP6) acupressure on labor pain and the length of delivery time in primiparous women.* **Tahmineh, Salehian.** 1, s.l. : Scientific Journal of Kurdistan University of Medical Sciences, 2011, Vol. 16.

710. *Effects of San-Yin-Jiao (SP6) Acupressure on Labor Pain, Delivery Time in Women during Labor.* **Lee, Mi Kyeong.** 6, s.l. : J Korean Acad Nurs, 2003, Vol. 33.

711. *Effects of LI-4 and SP-6 Acupuncture on Labor Pain, Cortisol Level and Duration of Labor.* **Asadi, Nasrin.** 5, s.l. : J Acupunct Meridian Stud, 2015, Vol. 8.

712. *Effects of LI4 Acupressure on Labor Pain in the First Stage of Labor.* **Hamidzadeh, Azam.** 2, s.l. : Journal of Midwifery & Women's Health, 2012, Vol. 57.

713. *The Effect of LI4 Acupressure on Labor Pain Intensity and Duration of Labor: A Randomized Controlled Trial.* **Dabiri, Fatemeh.** 6, s.l. : Oman Med J, 2014, Vol. 29.

714. *Effect of LI4 Acupressure on Labor Pain in the First Stage of Labor in Nuliparous Women.* **Kordi, M.** 3, s.l. : Journal of Hayat, 2011, Vol. 16.

715. *Pregnancy Guide.* **NHS 111 Wales.** [Online] 08 November 2017. [Cited: 08 August 2020.] https://111.wales.nhs.uk/livewell/pregnancy/whereyoucangivebirth/.

716. *Maternal outcomes and birth interventions among women who begin labour intending to give birth at home compared to women of low obstetrical risk who intend to give birth in hospital: A systematic review and meta-analyses.* **Reitsma, Angela.** s.l. : eClinical Medicine, 2020, Vol. 21.

717. *Perinatal or neonatal mortality among women who intend at the onset of labour to give birth at home compared to women of low obstetrical risk who intend to give birth in hospital: A systematic review and meta-analyses.* **Hutton, Eileen.** s.l. : eClinical Medicine, 2019, Vol. 14.

718. *Perinatal and maternal outcomes by planned place of birth for healthy women with low risk pregnancies: the Birthplace in England national prospective cohort study.* **Brocklehurst, P.** s.l. : BMJ, 2011, Vol. 343.

719. *What Doulas Do.* **Doula UK.** [Online] 2020. [Cited: 08 August 2020.] https://doula.org.uk/what-doulas-do/.

720. *The doula: an essential ingredient of childbirth rediscovered.* **Klauss, M.** 10, s.l. : ACTA Paediatrica, 1997, Vol. 86.

721. *Satisfaction in childbirth and perceptions of personal control in pain relief during labour.* **Hally McCrea, B.** 4, s.l. : Journal of Advanced Nursing, 1999, Vol. 29.

722. *Continuous support for women during childbirth.* **Hodnett , E.** 10, s.l. : Cochrane Database of Systematic Reviews, 2012.

723. *Social laughter is correlated with an elevated pain threshold.* **Dunbar, R.** 1731, s.l. : Proc. R. Soc. B, 2012, Vol. 279.

724. *Massage or music for pain relief in labour: A pilot randomised placebo controlled trial.* **Kimber, L.** s.l. : European Journal of Pain, 2008, Vol. 12.

725. *Does regular massage from late pregnancy to birth decrease maternal pain perception during labour and birth?—A feasibility study to investigate a programme of massage, controlled breathing and visualization, from 36 weeks of pregnancy until birth.* **Mc Nabb, Mary.** 3, s.l. : Complementary Therapies in Clinical Practice, 2006, Vol. 12.

726. *Child birth in squatting position.* **Nasir, Ayesha.** 1, s.l. : JPMA, 2007, Vol. 57.

727. *Immersion in Water During Labor and Delivery.* **Committee on Fetus and Newborn.** 4, s.l. : American Academy of Pediatrics, 2014, Vol. 133.

728. *Waterbirth – Safety and Procedures.* **The Association of Radical Midwives.** [Online] [Cited: 22 August 2020.] https://www.midwifery.org.uk/articles/waterbirth-safety-and-procedures/#:~:text=Ruth-,Water%20Temperature,and%20contractions%20may%20slow%20down..

729. *Coronavirus: Planning your birth.* **NHS.** [Online] [Cited: 19 October 2020.] https://www.england.nhs.uk/coronavirus/wp-content/uploads/sites/52/2020/05/C0441-maternity-leaflets-cv19-planning-your-birth.pdf.

730. *Analgesia in labour: alternative techniques.* **Porter, Jackie.** 7, s.l. : Anaesthesia & Intensive Care Medicine, 2004, Vol. 5.

731. *Managing Labour Pain.* **Mid Cheshire Hospitals.** [Online] NHS. [Cited: 24 August 2020.] https://www.mcht.nhs.uk/information-for-patients/departmentsandservices/maternity/labour-and-birth-information/managing-labour-pain/#:~:text=If%20pethidine%20or%20diamorphine%20are,baby%20drowsy%20for%20several%20days..

732. *Having a Regional Anaesthetic.* **Northern Lincolnshire and Goole.** [Online] NHS. [Cited: 27 August 2020.] https://www.nlg.nhs.uk/content/uploads/2014/04/IFP-0652.pdf.

733. *Headache after an epidural or spinal.* **University Hospitals Coventry and Warwickshire.** [Online] NHS, April 2020. [Cited: 27 August 2020.] file:///C:/Users/Attilio/Downloads/Headache%20after%20an%20epidural%20or%20spinal%20infection.pdf.

734. *Caesarean section.* **NHS.** [Online] 27 June 2019. [Cited: 04 September 2020.] https://www.nhs.uk/conditions/caesarean-section/.

735. *Delivery mode and gut microbial changes correlate with an increased risk of childhood asthma.* **Stokholm, Jakob.** 569, s.l. : Sci. Transl. Med, 2020, Vol. 12.

736. *A meta-analysis of the association between Caesarean section and childhood asthma.* **Thavagnanam , S.** s.l. : Clinical & Experimental Allergy, 2008, Vol. 38.

737. *Effects of acupressure, gum chewing and coffee consumption on the gastrointestinal system after caesarean section under spinal anaesthesia.* **Kanza Gül, Derya.** s.l. : J Obstet Gynaecol, 2020.

738. *The natural caesarean: a woman-centred technique.* **Smith, J.** 8, s.l. : BJOG, 2008, Vol. 115.

739. *Use of acupuncture during labour.* **Carr, David.** s.l. : The Practising Midwife, 2014.

740. *Prenatal Acupuncture and Serum Prostaglandin E2 Levels During the First Stage of Labor.* **Zeisler, H.** s.l. : Geburtsh Frauenheilk, 2000, Vol. 60.

741. *Randall, Wendy. After your 'waters break'.* **Oxford University Hospitals.** [Online] NHS, April 2020. [Cited: 7 July 2021.] https://www.ouh.nhs.uk/maternity/documents/after-your-waters-break.pdf.

742. *The Apgar Score Has Survived the Test of Time.* **Finster, Mieczyslaw.** s.l. : Anesthesiology, 2005, Vol. 102.

743. *Mastering the golden minute.* **deRegnier, Raye-Ann.** s.l. : The Journal of Pediatrics, 2016, Vol. 178.

744. *Delayed Cord Clamping in Very Preterm Infants Reduces the Incidence of Intraventricular Hemorrhage and Late-Onset Sepsis: A Randomized, Controlled Trial.* **Mercer, Judith.** 4, s.l. : Pediatrics, 2006, Vol. 117.

745. *Effects of delayed cord clamping in very-low-birth-weight infants.* **Oh, W.** s.l. : Journal of Perinatology, 2011, Vol. 31.

746. *Effect of delayed versus early umbilical cord clamping on neonatal outcomes and iron status at 4 months: a randomised controlled trial.* **Andersson, Ola.** s.l. : BMJ, 2011, Vol. 343.

747. *Effect of Delayed Cord Clamping on Iron Stores in Infants Born to Anemic Mothers: A Randomized Controlled Trial.* **Gupta, Rajesh.** s.l. : Indian Pediatrics, 2002, Vol. 39.

748. *Effects of Delayed Umbilical Cord Clamping vs Early Clamping on Anemia in Infants at 8 and 12 Months. A Randomized Clinical Trial.* **Ashish, K.** 3, s.l. : JAMA Pediatrics, 2017, Vol. 171.

749. *Effect of Delayed Cord Clamping on Neurodevelopment at 4 Years of Age.* **Andersson, Ola.** 7, s.l. : JAMA Pediatr, 2015, Vol. 169.

750. *Umbilical Cord Milking Versus Delayed Cord Clamping in Preterm Infants.* **Katheria, Anup.** 1, s.l. : Pediatrics, 2015, Vol. 136.

751.   *Milking Compared With Delayed Cord Clamping to Increase Placental Transfusion in Preterm Neonates: A Randomized Controlled Trial.* **Heike, Rabe.** 2, s.l. : Obstetrics & Gynecology, 2011, Vol. 117.

752.   *Fetal Effects of Primary and Non-primary Cytomegalovirus Infection in Pregnancy: Are we Close to Prevention?* **Ornoy, Asher.** s.l. : IMAJ, 2007, Vol. 9.

753.   *Perinatal outcomes following mid trimester detection of isolated short foetal femur length.* **Smith, M.** 5, s.l. : Journal of Obstetrics and Gynaecology, 2018, Vol. 38.

754.   *Interferon lambda protects the female reproductive tract against Zika virus infection.* **Caine, Elizabeth,** et al. s.l. : Nature Communications, 2019, Vol. 10.

Index

caffeine 43, 126, 128, 137, 145, 149, 161

calcium 12, 47, 51, 56, 113, 137, 145, 149, 150, 151, 155, 161

carbohydrates 9, 12, 30, 31, 125, 127, 129, 136, 141, 145, 156

carbon monoxide (CO) 114

carpal tunnel syndrome 51

castor oil 187, 214

cervical plug 8, 172, 205, 226

chemicals 10, 141;
  reducing exposure to 102, 138

chickenpox 12, 39

Chinese herbs Ch 8;
  benefits 76
  dosages 78
  effects 77
  history 75
  how to take 78
  safety 76
  timing 78

Chinese medicine, Ch 6;
  blood 67
  jing 68
  qi 65
  yin and yang 64

chlorella 154

choline 130, 146

chorionic villus sampling (CVS) 36, 94

chromium 154

chromosomal screening 34

clary sage 164, 188, 214

clothing 99, 223

clotting see thrombophilia test

cod liver oil 92, 144, 150, 161

coenzyme Q10 159

cold;
  food 124, 139
  weather 99, 242

conception 153, 169, 184

constipation 30, 48, 77, 149, 216, 221

contraction stress test (CST) 37, 238

copper 141, 146, 149

corticosterone 26

corticotrophin-releasing hormone (CRH) 23

cortisol 26, 73, 204, 226, 228

cortisone 26, 238

cosmetics 92, 106, 110, 113

cottonroot 187, 189, 214

COVID-19 212;
  test 40
  vaccine 89

cramps 7;
  leg 51
  stomach 30

cytomegalovirus (CMV) 37, 76, 238

D

dang gui see dong quai

deep vein thrombosis (DVT) 60, 229

delayed cord clamping 234

depression 42, 45, 56, 73, 76, 79, 87, 88, 154, 218

DHA *see* docosahexaenoic

diabetes *see* gestational diabetes mellitus

dichlorodiphenyldichloroethane (DDD) 105

dichlorodiphenyldichloroethylene (DDE) 105

dichlorodiphenyltrichloroethane (DDT) 105

diet, Ch 12;
cravings 9, 122, 126, 130
ideal 125, 127
optimising 124

dieting 132, 133, 140

discharge 8, 41, 226, 235, 240

docosahexaenoic (DHA) 92, 131, 132, 133, 136, 144, 146, 150

donating blood 100

dong quai 187

doppler ultrasound 30, 53, 58, 59, 60, 175

down's syndrome 29, 34, 35, 238, 239

doula 185, 209, 211, 231

E

eclampsia 238

ectopic pregnancy 238

edwards' syndrome 29, 34, 35, 239

eicosapentaenoic acid (EPA) 131, 133, 134, 136, 144, 147, 150

electromagnetic waves (EMWs) 115

embryo 20, 22, 27, 28, 94, 96, 157, 169; development 170

energy 7, 15, 25, 42, 45, 51, 54, 56, 70, 71, 72, 74, 78, 94, 96, 97, 98, 99, 124, 125, 130, 136, 137, 139, 142, 146, 153, 156, 157, 159, 173, 203, 227, 230;
see also qi

environment, optimising Ch 11

epidural block *see* pain relief

essential fatty acids (EFAs) 54, 125, 131

essential oils 162, 164, 165

evening primrose 158, 188

exercise 66, 67, 95, 98, 140, 141, 203, 223

external cephalic version (ECV) 181, 197, 239

F

fallopian tubes 7, 239

false unicorn 159

fats 129, 132, 133, 156, 240

fertilisation 153, 170, 171, 184

flaxseed oil 133

flavonoids 153, 161

foetal growth restriction (FGR) 52

foetal well-being test 36

folic acid (vitamin B₉) 58, 91, 93, 147, 149, 156, 161

foods;
  avoid 124, 126, 128, 130, 136, 139, 145
  cold 124, 125, 129, 139
  groups 125, 129
  hormones in 103, 106
  hot 124, 125, 129, 138
  packaging, hormones in 109, 116
  see also phytoestrogens 140
  progesterone affecting 140
  soya 128, 142

footwear 99

fossil fuels 112, 113

free radicals 115;
  see also antioxidants

frustration *see* stress

G

general anaesthesia *see* pain relief

genetics 196;
  see also chromosomal screening

genistein 142

gestational diabetes mellitus (GDM) 54

glucocorticoids 26

glyphosate 104, 111

green tea 10, 161

group B streptococcus (GBS) 38, 140

H

haemorrhoids 48, 76

hair loss 11, 155

harmony test 34, 35, 36, 94, 175, 239

headaches 45, 46, 49, 98, 114, 205, 216, 218

heartburn 43, 44, 73, 77, 84, 124, 131, 139, 149

heavy metals 103, 112

herbicides 92, 104

herbs *see* Chinese herbs

high-density polyethylene (HDPE) 118

home birth 207, 227

hormones 20;
  household 106
  in cosmetics 110
  in food 103
  in food packaging 116
  in water 106
  sexuality 120

human chorionic gonadotrophin (hCG) 12, 20, 21 (table), 28, 35, 83, 94, 170, 239

hyperemesis gravidarum 43

hypertension 33, 44, 46, 47, 51, 58, 60, 135, 154, 185, 218

polybrominated diphenyl ethers (PBDEs) 106, 107, 108, 111

polychlorinated biphenyls (PCB) 105, 106, 108, 111

polycyclic aromatic hydrocarbons (PAHs) 112

polyethylene terephthalate (PETE or PET) 118

polyfluorinated chemicals (PFCs) 106, 108, 111

polyhydramnios 54, 59, 60, 76, 202

polylactic acid (PLA) 118, 119

polypropylene (PP) 118

polystyrene 118

polyvinyl chloride (PVC) 118

poor memory 13, 155

pregnancy dictionary 237

pregnancy mask see melasma

pre-eclampsia 13, 32, 33, 34, 46, (table) 47, 52, 54, 58, 61, 135, 145, 154, 159, 160, 185, 186, 202, 241

pregnancy gingivitis 56, 140

preterm birth 40, 86, 100, 113, 116

probiotics 48, 139, 149, 191

progesterone 12, 21, 22, 25, 48, 103, 105, 106, 112, 120, 171, 172, 203, 238, 241, 242;
see also progestins
foods and 140

reduced 112

progestins 22, 242

prolactin 9, 24, 25, 242

prostaglandin E$_2$ (PGE$_2$) 160, 190, 226

protein 22, 45, 46, 47, 54, 55, 94, 125, 230, 134, 136, 150, 155, 179;
initiate labour 192
test 32, 241, 242

pudenal analgesia see pain relief - local block

pyrroloquinoline quinone (PQQ) 150

Q

Qi 65;
see also energy

R

raspberry leaf 188, 214

red meat 129, 135, 153, 154;
replacement 150

relaxin 25, 238, 242

rhesus disease 30, 31

S

SAFE test 34

salt 126, 135, 148

scarlet fever 38

selenium 135, 160

sense of smell 7, 10

shepherd's purse 189, 215, 234

shingles 39

uterus 7, 12, 20, 21, 22, 24, 30, 35, 41,
49, 57, 59, 60, 65, 73, 96, 98, 169,
(figure) 170, 171, 180, 181, 185, 202,
219, 221, 222, 224, 235, 238, 239,
241, 242;
avoid 94, 96
blood flow to 67, 68, 70, 73, 93, 99,
100, 140
changes in size 11
contractions 154, 181, 188, 190, 214,
233
dilation 227, 230

V

vaccines 88, 91

vagina stretching 200

valerian 189, 215

varicose veins 14, 61, 213

vasa previa 59

veganism 23, 133, 134, 135, 137, 216

vegetarianism 23, 133, 134, 135, 136,
150, 156, 163, 216

vernix caseosa 178, 180, 182, 233

vitamins;
baby 153
mother 145

vitamin A (retinol) 128, 144, 145, 150,
161

vitamin B$_1$ (thiamin) 44, 156

vitamin B$_2$ (riboflavin) 156

vitamin B$_5$ (pantothenic acid) 157

vitamin B$_6$ (pyridoxine) 133, 156, 157

vitamin B$_{12}$ (thiamin) 58, 135, 150, 156,
216

vitamin C (ascorbic acid) 157, 161

vitamin D 91, 93, 129, 151

vitamin E 157, 161

vitamin K 151

vulval varicosity 15

W

water 43, 48, 49, 55, 59, 94, 126, 129,
138, 139, 162, 163, 165;
containments in 83, 103, 105, 106,
109, 113, 117

water birth 201, 206, 210, 212

weeks;
week by week 169
going over 40 weeks 184

weight 8, 24, 25, 133, 211, 237;
baby's 13, 27, 29, 31, 37, 50, 52, 86,
97, 99, 100, 106, 107, 109, 110, 112,
133, 138, 146, 153, 179, 180, 181,
239, 240, 242;
controlling 73, 130, 140, 154

whooping cough 89, 90, 180, 241

Y

yang 64, 65, 66, 125, 203, 242

yin 64, 67, 68, 97, 125, 153, 240, 242

Make fertility friends on

My Fertility Forum

The leading fertility network UK and USA.

Register today and make new fertility friends, gain emotional support, write your own blog and learn more about how to improve your pregnancy and labour.

Download the new Apple and Android app for FREE and keep updated while on the move.

My Fertility Forum

www.myfertilityforum.com

Printed in Great Britain
by Amazon

19481971R10173